Stock Trading Wizard

Advanced Short-Term Trading Strategies
for Swing and Daytrading

● ● ● ● ● ● ● ● ● ● ●

Tony Oz

Tony Oz Publications
Laguna Hills, CA

Copyright © 1999 by Tony Oz. All rights reserved. Except as permitted under the United States Copyright Act of 1976, no part of this publication may be reproduced or distributed in any form or by any means, or stored in a data base or retrieval system, without the prior written permission of the publisher.

Published by Tony Oz Publications, Laguna Hills, CA.

ISBN 0-9673862-0-9

Printed in the United States of America.

To My Wife Jodi, and My Son Jordan,

You have made my life complete.

I love you both.

Disclaimer

This book is to be used for informational purposes only and without warranty of any kind. The materials and information in this book are not, and should not be construed as an offer to buy or sell any of the securities named in these materials. Trading of securities may not be suitable for all users of this information. Both day trading stocks and investing in the stock market in general have large potential rewards. However, they both have large potential risks involved in which you can lose all your money. You, the reader, and not Tony Oz or Tony Oz Publications, are solely responsible for any losses, financial or otherwise, as a result of trading stocks. Under all circumstances, you the reader, and not Tony Oz or Tony Oz publications, assume the entire cost and all risks involved with trading any stock based on strategies illustrated in this book. **Past performance is not indicative of future results.**

Table of Contents

Section One, About the Stock Market

Investment/Trading Objectives	2
The Stock Market	2
Exchange Market	2
OTC-NASDAQ	3
Risks	3
Factors Affecting the Stock Market	4
General Market Psychology	5
Indexes	5
Supply and Demand	6
Supply and Demand in the Stock Market	7
Bid and Ask	8
Spread	10
Traditional Order Entries to Start a Position	10
Market Orders	10
Limit Orders	10
Stop Orders	11
Stop Limit order	12
Mental Stops	12
Traditional Order Entries to Exit Positions	12
Market Orders	12
Limit Orders	12
Stop Loss Orders	12
Mental Stops	13
Trailing Stops	13
Where to Set Stops	13
Short Sale	14

Section Two, Technical Analysis

Basics of TA	18
Volume	19

Identifying the Trend	20
Support and Resistance	25
Trendlines	30
Moving Averages	34
Using Moving Averages in Trading	36
Breakouts	39
Buying Stocks After Consolidation	41
Characteristics of Price Movements	48
Technical Price Patterns	50
Double Bottom	50
Double Top	51
Head and Shoulders	53
Reverse Head and Shoulders	54
Cup and Handle	54
Trading in a Channel	56
Continuation Patterns	60
Triangles	60
Flags	62
Wedges	63
Stair Stepping	64
RSI	65
Using Intraday Chart	66
Technical Analysis Summary	68

Section Three, Introduction to Level II

Bid and Ask	70
Multiquote Window	73
What Does Level II Tell Us?	75
The Big Market Makers	79
Who is the AX?	80
Time and Sales Print Report	81
Using Time and Sales with Level II	82
Illustration of an AX in Action	83
Dynamics of Level II	88

Section Four, Advanced Order Execution Systems

SOES	92
SelectNet	95
SelectNet Preference Orders	95
ECNs	97
Playing Market Maker	101
More ISLD Stuff	102
Arca	104
Market Maker's Tricks	105
Which Execution System to Use?	107

Section Five, Trading For a Living

Research	112
Trading Strategy	113
Trading Strategy Table	115
Execution	116
Trade Records	116
Trade Records Table	118
Ego	119
Money Management	119
The Sweeping Philosophy	121
Winning Streaks	121
Losing Streaks	122
You Don't Have to Trade Everyday	124
Dealing With Pressure	125
Supervising Your Trades	125
Finding Stocks to Trade	126
Real Time Scan Formulas	126
Learning Curve	132
Paper Trading	133
Chat Rooms	133
Secrets to Successful Trading-What Does it Take?	134
Expensive Stocks Vs. Cheap Stocks	136
Capital Preservation	137

Trading Strategies, Buying Points, Where and How	137
Daytrading Vs. Swing Trading	140
Adaptation	141
Buyers/Sellers Remorse	141
Cost Averaging for Long Term Growth	142
Taxes	142
Mastering the Trading Game	143

Section Six, Daytrading Case Study

Yahoo! Case Study	146
Observation Phase	147
Taking Action	149
Sitting in the Trade	150
Market Makers Playing Games	151
Modifying the Strategy Behind the Trade	154
The Breakout	156
Trailing a Stop	158
Selling 1/2 of the Position	162
Bouncing Back up	163
Closing the Position	164
The Next Trading Day	167

Appendix A

Market Indexes	169
Industry Indexes	169

Appendix B

Trading Station Setup	171

Glossary   172

About the Author	187

Acknowledgements

Thanks to my wife Jodi, Russell and Julie Paris, Noriko and Bruce Carnes, for your hard work and dedication. Thanks to Ted Murphy, Tim Bourquin, Len Cohen, Scott Webster, Jerry Rabenberg, Steve Moebius, Baron Robertson, Sibrag, Spacegold, Ces, William Zhu, and Kevin Britko for your friendship. Thanks to Townsend Analytics, Janice Kaylor, Danilo Torres, Mary Heim, The BBC, and the crew at CNBC for all your help. Thanks to all the members of Daytraders of Orange County and special thanks to all my students. You have inspired me to write this guidance book for you. I feel that I owe so many professionals in the industry a debt of gratitude. Thanks to all the members of the Market Technicians Association. Thanks to Mr. Katz, Linda Raschke, John Bollinger, Paul Umansky, Charlie Hampton, and to all the ones I forgot, please forgive me.

Section One

About The Stock Market

Investment/Trading Objectives

It is important to determine your investment/trading objectives as it varies for each individual. The objectives of a married 28 year old with a newborn baby are totally different than the objectives of a 50 year old looking to retire and, of course, both are totally different than the objectives of a 23 year old who is single. It is important to define the financial responsibilities one has in order to better manage his/her money. Before you start, write down your objectives and goals as an investor along with your present and future financial responsibilities.

The Stock Market

What is the stock market? The stock market is a marketplace where buyers and sellers meet. The item that is being sold is a piece of paper which represents ownership in a company. Professional traders see the stock market as nothing more than letters and numbers changing rapidly. My definition of a stock is four letters (in the NASDAQ stock market) followed by a number. The four letters being the ticker symbol which remains the same (it does not change unless the exchange removes it from being listed) and the number being the price per one share (unit) of that stock. The price (the number) will dynamically fluctuate during trading hours in direct relationship to ... SUPPLY and DEMAND.

The Exchange Market

The Exchange Market is a place where buyers and sellers come together to trade. The best known and largest exchange is the New York Stock Exchange (NYSE). The NYSE is a large room with many trading posts where trades take place. Each post has a specialist who handles specific securities. He can act as a broker's broker and make commissions on the trades, or he can buy and sell out of his own account, hence, creating a market in that specific security. The NYSE is not directly involved in the actual transactions (trades) but acts as a police officer enforcing certain rules to ensure fairness. The NYSE sets the policies of rules and regulations and decides which stocks are eligible for listing, and which firms can become members of the exchange. The NYSE approves specialists as well. There are many restrictions on the specialists in order to make a fair marketplace. One important restriction a specialist has is that he may not cross orders without first offering the stock higher than his Bid. For example, if a specialist has an order to buy 1000 XYZ at 20 1/2 from one broker and an order to sell 1000 XYZ at 20 1/2 from another broker, he must ask 20 9/16 or more (or lower his bid to 20

7/16 or less) in an attempt to get a better price prior to crossing the orders.

Over The Counter – NASDAQ

The NASDAQ is different from the NYSE because the exchange has no physical location nor trading posts. This exchange is 100% electronic and the specialist here is replaced with Market Makers (MM.) These Market Makers are individual firms willing to make a market. The Market Maker is similar to a specialist on the NYSE, but he acts as a dealer, not as a broker. In general, the Market Maker has a position in a particular stock and sells out of his own inventory. Market Makers make their money from a markup or markdown rather than from commissions. The Market Maker regularly publishes Bid and offer quotes and is ready to buy or sell the stock at the quoted prices. These quotes can be seen on a Level II screen.

Risks

When we talk about risk, we refer to the possibility of a loss. Risk cannot be measured in exact numbers, but we can look at some factors which affect the risk of investing in stocks or trading them. It is important to remember that the possibility of a loss is always present, and that the stock market does not provide us with a guaranteed way to make profits.

General stock market risk is always present. A stock market crash can occur on any given day without prior notice. If this was to happen, all stocks would most likely trade significantly lower. The first risk to consider is the general market risk. This risk is derived from numerous variables that affect the market, such as new government policy (a capital gains tax hike, interest rate hike, etc.), we have no control over.

The next risk is an industry risk or sector risk. Certain sectors/industries can be on fire one day and ice cold the next. Stocks move with the sector (industry) they belong to. If you look at the bull market we had in tech stocks and compare it to the oil drilling stocks in the period of time from October 1997 to January 1999, you will see that the NASDAQ 100 index was up 89% in 15 months, while some of the drillers (such as Marine drilling) were down as much as 83% in the same period of time. So the sector a stock belongs to represents the next risk to be considered.

Volatility represents another risk; this risk is also known as beta. Some stocks are more volatile than others. Consequently, they represent higher risk. That is not to say that low beta stocks (less volatile) represent lower risk at all time, because you also have to factor in the potential returns. In certain environments, low beta stocks can gap down big and become more volatile than other high volatility stocks. However, generally speaking, low beta stocks are considered to have less risk than high beta stocks according to the experts. Interest rates or monetary policy represent another risk factor. In a rising interest rate environment, stocks will not be as attractive, and more likely than not, they will decline and vice versa. Other risks to consider are inflation, domestic economy, world economy, etc. These are the main risks connected to investing in the stock market. In short, investing in the equity market is risky, because there is a possibility of a loss. Volatility, government policies, and inflation contribute to the risk. However, the risk is not the same for all stocks and it is dependent on which sector or industry they belong to, and their relative beta (volatility). Stocks are considered a relatively high risk form of investment, however, overall, the stock market has been the best investment vehicle for long term investments. I think it will remain the best long-term investment for centuries to come. Remember, there is an added risk factor to trading on margin and short-term trading.

Factors Affecting the Stock Market

The first factor that comes to mind is the changes in the structure of the market. For instance, the new wave of online investors has contributed to a growing interest in the U.S. equity market. In fact, I was contacted three times in the last month by major broadcasting companies, which were doing a special feature on online trading. ABC did a special feature on Good Morning America. This did not come as a big surprise, as I knew the domestic online trading boom was in 5th gear. The one that surprised me was the latest e-mail I received, which I am including here: *"I am a television researcher in England. We are making a television series on the global economy for BBC television, in which we will follow various types of investors during 1999 as they respond to the changing economy. We are particularly interested in looking at the "day trading" phenomenon which seems a very exciting development and is sure to spread throughout the world."* This really caught my attention because the online trading virus is spreading globally. This is definitely the biggest factor affecting the stock market right now. Other factors which affect the stock market are economy, business activity, technology, and investor psychology.

General Market Psychology

Investor psychology plays a major role in the volatility of the stock market. By volatility, I refer to the dynamic price swings stocks and indexes show during the trading session. The latest psychological effects come from new investors and players listening to stories of how their friends have made a "killing" buying XYZ shares 7 years ago at $4 and now they trade at $150. These new investors who were "left out" want in now, and they want to make all the money they "missed" in a short period of time. This has fueled the stock market over the last 4 years, and no one knows when it will stop. Investor psychology plays a major role in what will become a hot sector and which hot sector will cool down. The best example I can think of is the run up in prices enjoyed by the Internet stocks in 1998 and in 1999. When almost every analyst was saying Yahoo, Amazon and America Online were overvalued in March of 1998, investors thought differently and were scooping up shares of these companies with a big shovel, causing them to double in price again and again and again. Another example is the performance of big cap stocks in comparison to small cap stocks. Investors like the big companies. These are the companies they are familiar with. Therefore, they will buy those stocks. To summarize this section, I will compare the stock market to fashion. One season leather is "in", the next season it is flannel they want. The consumer determines the colors and patterns to be "in" that season and it is the same in the stock market. Investor psychology determines the hot and cold stocks. Similar to fashion, the stock market is always changing as investors search for the greatest profit potential.

Indexes

An index is an average of a basket of stocks. The most well known index is the Dow Jones Industrial Average. This average contains a basket of 30 stocks that changes in value as the stocks in this average fluctuate in price. Traders use the indexes to get an overall feel for the direction the broader market is going in. The most important aspect of trading is to know the overall direction of the market. There are different indexes which track different markets and different sectors. It is extremely important to know the sector a stock belongs to, before you trade that stock. Most indexes are also cap weighted, which means that the bigger the market cap of a stock in the index, the bigger part of the index it will be. A big company like Microsoft will have a bigger effect on the NASDAQ 100 index than a small company in the index. If Microsoft was to go up or down sharply, it will have a bigger effect on the overall value change of the index. There is a list of the different industry indexes including their symbols in Appendix A.

Supply and Demand

Just like any business in the free market that sells goods or services, stock prices are affected by supply and demand. It is important you understand this. The rules of supply and demand are simple. If the quantity demanded is greater than the quantity supplied, prices will go up until there is an equilibrium, where quantity demanded is equal to the quantity supplied. What makes it all possible is GREED. For example, a plumber in the Los Angeles area was charging $75 to replace a water heater on January 15, 1994. On January 17, 1994 there was a big earthquake causing thousands of water heaters to break down and flood homes. The demand for plumbing services and water heaters increased; consequently, plumbers were charging $350-$850 to install a new water heater. And guess what, customers were paying that much and begging plumbers to come and fix their water heaters that week. Some may think it is immoral to take advantage of a situation like that, but it is exactly that greed that fuels a free marketplace, and it is the basis of our economy. Greed is good. Don't get me wrong, I am not a cold hearted beast. I could have chosen a nicer example painted in pretty colors, but I chose this one, because I think it is very similar to the stock market, where taking advantage of changes in supply and demand will put a few coins in your pocket for a rainy day. Of course there is another side to the coin which suggests that if the quantity supplied is greater than the quantity demanded, it will result in a sharp decline in prices. A good example to illustrate this point is a dairy farm. Let's say the industry, as a whole, produces 5000 units for sale per day. The quantity demanded is 5000 units and the price is $5.00 per unit. However, this year the cows are producing way over the normal 5000 units. As a matter of fact, this morning they produced 25,000 units. This is what will happen: Farmer John counts on this production to pay the rent but, there are no buyers. His wife is panicking and tells him to call everyone. "Sell at any price, we need some cash flow," she tells him. Farmer John calls Greedy Mike, trying to sell his milk. Mike tells Farmer John that he has Farmer Bob on the other line willing to sell him at $3.25 a unit. Farmer John consults his wife and decides to sell at $3.00, but by the time he gets back to Greedy Mike, Farmer Gene already offered Greedy Mike to sell his lot for $2.00 a unit. Farmer John knows that he has to sell at any price, or his production is worthless, as it will be spoiled. He tells Greedy Mike, just buy it at any price and he sells it all at $1.25 a unit. Remember this example as it relates directly to the stock market and panic selling. In panic selling situation, Market Makers will buy stocks from the public at rock bottom prices.

Supply & Demand in the Stock Market

To better understand the concept of supply and demand, we will feature a hypothetical example using XYZ stock to illustrate what makes a market in the stock. We will assume that there are only 5 stock holders in XYZ Corp. and that you and 3 other investors are interested in buying the stock.

Now let's say that John, Leslie, Mark, Bill and Andy own 100 shares of stock each and that you, Betty, Frank and Linda are interested in buying 100 shares each.

John is willing to sell his 100 shares at $150 a share, Leslie is willing to sell her 100 shares at $152 a share, Mark is willing to sell his 100 shares at $154 a share, Bill is not interested in selling his 100 shares right now (he is a long term investor), and Andy is willing to sell 50 shares at $160 a share and will hold the rest for long term investment.

Frank is interested in buying 100 shares at $145 a share, Linda is interested in buying 100 shares at $147 a share, Betty is willing to buy 100 shares at $148 a share, and you are interested in buying 100 shares at $149 a share.

The following table illustrates the current market (supply and demand) for shares of XYZ corp.

Demand	Supply
You 100 @ 149	**John** 100 @ 150
Betty 100 @ 148	**Leslie** 100 @ 152
Linda 100 @ 147	**Mark** 100 @ 154
Frank 100 @ 145	**Andy** 50 @ 160

This table shows four individuals who are interested in purchasing a certain number of XYZ shares at a certain price on the left column, labeled Demand. This column also represents the current overall demand for XYZ shares and the quantity demanded at the different price levels.

This table also shows four individuals who are interested in selling a certain number XYZ shares at a certain price on the right column, labeled Supply. This column also represents the over all supply for XYZ shares and the quantity supplied at the different price levels.

You may also notice that the 100 shares owned by Bill and the other 50 shares owned by Andy are not showing in the table as these individuals are not interested in selling those shares of XYZ right now.

What we can learn from this very simple situation is that there are 4 different individuals who are interested in buying XYZ shares at different prices and that there are 4 individuals who are interested in selling XYZ shares at different prices. The total number of shares (quantity) in demand is 400 shares and the total number of shares (quantity) in supply is 350.

Bid and Ask

There is so much confusion in understanding the Bid and Ask or "quote" on a stock that I feel it is important to explain it in simple terms. After a short while this will become second nature to you. Let's use the same XYZ Supply and Demand table to illustrate Bid and Ask.

Demand	Supply
You 100 @ 149	**John** 100 @ 150
Betty 100 @ 148	**Leslie** 100 @ 152
Linda 100 @ 147	**Mark** 100 @ 154
Frank 100 @ 145	**Andy** 50 @ 160

The column on the left shows the demand for the stock represented by the potential buyers (You, Betty, Linda and Frank). The column on the right shows the supply represented by potential sellers (John, Leslie, Mark and Andy.)

Let's take a look at the Supply column and read it from top to bottom. We will first look at John. John is willing to sell his 100 shares of XYZ at $150 a share. It is also true to say that he is **offering** his 100 shares of XYZ at $150 a share or that he is **asking** $150 a share for his 100 shares of XYZ stock. Next is Leslie and she is **asking** $152 a share for her 100 shares of XYZ stock followed by Mark who is **asking** $154 a share for his 100 shares of XYZ stock followed by Andy who is **asking** $160 a share for his 50 shares of stock. So, the **Ask** or **offer** price represents the price **sellers** are willing to sell their stock at.

Next, we will look at the Demand column and read it from top to bottom. The first potential buyer is You who is willing to buy 100 shares of XYZ at $149 a share. Since you are willing to pay $149 for 100 shares of XYZ stock, we can also say that you are **bidding** $149 a share for 100 shares of XYZ. Next is Betty who is **bidding** $148 a share for 100 shares of XYZ followed by Linda who is **bidding** $147 a share for 100 shares of XYZ followed by Frank who is **bidding** $145 for 100 shares of XYZ. So the **Bid** price represents the price **buyers** are willing to buy stock at.

We can now look at a new table for supply and demand for XYZ stock. We will change the label of **Demand** to **Bid** and change the label of **Supply** to **Ask**.

Bid	Ask
You 100 @ 149	John 100 @ 150
Betty 100 @ 148	Leslie 100 @ 152
Linda 100 @ 147	Mark 100 @ 154
Frank 100 @ 145	Andy 50 @ 160

The inside market for this example will be the best Bid and best Ask. It will be represented as so on a level 1 quote: XYZ Bid 149 Ask 150. The best Ask and best Bid make the inside market. In this case if someone wanted to buy 100 shares of XYZ at the market (using a market order to buy) he would get an order fill at $150 a share and if someone wanted to sell 100 shares of stock at the market (using a market order to sell) he would get a fill at $149 a share.

The common confusion that buyers are bidders and sellers are askers arises because of the traditional way we get a stock quote from our broker. For example, if Dan wanted to buy 100 shares of XYZ and called his broker for a quote, the broker would say: XYZ Bid 149 Ask 150. If Dan placed a market order to buy 100 shares of XYZ, then he will be filled at $150 a share. He would buy at the best Ask. So Dan was a buyer, yet he was not a bidder for the stock as he bought the stock at the best Ask. It is important to understand that when you look at a quote table, the bidders represent buyers or demand and the Ask represents sellers or supply.

Spread

Let's look at the same example of XYZ Bid and Ask (supply and demand) table.

Bid	Ask
You 100 @ 149	**John** 100 @ 150
Betty 100 @ 148	**Leslie** 100 @ 152
Linda 100 @ 147	**Mark** 100 @ 154
Frank 100 @ 145	**Andy** 50 @ 160

As you can see the best Bid is 149 and the best Ask is 150. The difference between the best Bid and the best Ask is called a spread. If we subtract 149 from 150 we get 1. Hence, the spread in this case is $1.00. If another bidder came in at 149 3/4 than the spread will 1/4 of a point (subtract 149.75 from 150.)

Traditional Order Entry to Start a Position

Market Order: This is an order to immediately buy or sell a security at the current market price. By "current" it means at the inside market (best Bid or Ask) or at whatever price the seller/buyer will be willing to fill you at, and "immediately" can mean up to 7 1/2 minutes at times and 5 points later (from my own experience). Never use a market order to buy a stock before or at market open. You are almost guaranteed to get a lousy fill. You may use market orders to buy stocks after the open, depending on the issue and its spread (the difference between the Bid and Ask). However, we recommend you try and avoid placing market orders at all times, unless you feel you have to use one. (Please note that the execution system you use or are able to use, your broker, etc., are variables that differ for all investors. Therefore, you must determine how you can enter a position in the best and most profitable manner according to all the variables and tools you have.) We will look at advanced order entry systems later in this book.

Limit Order: This is an order to buy or sell a stock at a specified price. For instance, let us look at the XYZ example again. You can enter an order to buy 100 shares at $146. You specify a price and the order can be executed only if the market reaches or betters that price. It is a conditional trading order designed to avoid the danger of adverse unexpected price changes. This is the type of order that should be used most often to enter positions. It is great to use on stocks with bigger than a 1/16 spread as well as extra volatile stocks. For example, let's look at XYZ quote.

Bid	Ask
Tony 100 @ 149	**John** 100 @ 150
Betty 100 @ 148	**Leslie** 100 @ 152
Linda 100 @ 147	**Mark** 100 @ 154
Frank 100 @ 145	**Andy** 50 @ 160

As you can see, the best Bid is 149 and the best Ask is 150. There is a spread of 1 point. You can place a buy order at 149 1/8 and now you become the best bidder. The XYZ quote will now read 149 1/8 X 150, if anyone wants to sell at 149 1/8 and no one is bidding better than you for the stock, you will most likely get a fill at 149 1/8. There is no golden rule here but remember that by placing your limit order in between the spread, you are taking the risk of missing it, entirely, if the stock moves up and no one sold you any shares at 149 1/8. The biggest problem with limit orders is when a stock starts moving fast and you miss the entry price. If you are still interested in getting in the position even at a slightly higher price, you have to cancel your order and re-enter an order at a higher price. Sometimes, it will just keep running away from you. Try not to chase it. If you really want to get the position in the first place, you can enter a limit order at 1/16 or 1/8 above the best Ask. You would most likely get a price improvement and not miss it if it's going to run. (Use this strategy only with stocks that have a maximum spread of 1/8. You must be careful when you trade stocks with bigger spreads, because there is a higher risk involved.)

Stop Order: This is an order to buy or sell at the market when a definite price is reached, either above (on a buy) or below (on a sell) the price that prevailed when the order was given. Let's say XYZ is at 150 on the Ask, and we want to buy the stock if it goes over 153, so we enter a stop buy order as so: Stop buy XYZ 153 1/16. If XYZ Ask hits 153 1/16, our order becomes a market order to buy XYZ at the best available price. Please note that because it is a stop buy market order, we can get a fill anywhere. If XYZ runs up to 160 in 2-3 minutes we could very possibly get a fill at 160. I like to use either a mental stop buy order or a stop limit order.

Please note that not all brokers offer stop orders and some might offer a limited variety of stop orders that might not be complete (like availability only on NYSE issues or only on NASDAQ issues.) Check with your broker.

Stop-Limit Order: This is a stop order that designates a price limit. The stop-limit order becomes a limit order once the stop is reached. Let's use XYZ as an example again. We want to buy XYZ if the stock price goes over 153, so we will enter a stop buy limit order to buy XYZ 153 1/16 (the order will get activated when XYZ Ask hits 153 1/16). In the second price field or "limit" field we will enter the maximum we are willing to pay for it, let's say 154 1/4. So if XYZ hits 153 1/16 on the Ask, our order to buy XYZ at 154 1/4 will be sent in. We can get a better price if it is available, we can get it at 154 1/4 or we could still miss it if there are buyers in front of us. Many times we could miss it and get a fill on a price snap back.

Mental Stop Order: This type of order is used by investors who follow the market tick by tick. For example, once a stock has reached the price target where you think there is a breakout, you can enter a limit order to buy it. Example: XYZ is at 149 x 150, you set a mental stop buy order at 152 15/16. XYZ is moving up, and it hits 152 5/8 x 152 15/16. At this point, you have a few options. Enter a market order to buy, Enter a limit order to buy at 152 15/16 -153 1/4, or try to split the spread and enter a limit order to buy at 15211/16-152 7/8. You must predetermine it and act quickly. Many data vendors' software have built in alarms where you can set prices for stocks both on the upside or downside, and once a certain price is met, the alarm will alert you to it. You must have a predetermined strategy for the trade, so you can quickly enter an order once the alarm goes off.

Order Entry to Exit an Existing Position

Market Order: This is a way to sell if you really want out!

Limit Order: You can place a limit order at your target exit price. For instance, let's say you are long XYZ at 150 and you want to sell at 153. You can enter a limit order to sell XYZ at 153. If your price hits and someone is willing to buy it from you at 153, then your limit sell order will be filled.

Stop Loss Order: Use this type of order to limit your loss in a position or to lock in profits if a stock you are holding is turning against you. There are many pros and cons to this system and the price in which to set these orders at. If you cannot follow the market every minute of the day, then this strategy can save you a fortune. Let's say that you bought XYZ at 150. Before you enter the trade you must determine what is the maximum loss you are willing to take if XYZ turns south on you. It is an important aspect of money management. So, let's presume that you think there is support for XYZ at 148 and 145. You may place a stop loss order at 147 1/2 which means that if

XYZ bids 147 1/2, then your sell order will be sent out. (Please note that we feel that entering a stop loss market order or a stop loss limit order with 3 points cushion could save you a lot of money if a stock is falling down really hard, but a lot depends on your broker and execution.) Hopefully, you got out at 147 1/2 and limited your losses to 2 1/2 points in this case. If you do follow the market with every tick, then Mental Stops are another way to go.

Mental Stops: This is a tool used to limit a loss on a certain position when you trade a stock and follow it in real time throughout the day. Instead of setting a stop loss order with your broker in advance, you enter a sell order when the stock you are trading has dropped to a level that is at the maximum loss you are willing to take. Exercising your mental stop will let you exit the position at a mentally predetermined price (unless the stock keeps falling down faster than you can put a sell order in).

Trailing Stops: These are used when you have a profit in your position. After assessing the potential upside of your holdings, you can place trailing stops as the stock moves higher. You increase the stop price as the stock moves up so if the stock turns around and goes south, you will be stopped out with a profit in your hands. A smart trader once said, "You will never go broke taking profits."

Where Should You Set Your Stops?
It depends on the stock you are trading with a few golden rules:

1. Never let a profit turn into a loss!!! If you are in the money (stock price is higher than your entry price by 5/8 or more) set a stop at even (flat) so if the stock turns around and goes south, you will not lose. The psychological effect of letting a winning position turn around on you and ending with a loss is devastating. Try and avoid letting a profit turn into a loss.

2. Depending on stock price and volatility, I typically limit my loses to 3/8 of a point to 7/8 maximum loss. When I enter a position, I normally look to make 1 point minimum for every $20 I lay out (which is 5%.) I am not entering positions to make fractions and make my broker rich, however, there will be times to exit a position with a fractional gain.

3. This is very important: If you get stopped out of a position, it means that the stock you bought or sold short went in the opposite anticipated direction. It does not matter if it rebounded and continued moving in the original anticipated direction. When you use stops, mentally or electronically, you will get stopped out, and at times, you will be shaken out of your position. That is

okay, because you can always enter the position again, but if you take a major loss, your capital will shrink and it will be much harder to bring it back up. Remember protecting your capital is the number one goal.

4. It is a lot easier being looser on your stops when you have an in-the-money position. If a stock is showing you that it is strong and is going in the anticipated direction, keep riding it. Always evaluate the strength of your stock, (a.k.a. momentum) see where it is going.

Short Sale

Stocks go up and down. We all understand how we make money if we buy a stock at one price and sell it later at a higher price, that's pretty simple. Short selling is the same; we make a profit by selling a stock at a certain price and buying it at a lower price. The only difference is that we reverse the course of the action. When we go long, we buy a stock first and sell it after we bought it, hopefully at a higher price. When we take a short position, we first sell the stock and buy it after we sold it, hopefully at a lower price. Normally, we will say buy low, sell high. When we short stocks we say, sell high, buy low. The profit being made is the difference between the sale price and purchase price in both cases.

Why would a trader short sell a stock? A trader short sells a stock when he thinks the stock is going to decline in price. He hopes to take advantage of declining stock prices to make a profit. If you plan on trading for a living you must learn how to short stocks successfully, as you need to play both sides of the market. If you only play the long side, exclusively, you will deny yourself the opportunity to improve your performance. There are times when short selling stocks yields great returns. Many traders do not feel comfortable shorting stocks, they think it is un-American to short stocks. If you feel this way, it will be harder for you to take a full advantage of the ups and downs in the stock market.

What takes place when you short sell a stock? First, it is important to understand that you think a stock is going to decline in price and you want to profit from it. Let's say that XYZ is trading at 55 and you short sell it at 55. The stock goes down to 51, and you want to close your position. You will now buy the stock at 51 and **cover** your short. Congratulations, you have just made a 4 point profit on your trade, 55-51=4. You may wonder how was it possible to sell XYZ when you did not own the stock. This is how it works. You borrow the stock from your broker, if he has it available, and you simply sell it. When you want to close your position, you buy the stock and return it to your broker. Now, you have covered your short position. You will have a profit or a loss equal to the difference between the sale price and the purchase price times the number of shares you traded.

Rules and regulations:

1. You must have a margin account.
2. Your broker must have the stock, so you can borrow it.
3. A short sell order must be executed on an uptick. This means that the stock must tick up higher for your order to short sell a stock to be executed. This rule was set to prevent short sellers from manipulating the market.

There are different short selling strategies exercised by daytraders. These can be based on technical or fundamental changes. The important thing to understand is that a trader must learn the art of playing both sides of the market. That is, making money when stocks go up in price and making money when stocks go down in price. Short term traders short sell stocks because they know that stock prices don't always go up, and if a bear market starts, the only way to make money will be to short the bear market rallies. There are 4 things to remember about short selling stocks.

1. Do not short sell a stock in a hot sector.
2. Do not short sell a stock because you think it is overvalued.
3. Do not short sell a stock because you would have loved to own it when it was 1/20 of the price it is trading at now.
4. Never ever short sell a moonrocket, a stock that is going vertical in price as if it is going to the moon. If you do, it can send you to the cleaners very fast. Would you stand in front of a runaway train? I didn't think so.

Section Two

Technical Analysis

Charts used in this section are provided by RealTick™ III and are used with the express written permission of Townsend Analytics, Ltd. RealTick™ III is a trademark and copyright of Townsend Analytics, Ltd.

Basics of Technical Analysis

Technical analysis is used to determine supply and demand for a stock. It is done by analyzing the behavior of a stock over a period of time, which can be one day or even 200 years. In other words, we analyze past price behavior of a stock over any period of time to see where we think it could go next. The results are plotted into a chart which illustrates the prices a stock traded in over the given period of time. There are different ways to record the data in a chart format. We will focus on "bar charts." In a bar format we record the price data simply by drawing a straight vertical line for the price range a stock traded in. The simplest bar chart will include price and time. Price will be on the Y axis and time will be on the X axis of the chart. Look at the example below as it shows a price study of 20 days for Sportsline USA, Inc.

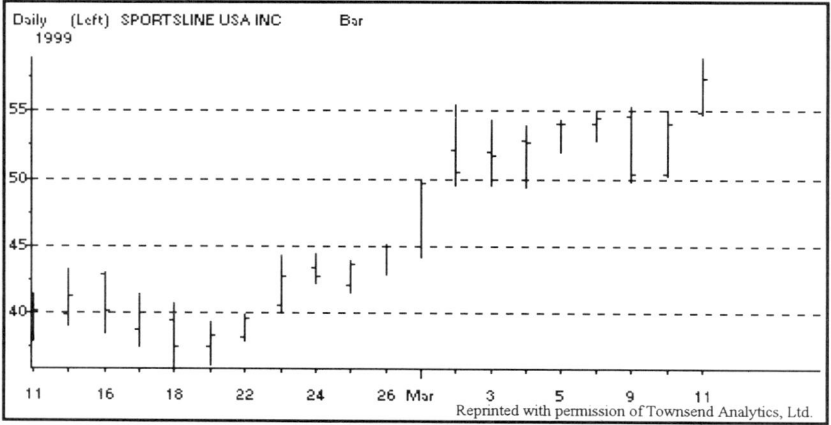

The bars seen on the chart represent the prices Sportsline traded at, that day. Each bar shows 4 different price fields for any given day. These price fields include the **opening** price, the **high** price of the day, the **low** price of the day and the **closing** price of the day.

Opening price– This is the execution price of the first trade of the day.
High– This is the highest price point that the stock traded at that day.
Low– This is the lowest price the stock traded at that day.
Closing Price– This is the price of the last trade of the day.

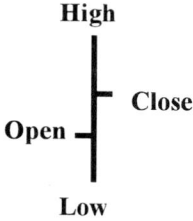

The length of the bar is the **trading range** of a stock for a given day. Trading range is the difference between the high and the low of the day. So if the high was 58 and the low was 55 then it is also true to say that the trading range was 3 points (55 to 58.) We draw a vertical line from the low price of the day to the high price of the day. We also indicate the opening price and the closing price, and that creates one bar for a bar chart. Remember that the time period can be different so a bar will represent the trading range for that period of time. If a bar represents one day of trading then we call that chart a **daily** chart. In some charts, a bar can represent prices for one week, one month, or even one year. If a bar represents one week of trading prices, then we call that chart a **weekly chart**. If a bar represents one month of trading prices, then we call that chart a **monthly chart**. There are many other technical studies and indicators that can be added to bar charts. These technical studies also represent price behavior and many times are derived from averages of prices over a period of time. We will look at some technical studies later in this manual. The only technical study that I want to include now is Volume.

Volume

Volume in charts represents the total number of shares traded on a stock in a given period of time. There is a relationship between the number of shares (volume) traded on a stock to the present price behavior, and it can forecast future price behavior as well. In this segment we will illustrate the way we plot volume into a bar chart. The chart below is a bar chart for Infoseek Corp. We can see the volume (number of shares traded) for each of the days displayed as a bar on the bottom part of the chart.

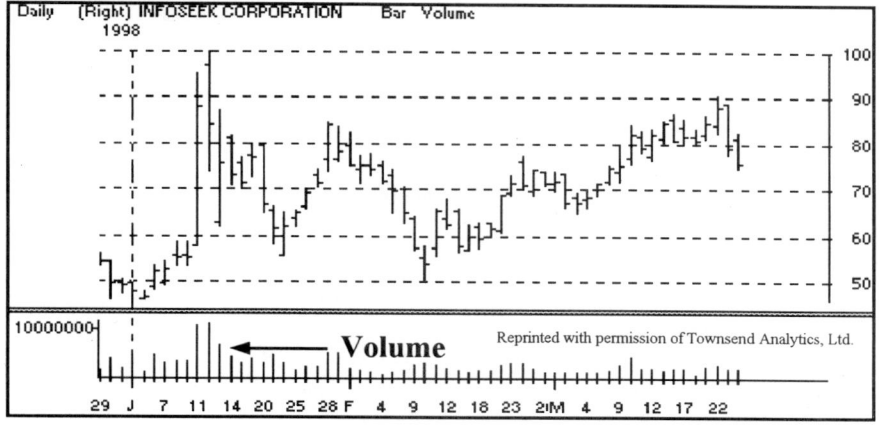

You may notice that the volume bars appear in a broader range and do not have as many intervals as the price bars do. What traders look for is a general level of volume. They will compare the volume of a given day to past volume numbers. It is very rare to find many intervals to scale the levels of the volume, so we need to look at the length of the volume bars relative to other volume bars from previous days. There is also a way to look at average daily volume over a period of time, such as 20 days. This number will be the total of 20 bars divided by 20 days in the period. Many times trader will use this number when comparing the latest volume bar. For instance, if a stock traded a total of 25,000,000 shares in the last 20 days it will also be true to say that the 20 day average volume for the stock is 1,250,000 a day. If the same stock traded 2,500,000 shares today then we can say that it traded twice its 20 day average volume. The thing to remember is that we first look at the price behavior of a stock. Next, we look at the volume for help in explaining certain patterns and changes in supply and demand, and we try to determine if we can see what the near term future and/or long term future for the stock is. However, before we elaborate on it any further, we first must learn about the overall trend a stock has and its different levels of price support and price resistance.

Identifying the Trend (Overall Price Direction) of a Stock

Stock prices go up and down continuously. The dynamics of these changes are determined by the rapid changes in supply and demand. When we use technical analysis to try and forecast future price changes for a stock, we must first determine the overall direction the stock is moving in. This is known as the **trend** of the stock. This is the simplest, yet most important element in chart reading. This should be the first thing to jump at you when you look at a bar price chart of a stock. There are 2 trends that should be easy to identify: an uptrend and a downtrend. An uptrend in a chart occurs when the price of a stock is trending (moving) higher over the studied period of time featured in the chart. A downtrend in a chart occurs when the price of a stock is trending lower over the studied period of time featured in the chart. The next illustration will show how to define the overall trend.

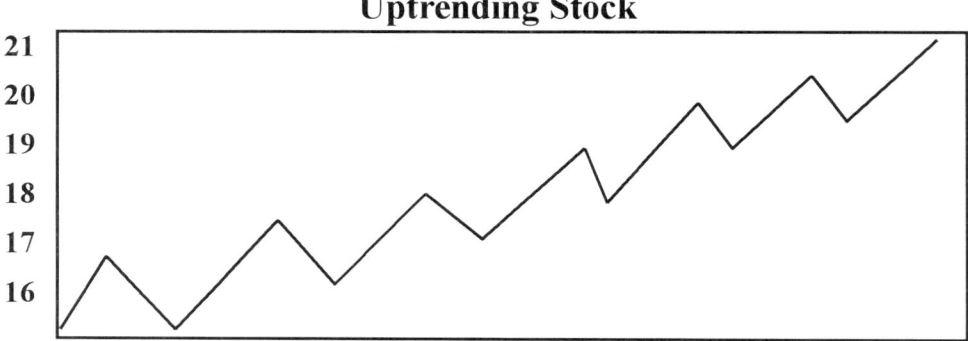

In this simple line chart we can see that the stock is moving to higher prices. The low price was around 16 and the latest price is around 21. Also note that we have rising bottoms and rising tops on the way up to 21. So the overall trend (price direction) for the period of time shown in this chart is up.

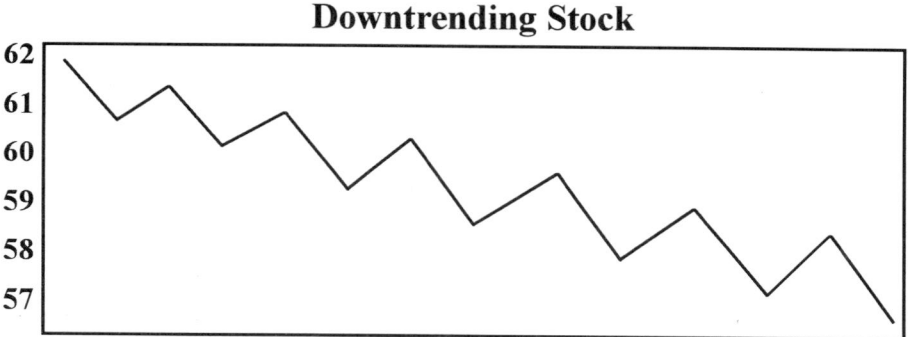

Downtrending Stock

In this simple line chart we can see that the stock is moving to lower prices. The high price was around 62 and the latest price is around 57. Also note that we have declining tops and declining bottoms on the way down from 62 to 57. So the overall trend (price direction) for the period of time shown in this chart is down. Let's look at some bar chart examples and identify the trend.

Dell 90-week Weekly Chart

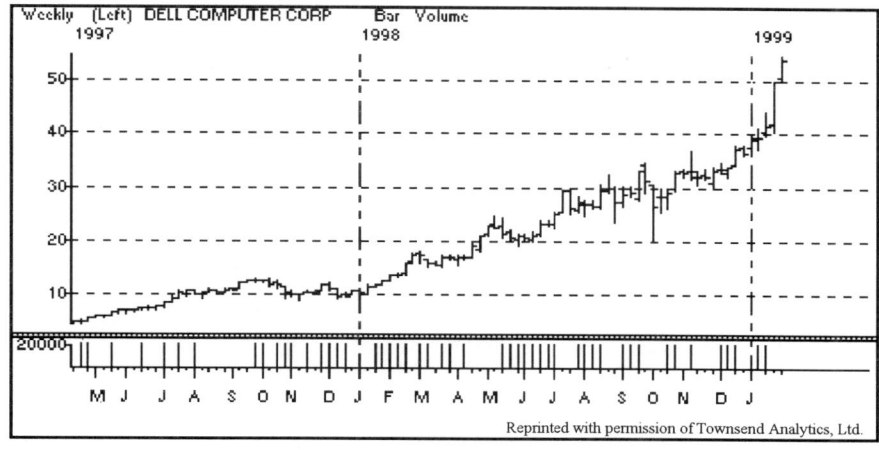

Cisco 80-day Daily Chart

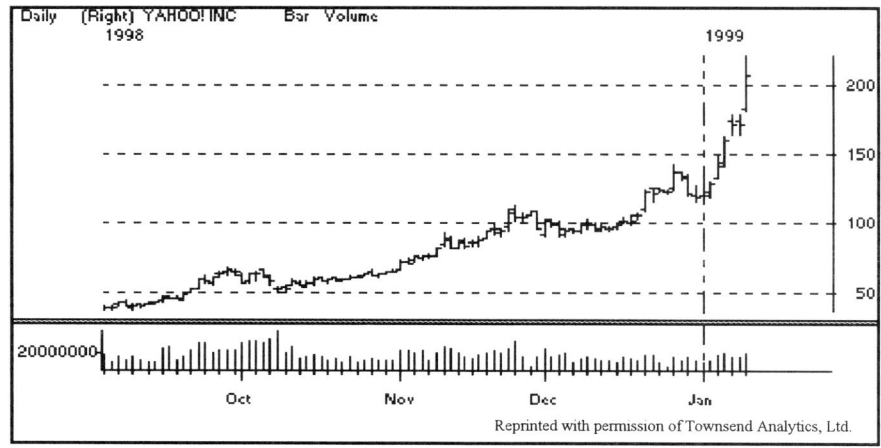

Yahoo 90-day Daily Chart

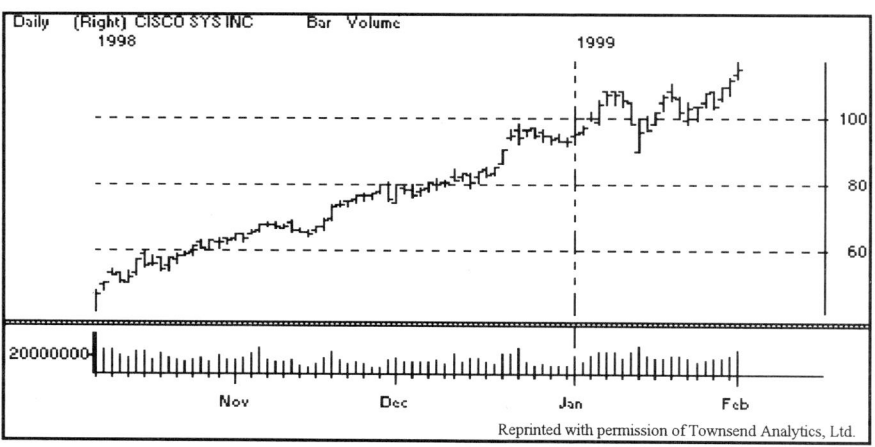

All of these charts are showing a clear uptrend. You should be able to recognize the ascending price direction immediately. You should also be able to identify the rising tops and rising bottoms as well.

Maverick 60-week Weekly Chart

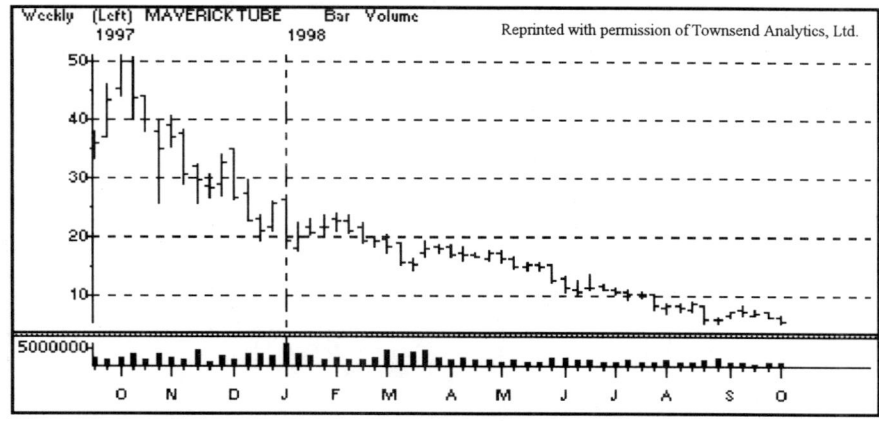

Pairgain Technologies 90-day Daily Chart

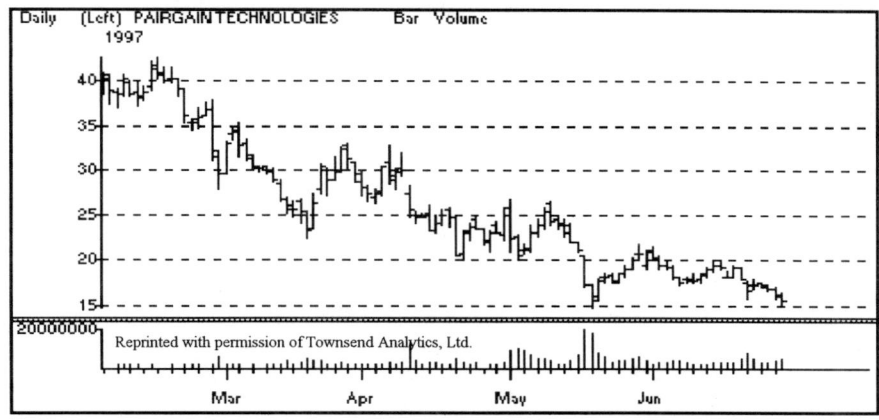

Marine Drilling 60-week Weekly Chart

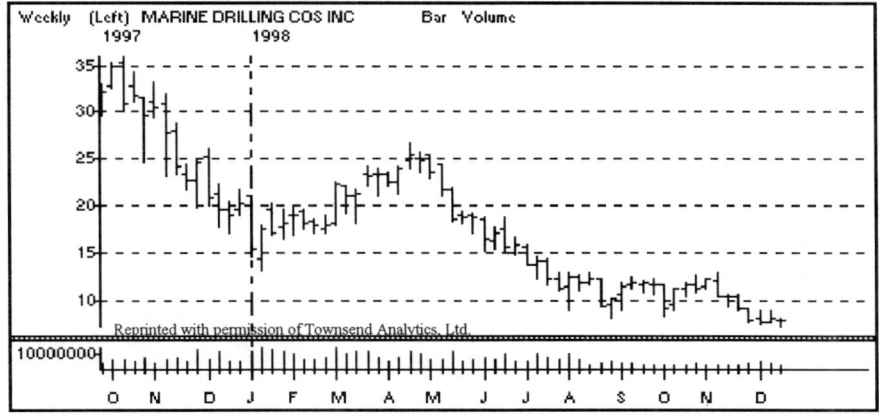

All of these charts are showing a clear downtrend. You should be able to recognize the descending price direction immediately. You should also be able to identify the declining tops and declining bottoms as well.

One more thing to keep in mind is that a stock can be in a short term downtrend while it is in a longer term uptrend and vice versa. It is important to study longer term trends and short term trends at the same time, as shown in the next example.

Microsoft 3 Month Daily Chart

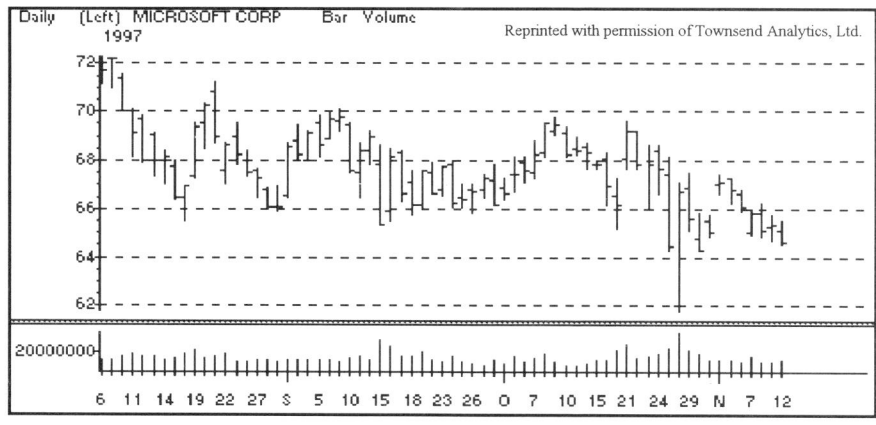

In this 3 month daily chart of Microsoft, we can see a decline in the price of the stock from 72 to as low as 62. The significant tops are declining and so are the significant bottoms. The short term (3 month) trend is down. However, it is important to look at a longer term chart to see a longer term trend.

Microsoft 60-week Weekly Chart

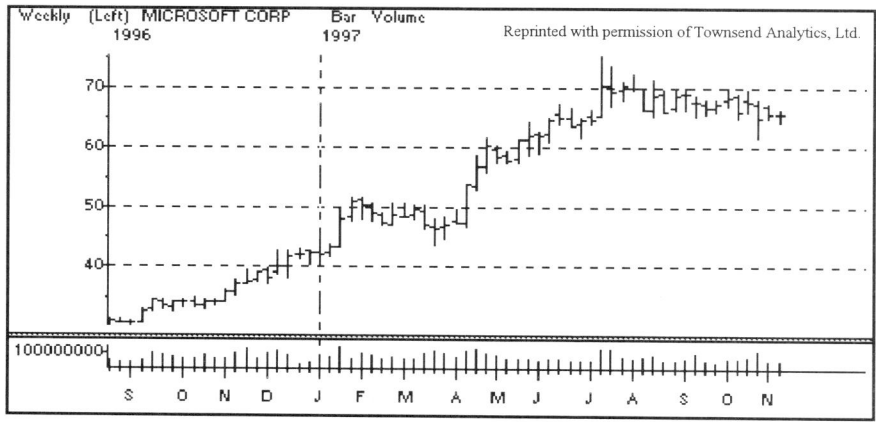

This 60-week, weekly chart shows that Microsoft is in a longer term uptrend. This is very important because you will need this information before you make a decision to trade the stock. The thing to remember is that the trend is your friend ... until it ends. It is important to practice chart reading, looking at longer term and shorter term charts. The first thing to determine is the long term trend followed by determining the short term trend. We will see how we incorporate the trend into our trading strategy later in the book. This brings us to our next task which is to look at price support levels and price resistance levels. We will explain the mechanics of drawing a trend line when we talk about support and resistance.

Support and Resistance

This is a key element in analyzing charts. The mechanism of price movement in a stock are attributed to supply and demand. How many shares are offered for sale versus how many shares are desired by buyers, at a given price, make the price go up and down. The fluctuations in the price of a stock are directly related to these factors and can be seen on a chart. The simplest way to look at it is by analyzing a one day price movement for a stock. We will use shares of XYZ in a hypothetical example. Let's say that XYZ opened its trading day at $102 a share. This says that the first trade of the day for XYZ was executed at $102 a share. During the morning, there were more sellers than buyers and the stock went down to $100 a share. This was the low price of the day XYZ traded at. At this point, more buyers were interested in purchasing the stock as the price was very attractive to them, so the quantity in demand was greater than the quantity in supply, causing XYZ shares to go up all the way to $105 a share. This was the highest price XYZ traded at. The scales change again and quantity supplied was greater than quantity demanded and sellers pushed the price of XYZ down to $103 where it closed the trading session. Let's chart this data and analyze it further.

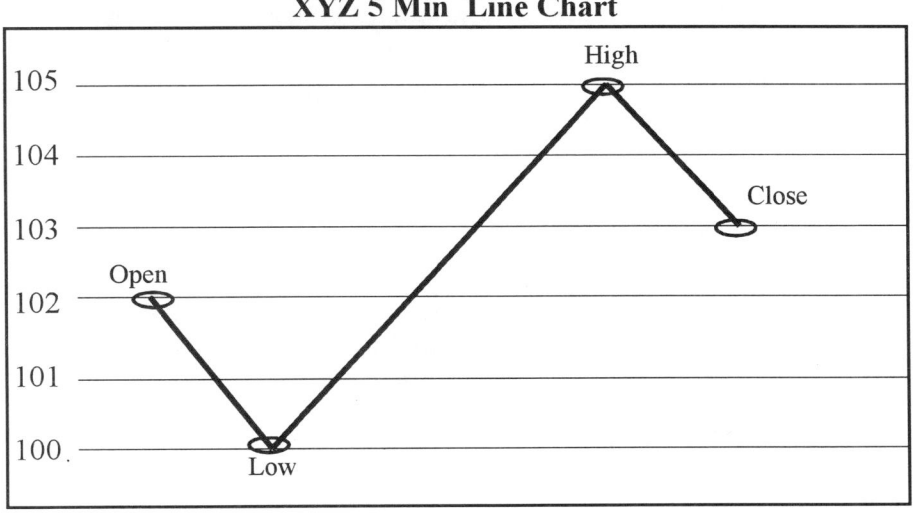

We opened trading at $102. Normally, this means that at the open of trading, that very first second, there was just as much interest from buyers to buy XYZ at 102 as there was from sellers willing to sell at $102. This, of course, changed and there were more traders willing to sell XYZ shares than there were traders willing to buy it. This caused the price of the stock to decline all the way to $100 a share. At this point, the momentum of the stock shifted. In other words, there was more quantity in demand than there was in supply and the stock started trading higher. This low point of the trading range where the momentum turned around is called a **support** level. In other words, at $100 a share there are more shares in demand than share-holders are willing to sell. This is why the stock held the price of $100 a share and did not trade any lower. So the support level indicates a price level where the quantity in demand is greater than the quantity in supply. We call it support because investors supported the price of a stock at that point and prevented it from going lower. Let's go back to our example and look at the run up of the price from $100 a share to $105 a share. After finding a bottom (support) at $100 a share, there was more interest in buying XYZ shares than there was of selling it. This caused the price of the stock to go all the way up to $105 where it made the high point of the trading range for the day. At this point, the momentum shifted over again as the scales changed. There were more shares offered for sale by traders than other traders were interested in buying, and this, of course, caused the price of the stock to decline. In other words, XYZ stock was being bought by enthusiastic traders all the way up to $105. When the stock hit $105, there were more shares being offered by sellers than buyers wanted to buy, so the stock turned around at $105 a share. This is called the **resistance** level. It is called resistance because sellers of the stock are preventing the stock from moving higher, so this excess quantity in supply causes resistance for the stock to go higher in price. Indeed, the greater quantity in supply caused the price of the stock to decline all the way down to $103 where the stock last traded before the close of the trading day. When we look at this simple, one session of trading example, we know two things going into the next day of trading:

1. XYZ has support at $100 a share.
2. XYZ has resistance at $105 a share.

We look at support and resistance levels the same way no matter how long a period of time they cover. Let's look at more examples:

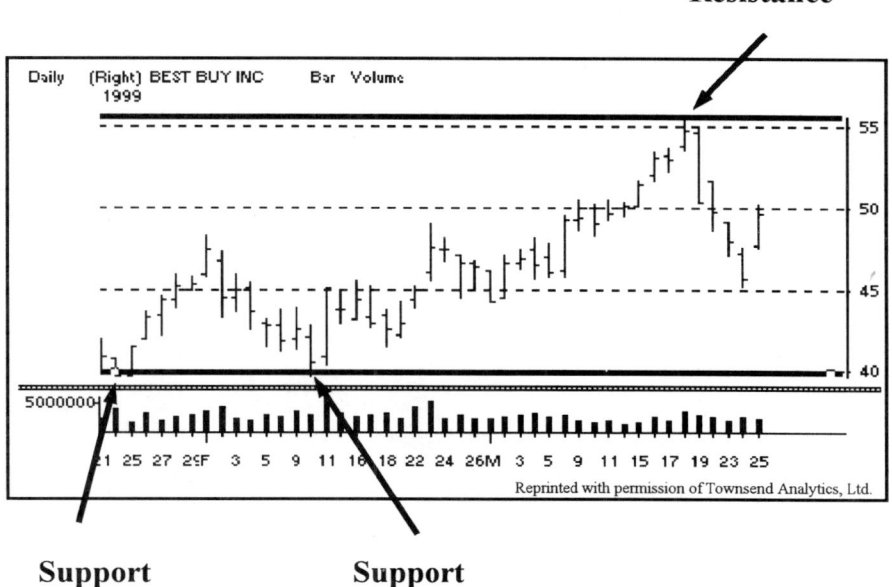

Best Buy has a support level at around $40 a share, and the price of the stock held (was supported) twice at $40, as seen in the chart. The stock ran up from 40 to 55, where it turned around. The $55 a share level represents the current resistance for the stock.

It is important to remember the following: Support represents a price level where the quantity demanded is higher than the quantity supplied because the majority of stock traders feel that the stock will move higher from the price the stock is currently trading at. Resistance represents a price level at which the quantity in supply is greater than the quantity in demand because the majority of stock traders feel that the price of the stock will decline and move lower than the price it is trading at. However, stock traders' and investors' psychology changes rapidly with time. This causes penetration through the resistance and support levels which are significant signals to the change of supply and demand. These changes will trigger buy and sell signals for both short term and long term traders. We will study these changes in later examples but first we need to learn a few more things about support and resistance.

As seen in the previous examples, the absolute high price point a stock traded at represents resistance, and the absolute low price point a stock traded at represents support. These are also known as the primary resistance and support levels. It is also important to study secondary technical support and resistance levels and psychological support and resistance levels.

In the next few examples, we will look at such support and resistance levels. When we look at a chart, we first try to identify the trend. Next, we look for primary support and resistance price levels followed by secondary support and resistance levels. Let's look at the chart below:

Cisco Systems 100-Day, Daily Chart

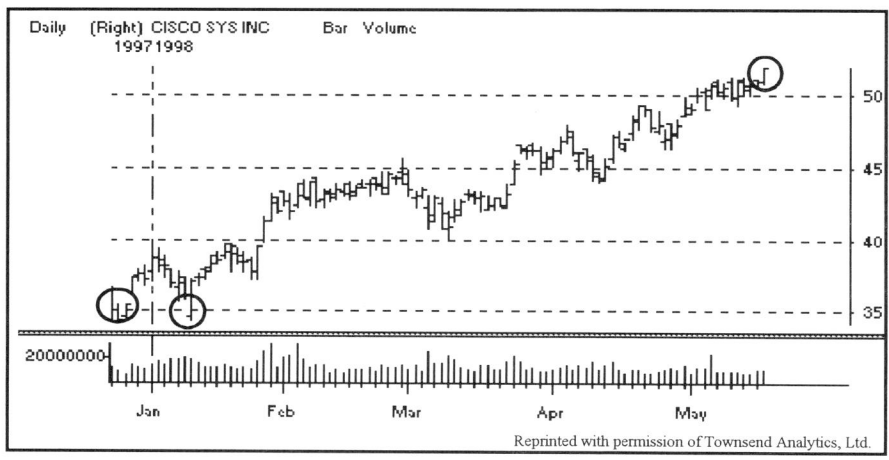

1. Identify the trend. The stock is rising in price as the bottoms are rising and the tops are rising as well; consequently, it is in an uptrend.
2. Primary support level is around 34, and primary resistance is around 53 represented by the circles on the chart (absolute top and bottoms).
3. Now we look for secondary support and resistance.

When we have an uptrend like this example, and a stock has just pulled back from the high it made recently, we can't really find secondary resistance, so resistance remains at 53. We can however find levels of secondary support in this chart. We know that the primary support is at 34, however, Cisco has traded all the way up to 53 and if it was to pull back here, where could we expect it to go. The question is: "At what price will Cisco be attractive to buyers, which will cause the stock price to increase again?" Believe it or not, these levels will be found at past resistance levels.

Resistance becomes support: Once a stock has managed to **successfully** break through a resistance level and go up in price, that resistance level becomes support. The logic is that the tables have turned around as more buyers stepped in and took the resistance level out. If prices were to decline back to that point, then interest from buyers should still be there. Let's look at the same chart again and see how resistance became support.

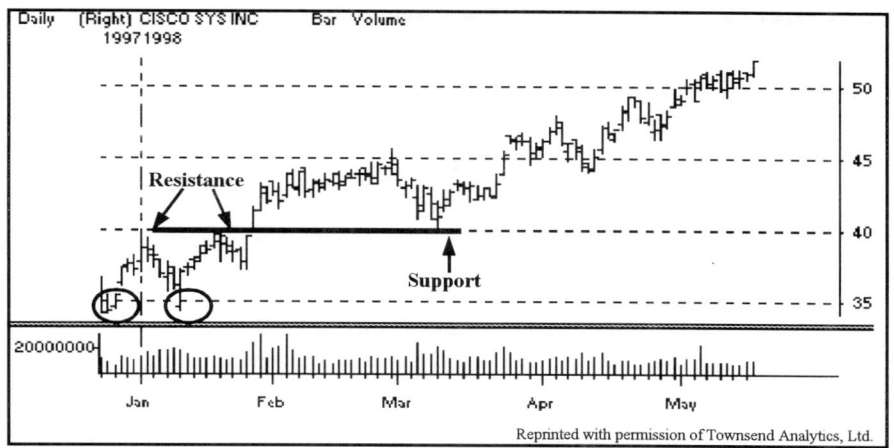

Look at the chart from left to right. In January, Cisco Systems traded up from 34 to 40 where it met resistance. It then turned around and traded down to 34 where the primary support (marked by the circles on the chart) held. Next, Cisco traded back up to 40 again, where it met resistance for the second time. The 40 level was not penetrated and the stock turned down again. On the third attempt, in late January, Cisco succeeded in penetrating through the resistance and traded over 40 for the first time and climbed up to 45+. In March, Cisco pulled back in price and guess at which price it held and never looked back again …. If you said 40, you got it right. This example illustrates how the previous resistance at 40, once successfully penetrated, became support later in the future. Notice that it took Cisco three attempts to get through 40 which means that this price level presented a strong resistance level for Cisco, and that strong resistance became strong support in March as Cisco did not go lower than 40. In fact, in the following 11 months, Cisco almost tripled in price.

This is how this opportunity would have presented itself before it actually took place:

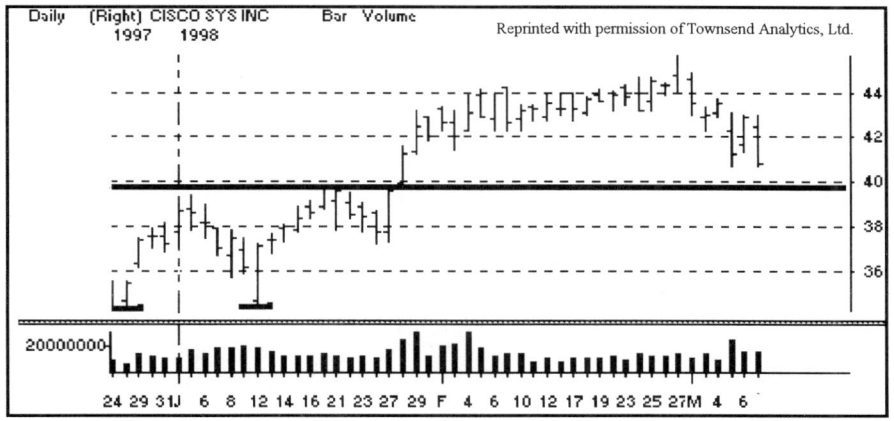

1. Stock is in an uptrend.
2. Primary support is at 34, primary resistance is at 45 1/4.
3. Secondary support is at 40

Strategy: Buy at 40 1/8. Great play! Hindsight is always 20-20. It is important to recognize secondary support and resistance levels.

Trendlines

We talked about uptrending stocks and downtrending stocks. A trendline is a straight line drawn below the bottoms in a stock that is rising in prices, or over the tops in a stock that is declining in prices as shown in the following examples.

Cisco Systems 90-Day, Daily Chart

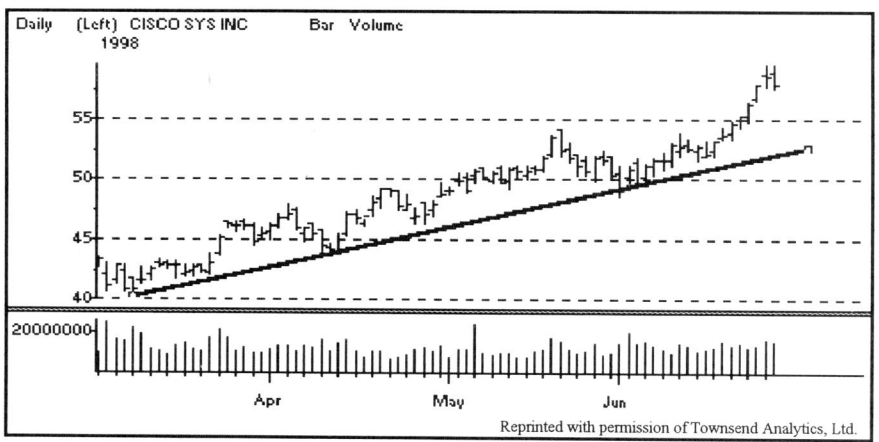

Cisco Systems is moving up in price, the bottoms and tops are rising. We draw a straight line under the significant bottoms to get the trend line. This is important in case a stock breaks through its trend line as it might signal a change in the trend.

Pairgain Technology 60-Day, Daily Chart

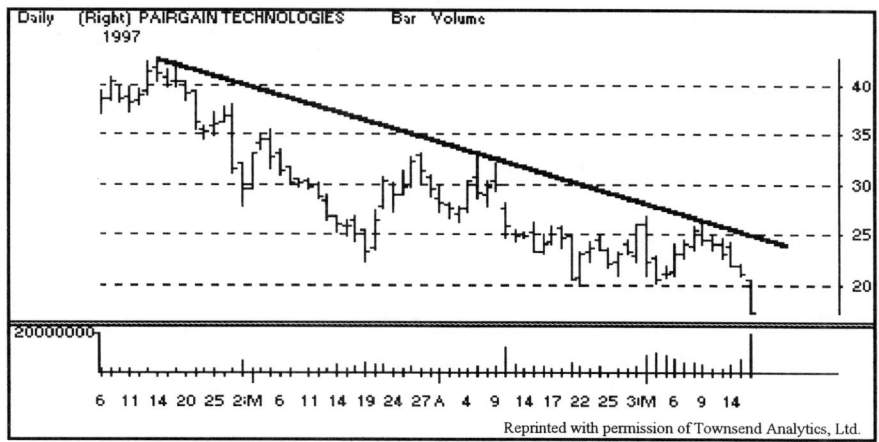

Pairgain Technology is declining in price. The tops are declining and so are the bottoms. We draw a straight line over the tops. This is how we get the trendline for a stock in a downtrend.

In February of 1997, Pairgain started a major downtrend. The chart above shows the beginning of the trend. In the next example, we will look at a longer term chart of Pairgain Technology. Note: The initial downtrend displayed in the 60-day chart is identified as the first downtrend in the longer term chart below.

Pairgain Technology Case Study

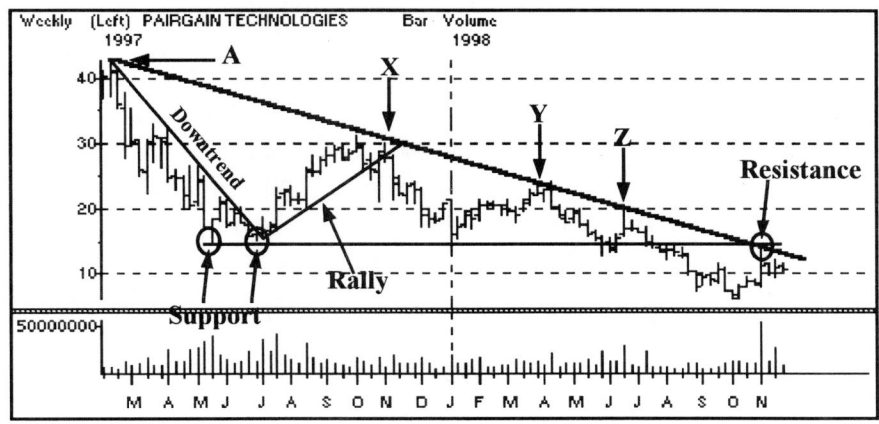

If we read the following chart from left to right starting at the high price point (A), around 42, we can see that the stock has declined in price to about 15. At this level, the stock found support and bounced back up to 22. However, it still remained in a downtrend and went back down to test support at 15 again. The trendline drawn over the tops was resistance for the stock. If you look at the move down from 42 to 15, you can see that every time the stock tried to rally back up, it turned around at the trendline and went back lower, all the way to the second support circle at 15.

Once the support level held for the second time, at 15 or so, and the stock turned around and started a rally. The rally ended at point X and the stock declined in prices again.

Adjusting the trendline: Our original trendline shown in the previous chart and in the chart above (labeled downtrend) was successfully penetrated and the stock went on a short term uptrend. However, the overall trend remains down as we draw a straight line over the tops. The rally attempt topped at point X. Our new trendline will be a straight line going through points A and X. This is the new adjusted trendline.

Once we have adjusted the trendline, we can see how it became resistance for every rally attempt. Look at the Y and Z points on the chart, they fall exactly on the same trendline drawn through points A and X. **In a downtrending stock, the trendline is another resistance point** to consider.

Please note that the support levels, indicated by the two circles and the horizontal line, were successfully penetrated. This happened when the stock turned around at point Z and went down to 8 or so. On the last rally attempt from 6 to 15 the stock turned around at previous support levels. **Support, once successfully penetrated, became Resistance.**

If we look back at the two support circles, we can also see that Pairgain stock tried to penetrate below 15 twice. Both times, buyers were able to hold the stock price and a short term rally occurred. In this case, the $15 support level was tested again and held up successfully. The stock managed to break out of the downtrend it was in and rally. This will qualify for a short term double bottom pattern which will be discussed later in this book.

Cisco Systems Case Study

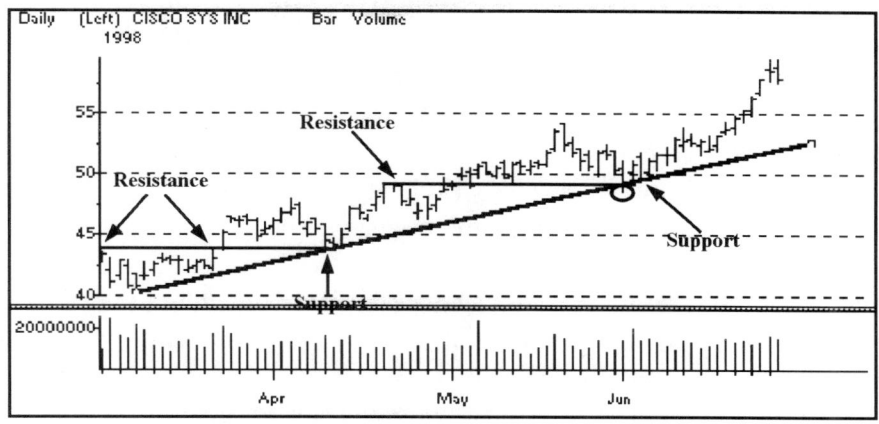

Reprinted with permission of Townsend Analytics, Ltd.

Let's look at Cisco Systems again and study the chart in more detail. Looking at the chart from left to right we see an uptrending stock. We drew a trendline through the bottoms.

In an uptrending stock, the trendline is another support point to be considered.

The 2 high points which were resistance for Cisco Systems became support once they were penetrated successfully, as shown by the horizontal lines.

If you examine the above chart carefully you can see that the trend line was penetrated (marked by the circle on the chart). However, it was not penetrated successfully and the trendline kept supporting the stock. I have chosen this example, because it illustrates that the trendlines are not perfectly straight and can be penetrated without causing a change in the direction of a stock. It is important to remember the difference between successful penetration and unsuccessful penetration. In hindsight, the small unsuccessful penetration marked by the circle was actually a buying opportunity.

Moving Averages

Moving averages are technical indicators that help us to identify both short term and long term direction (trend) of a stock. Many times they also represent support and resistance levels. A moving average is the average price of a security over a certain period of time. There are different moving averages that can be added as a technical study (indicator) to a chart. Most of which will vary in the time period in which the prices will be averaged over.

Simple moving average: This average is calculated by adding the stock prices for the period of time and dividing it by the period of time. For example, if we wanted to know the average price a stock was trading in the last 5 days, we would add the prices of the 5 days and divide them by 5.
Example: XYZ closed at 56 on Monday, 58 on Tuesday, 59 on Wednesday, 58 on Thursday and 61 on Friday. The average closing price for the five days will be calculated as so.
(56+58+59+58+61)/5
292/5=58.4
The average price is 58.4. You do not have to worry about calculating the average prices as most charting programs will do it for you. The important thing is to understand what that number stands for. Let's look at the chart below for an example of a simple moving average.

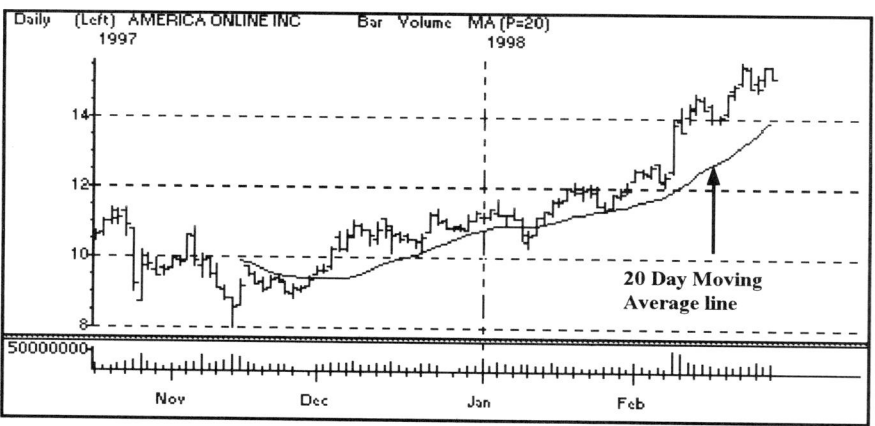

Reprinted with permission of Townsend Analytics, Ltd.

We have added a 20-day simple moving average to an America Online chart. The moving average appears as a line on the chart and indicates what the average price over the last 20 days was for America Online for each given day. You might have noticed that the moving average line is not present for the first 19 price bars on the chart (on the left side.) The reason for that is we need 20 days of price data to add in a 20-day moving average, so only on the

20th day, we will have enough data to plot in a 20-day moving average.

The simple 20-day moving average we used in the previous example averages the closing prices only. Many charting programs enable users to change the parameters of the moving averages. I will include a few examples of these parameter changes and show how they affect the moving average line.

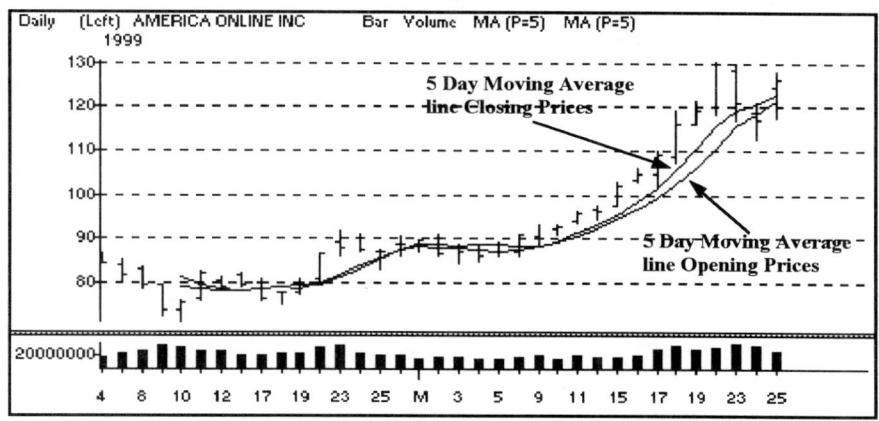

Reprinted with permission of Townsend Analytics, Ltd.

This example shows two 5-day moving averages, one is calculating the closing prices while the other is calculating the opening prices. Notice that the lines are connecting different price points. Many charting programs will allow you to use mid point, high price, low price, and day average price as parameters for moving averages. The most commonly used moving average calculates closing prices. This is the one that I use exclusively.

Moving Average is often abbreviated and is referred to as the **MA**. So a 20-day moving average is also called a 20-day MA.

Weighted Moving Average: Just like a simple moving average, a weighted moving average is averaging prices over a period of time. However, many times a simple moving average will lag in sending out buy/sell signals, so technicians have created the weighted moving average. This moving average weights the data in favor of the most recent periods.

Exponential Moving Average: This is another form of weighted moving average. This MA is favored by many technicians because it does not lag as much in creating buy and sell signals. It is important to remember that all moving averages are used with other indicators to confirm buy and sell signals.

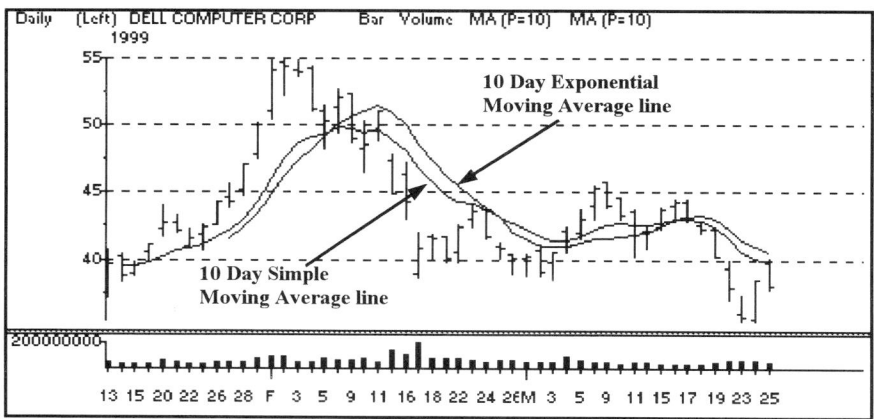

Reprinted with permission of Townsend Analytics, Ltd.

The chart above shows the different lines created by plotting a 10-day Exponential MA and a 10-day Simple MA. Although, both moving averages cover the same period of time, 10 days, and average the same closing price data, they differ from each other.

Using Moving Averages in Trading

The moving averages show the direction a stock moves in. There are 2 significant moving averages: a 50-day MA (10-week MA) and 200-day MA (40-week MA.) I also use a 10-day MA and a 20-day MA for short term trading. In general, **when a shorter term MA crosses over a longer term MA to the upside, and both slopes go up, it is a bullish signal** (the value of the shorter MA is greater than the longer MA). **When a longer term MA crosses over a shorter term MA to the upside, and both slopes go down, it is a bearish signal** (the value of the long term MA is greater than the value of the short term MA). It is also important to use other indicators to confirm these signals.

Buying a stock in its correction phase can occur at the 50-day MA and at the 200-day MA. We will look at some examples for this scenario. The changes in the price of a stock are attributed to supply and demand. Therefore, when I look at a 50-day moving average, it represents the average price investors were taking positions in a stock over the last 50 days. I look for a stock that is in a long term uptrend. I would like this stock to have come down in price from the high and trade at or near the 50 day MA. Many professional traders and institutional traders monitor for favorable securities that are approaching their 50-day or 200-day moving average. Many of them will become aggressive buyers at those levels.

Yahoo 100-day Daily Chart

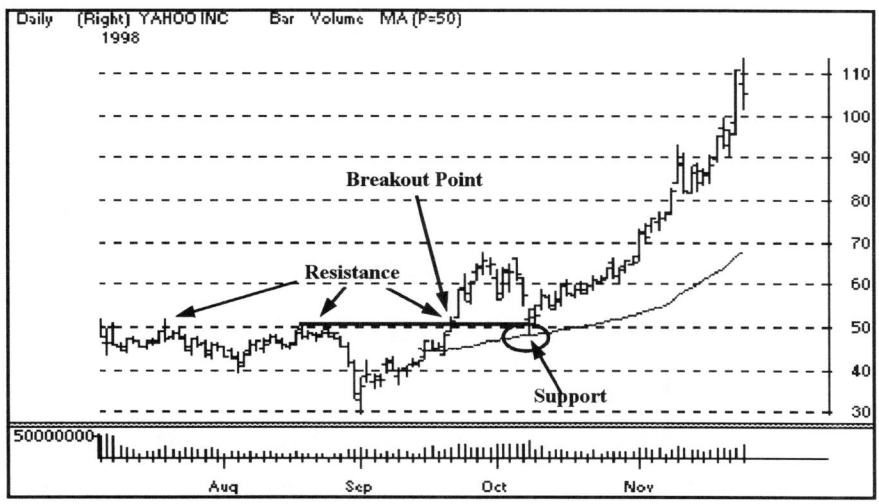

Reprinted with permission of Townsend Analytics, Ltd.

This is one of my favorite examples of how imperfect trendlines, support lines, and resistance lines are. However, they are great indicators and can be used successfully. If you take a close look at the Yahoo chart you can see that $50 was the resistance level on 3 different occasions. The stock finally broke out to the upside. It then corrected all the way down to $50, where the previous resistance was. In this case, the $50 level did not hold and the stock went as low as $48 1/2. Look at the area circled on the chart. This is where the 50-day moving average came to play and helped in supporting the stock. In fact, the stock closed over $52 that day and never looked back.

Cisco Systems 120-day Daily Chart

Cisco Systems represents the same buying opportunity repeatedly at the 50-day MA. In fact, it is a great price level for the long term cost averaging approach if you are bullish on Cisco. As you can see in the chart, the price did not touch the 50-day MA, but it did come close to it a couple of times. Buying Cisco Systems every time it came close to its 50-day MA would have been profitable in this case.

I have bought stocks many times right at the 50-day moving average. In fact, I did so three days ago for a profitable trade. Here it is:

Best Buy 100-day, Daily Chart

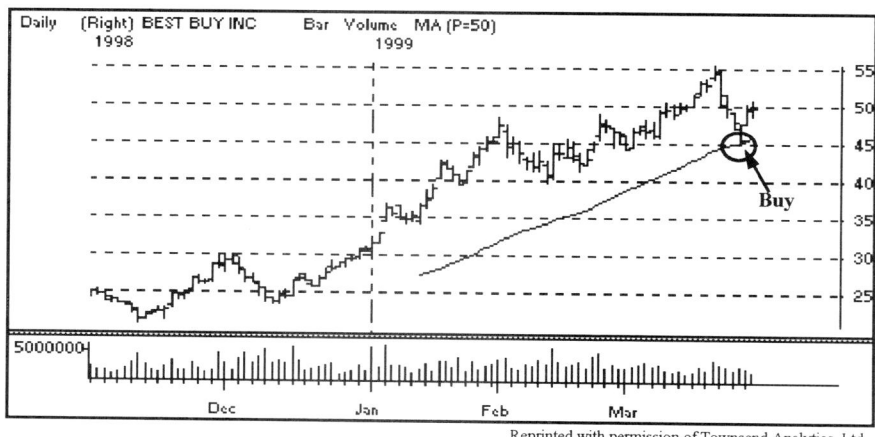

I entered Best Buy at 45 3/4 as it came down from 55 11/16 and hit the 50-day MA. The trade was good for 4 3/4 points in one day, 10%+.

I also remember another incident when I bought Best Buy at the 50-day MA.

Best Buy 100-day, Daily Chart

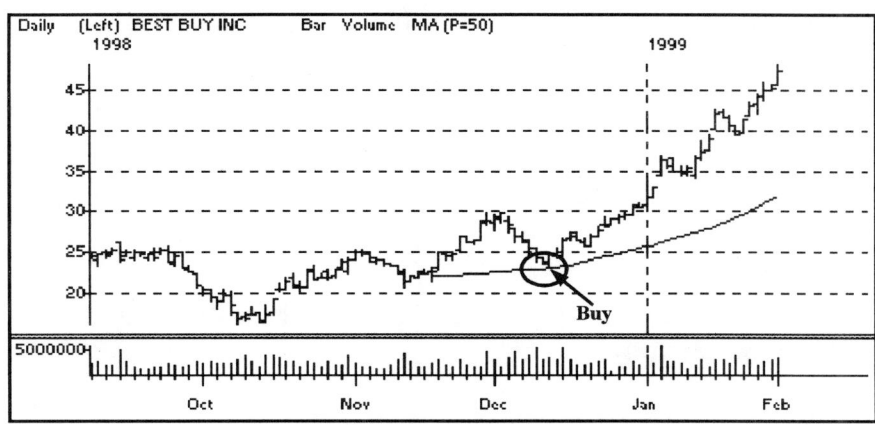

Reprinted with permission of Townsend Analytics, Ltd.

This was another successful trade buying Best Buy at the 50-day MA. In both cases Best Buy pulled back 20% off the all time high in a short period of time and hit its 50-day MA, where it turned back up.

These were all examples of support when an uptrending stock hit its 50-day moving average. If a stock is in a downtrend, the 50-day MA can be resistance for it and a good point to sell your long position or even take a short position in such a stock. Many traders choose to use a combination of moving averages that vary in the periods of time they cover. One reason is that volatility can cause sharp price movements and the longer term moving averages will lag at times. You need to experiment with each stock and see which average period works the best. I remember trading Pairgain Technology and shorting it successfully every time the stock moved above its 20-day moving average. This was true for a 3 month period of time. After that the stock declined so much that it was no bargain to short it anymore at those levels.

Breakouts

At this point, we have learned that supply and demand are the driving force behind stock prices. Supply and demand are directly related to investors' expectations and psychology. As these expectations change, a change in supply and demand will shortly follow. We have learned to recognize a trend of a stock and draw a trendline. We also learned what primary and secondary support and resistance levels are and how support can become resistance or resistance become support. It is important to master these elements of chart reading as they are the building blocks for successful chart interpretation.

Support and resistance levels paint the battle between bulls and bears as reflected by the overall expectations investors have. A successful penetration of resistance levels occurs when investors' expectations for investment returns rise. This is considered a **major change** in the expectations (outlook) for future price appreciation and it generates a strong buy signal. A successful penetration through support levels occur when investors' expectation (outlook) for future price appreciation decline and they want out of their position. This situation generates a strong sell signal.

A bull breakout occurs when a stock penetrates a previous resistance level successfully.

A bear breakdown occurs when a stock penetrates through its previous support level successfully.

It is also important to understand the psychology behind bull and bear breakouts because they represent a paradox to the buy-low sell-high philosophy. When I look to buy a stock, I first want to know that there is demand for it out there, because more likely than not, if demand is present, the stock will increase in price. If this is the case, then I have 2 choices. Buy the stock as it is going up or wait for a correction (pull back in price) which might never occur. I think this is a very important segment in successful trading, so I will include many examples to illustrate how buying a stock when it breaks out to the upside, or short selling it when it breaks through support to the downside, can be very profitable.

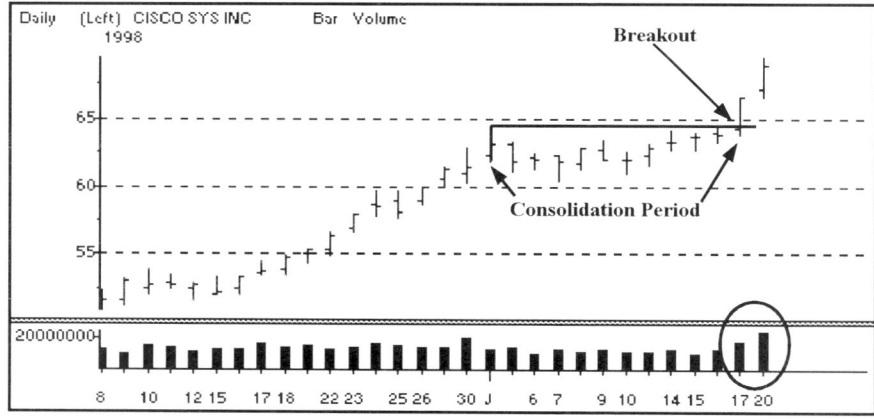

Reprinted with permission of Townsend Analytics, Ltd.

The chart above shows how Cisco Systems is breaking out through its previous resistance level, after a 2-week consolidation period, on better than average daily volume. This is a great example of a high percentage long play. These three key elements must be present in a high percentage breakout play:

Successful **penetration of resistance** after a **consolidation period** on **greater than average daily volume**.

Buy Stocks as They Make New Highs After Consolidation

What happened to buy-low sell-high? Just remember this; the new high of today could very well be the 52-week low a year from now. It is often the hardest thing to explain as many experts call it the paradox of the stock market. Let's take a closer look at it. When you purchase almost anything in real life, you will get exactly what you paid for it. Hence, when you buy a stock that is making new highs, you are buying something with great demand, and it will, more likely than not, appreciate in price. Think of it this way, if a stock is going to have a great run, it must make new highs, often enough, all the way to the eventual top. Once you research a company and find it to be fundamentally strong, in a bull market, then buying that stock when it makes a new high, after a reasonable consolidation, is like a "free lunch," if there is one on Wall Street. This breakout will be the next support level for your stock. Please look at the following patterns which illustrate buying stocks as they make new highs.

Example 1

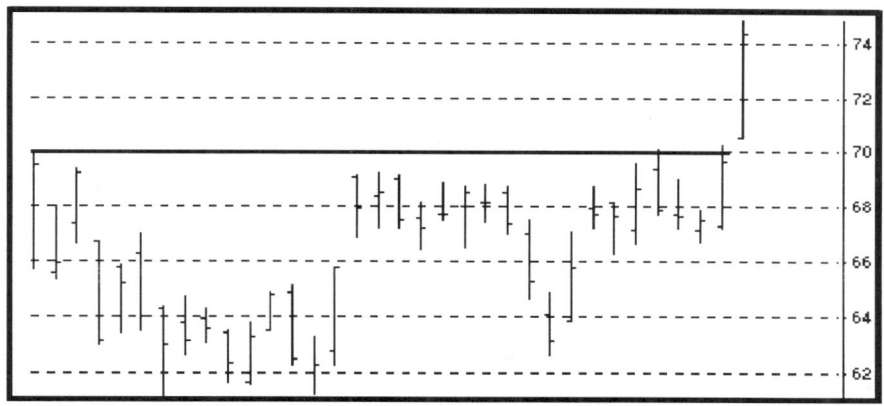

Reprinted with permission of Townsend Analytics, Ltd.

Example 1 is showing a security that made a new high at $70 a share or so (at the left end of the chart) and consolidated for 33 trading days. The horizontal line drawn over the top of the $70 price shows the resistance level. It then penetrated through the previous resistance and is generating a strong buy signal.

Result of Example 1

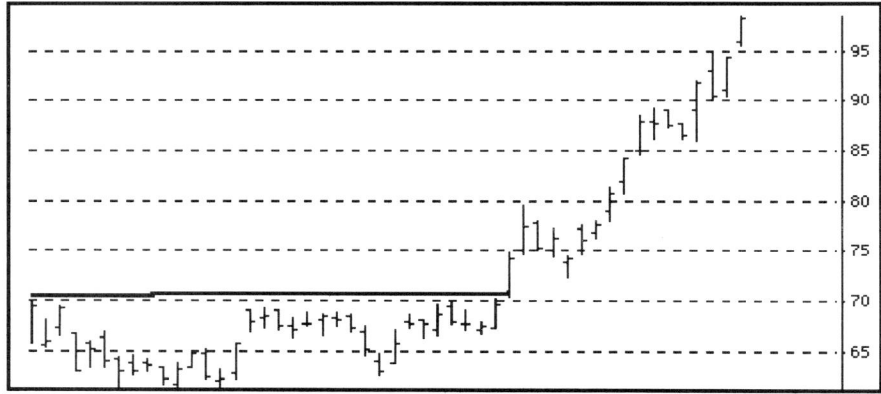

In this case, the stock went up to $98 a share in 17 trading days. This is a possible return of 39% in 3 weeks. In a bull market buy stocks as they make a new high after a 20+ day consolidation period. Remember this pattern. It is the easiest, most profitable trade you can make.

Example 2

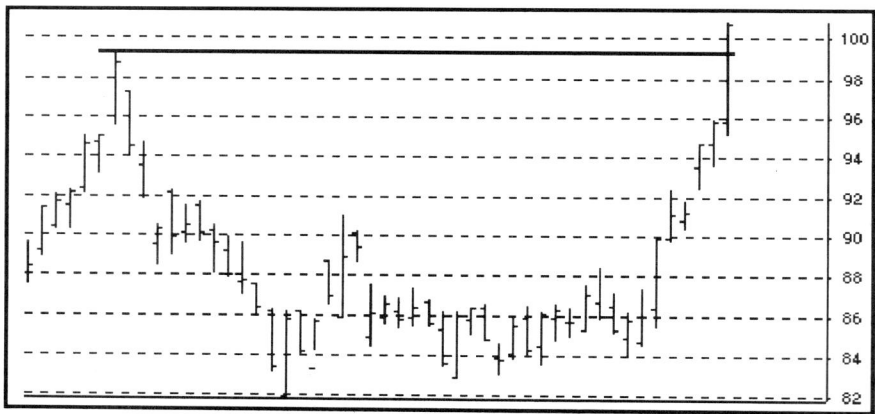

Example 2 is showing a security that made a new high at $97 a share (at the left end of the chart) and consolidated for 42 trading days. The horizontal line drawn over the top of the $97 price shows the resistance level.

Result of Example 2

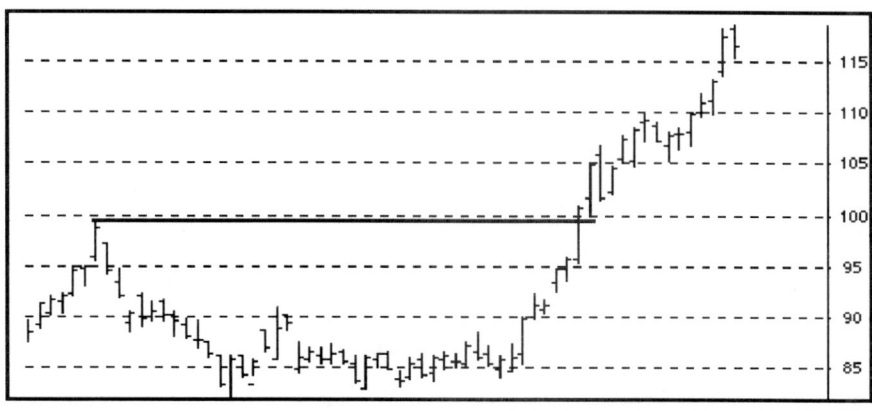

Reprinted with permission of Townsend Analytics, Ltd.

In this case, the stock went up to 119 in 14 trading days, a possible return of 20% in 3 weeks.

Example 3

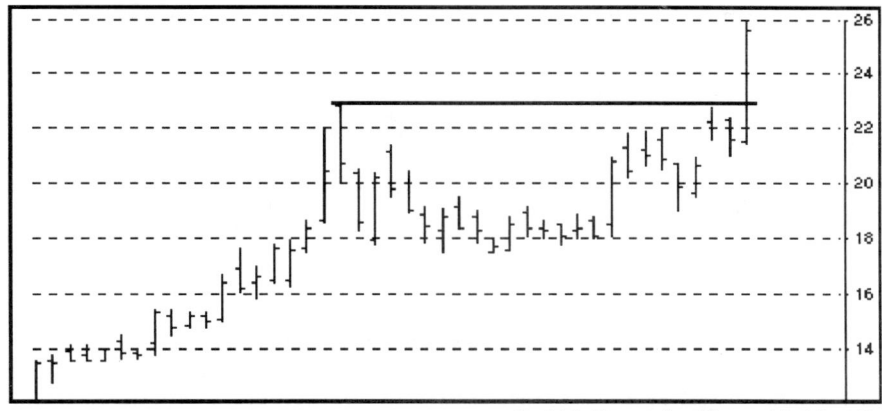

Reprinted with permission of Townsend Analytics, Ltd.

Example 3 is showing a security that made a new high at $23 a share (at the left end of the chart) and consolidated for 24 trading days. The horizontal line drawn over the top of the $23 price shows the resistance level.

Result of Example 3

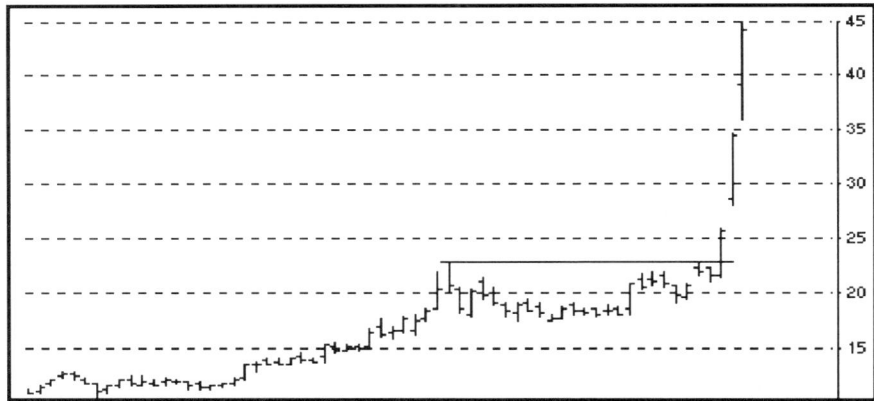

In this chart, the stock went up to 45 in three trading days, a possible return of 94% in three days. Not too bad for three days. Memorize these patterns, they are the easiest ones to find and the possible short term returns are rewarding.

Example 4

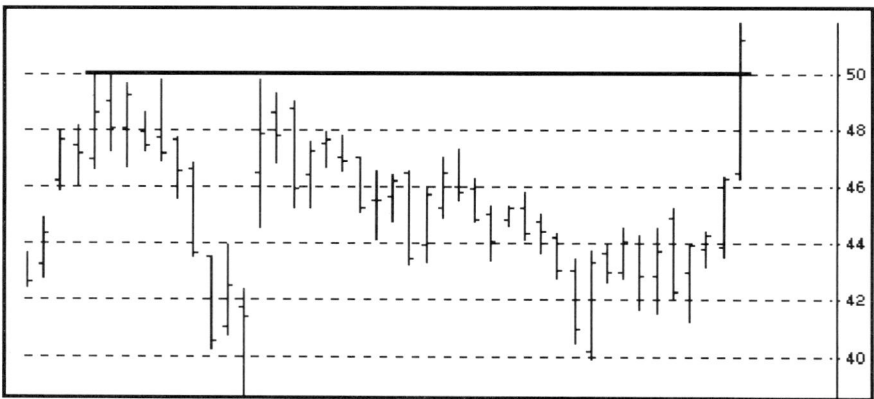

Example 4 is showing a security that made a new high at $50 a share (at the left end of the chart) and consolidated for 38 trading days. The horizontal line drawn over the top the $50 price shows the resistance level.

Result of Example 4

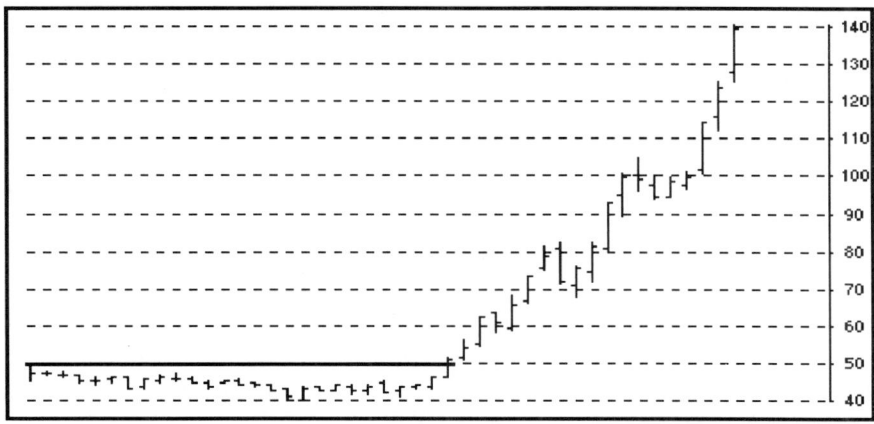

Reprinted with permission of Townsend Analytics, Ltd.

In this case, the stock went up to 140 in 18 trading days, a possible return of 178% in 18 days. Memorize these patterns, they are the easiest ones to find and the possible short term returns are rewarding. This one was a huge winner.

All of these examples show a stock breakout through its previous resistance levels to make new, all time, highs. It is important to have a consolidation period prior to the big move and we would like to see better than average daily volume, when the stock breaks out. These patterns generate great candidates both for a short term, and a long term hold. The significance of these breakouts is the fact that there is a **CHANGE** in supply and demand caused by the various changes in expectations investors have, for the underlying issue. In many cases, a breakout to a new all time high, after a long (6 weeks or longer) consolidation, can be a beginning of a new leg up for a stock that can last 3-6 months or even years. I have played many of these breakouts successfully in my trading years. The only thing I would have done different, if I could go back in time, is to hold some of the stocks I was in for a longer (much longer) period of time.

The easiest trading opportunity exists in stocks that are making new highs after consolidation, because it is easy to identify the chart pattern. The second easiest pattern to recognize is stocks that are making a new low after consolidation. These are to be considered as a sell. Let's look at some examples.

MRV Communications Daily Chart

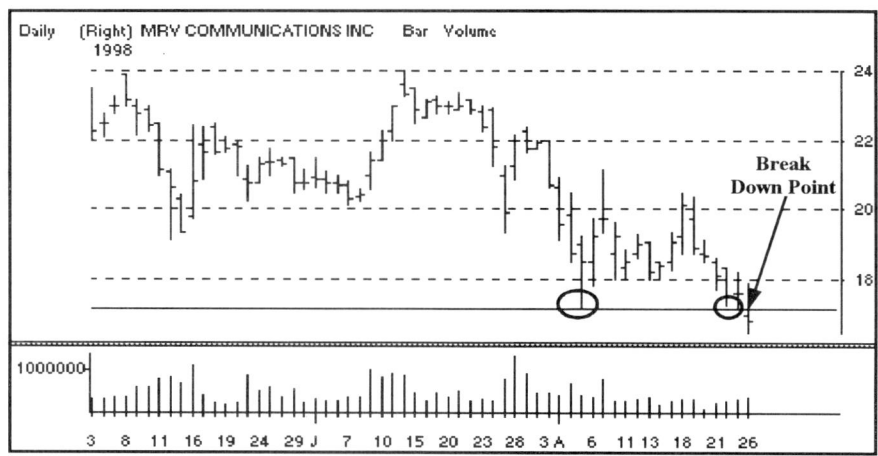

This chart shows how MRV Communications broke down to new lows. Please note that the support level held the prior two trading sessions and was finally penetrated through. This generated a strong sell signal. Let's look at the next chart to see what happened following the break down. **A breakdown is penetration of a stock price through its support level,** as it is **breaking down through support**.

MRV Communications Daily Chart

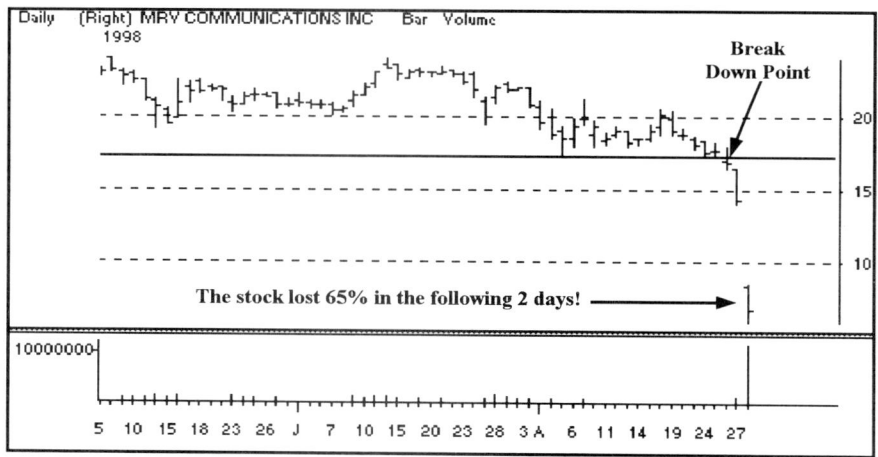

If you acted on the sell signal in this case you would have profited (or prevented a huge loss.) Bear breakdowns are just as significant as bull breakouts because they also show change in supply and demand caused by changes in investors' expectations. In this case it is safe to say that sellers were rushing to sell out their positions, but buyers were scarce.

A breakdown through support level is a sell signal as shown in the following charts.

Trico Marine Weekly Chart

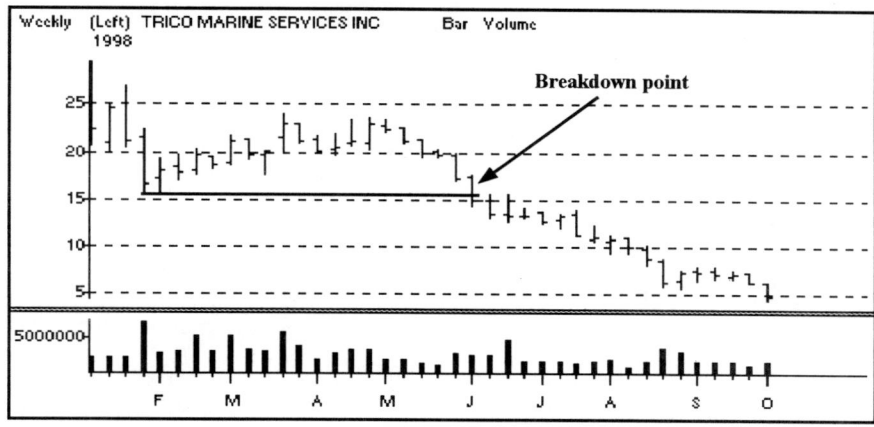

Reprinted with permission of Townsend Analytics, Ltd.

Ascend Communications Daily Chart

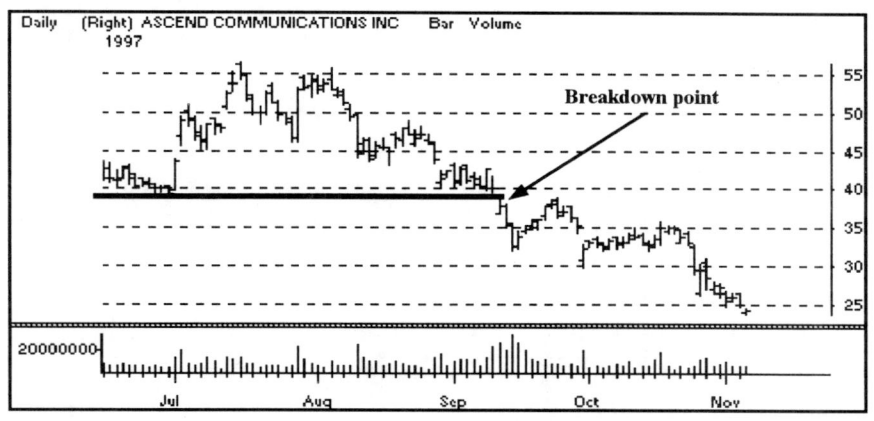

Reprinted with permission of Townsend Analytics, Ltd.

3 COM Daily Chart

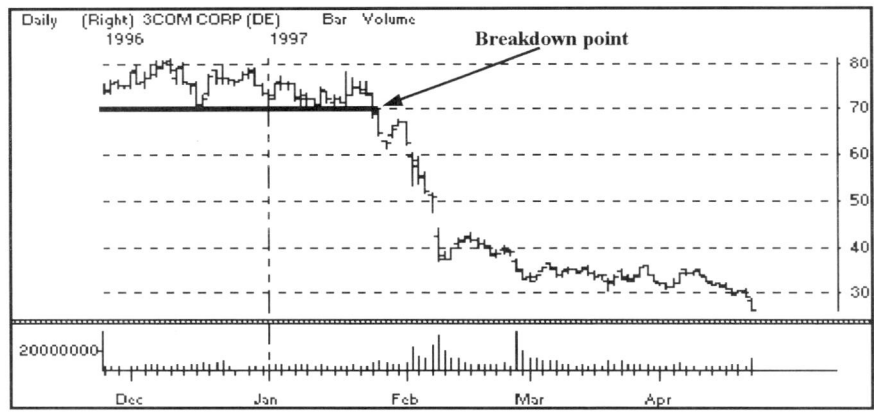

Reprinted with permission of Townsend Analytics, Ltd.

This last example of 3 COM breakdown is an exception because it did not breakdown to new lows at the breakdown point. However, it did breakdown through support at 70 after 10 weeks of consolidation in the same price range. 3 COM was a high flyer and as soon as investors' expectations changed it sold off sharply. Remember, this can happen to any high flying stock.

Characteristics of Price Movement

A stock fluctuation in price is determined by supply and demand. Supply and demand mirror overall investors' expectations. Short term expectations may differ from long term expectations. A sharp change in stock prices reflect a major change in investors' expectations. We have illustrated how a stock is viewed by investors in terms of the trend of a stock, support level prices, resistance level prices, and consolidation periods. We also showed how a change in investors' expectations will cause a stock to break out over its previous resistance level or break down through its previous support level. When we look at a study of stock prices on a chart we can identify tops and bottoms, consolidation periods, and the direction of a stock. Most stocks will have the following characteristics of price movement illustrated in the following chart.

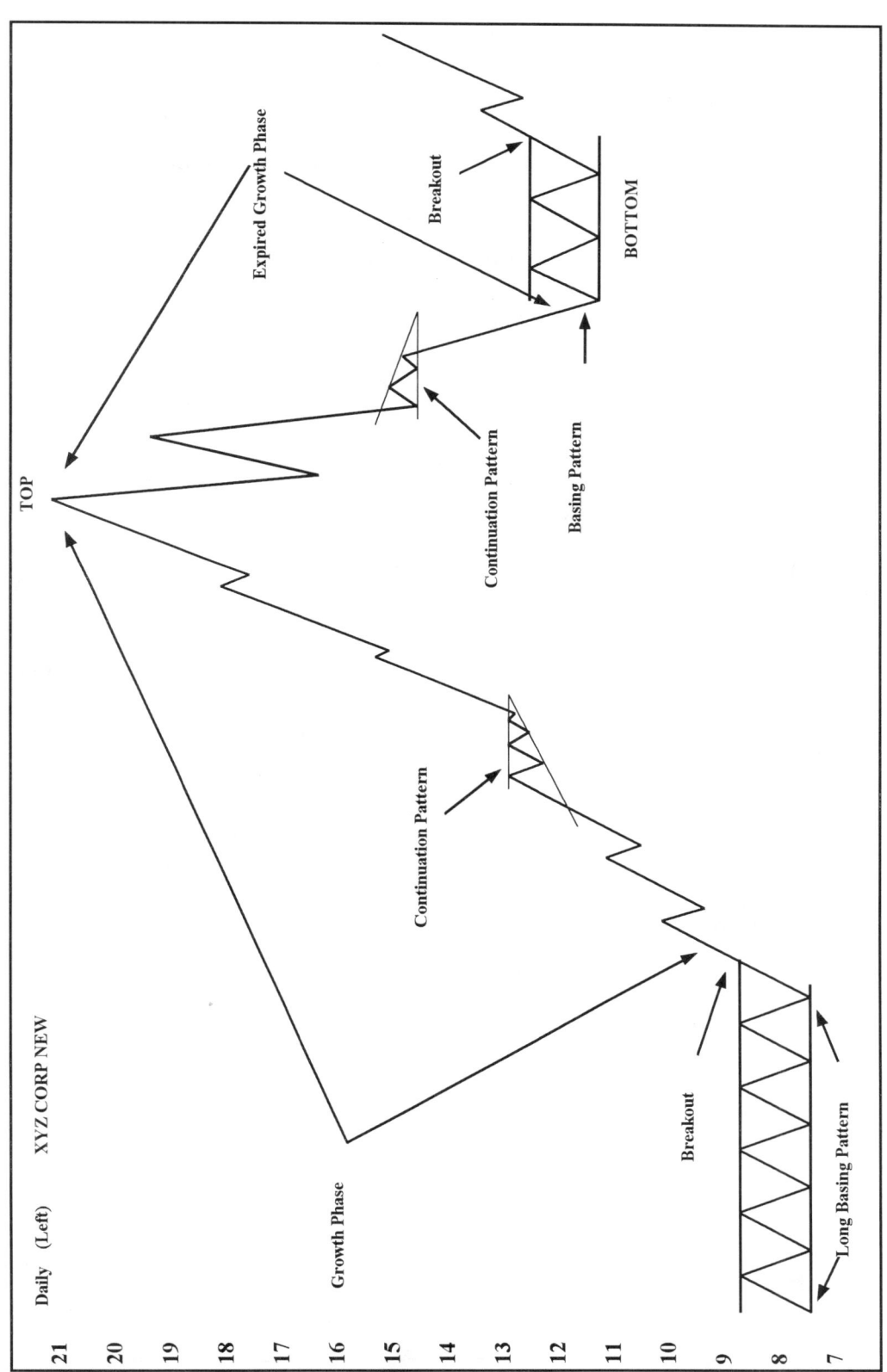

The previous hypothetical example using XYZ stock illustrates the typical price progress a stock will go through. It begins with a long basing pattern, as the stock consolidates (accumulated by investors). When the stock breaks out of the basing pattern it moves into its growth phase. It is normally a good time to buy the stock at the point it enters its growth phase indicated by the breakout from the basing pattern. The growth phase is an uptrend for the stock. Many times there will be a pause in the climb up as a continuation pattern forms before going all the way to the absolute top. A sell signal is given when the stock enters its expired growth phase as it will be trending down. There will be a pause in the decline as a continuation pattern forms before going all the way down to the absolute bottom. Now, the cycle can start over again, as the stock is basing. There are different patterns which are common for tops and bottoms as well as continuation patterns. We will learn how to identify these patterns and profit from them.

Technical Price Patterns

Now that we know more about trendlines, support levels and resistance levels, we can look at more technical price patterns (chart patterns) that occur repeatedly. Each of the patterns illustrated in the following examples is very significant and predicts the future price direction a stock has. Pay close attention to the characteristics of these patterns and learn to recognize them on a chart. We will go over trading strategies for these patterns in the "Trading Strategy" section.

Double Bottom

This pattern is formed when a support line holds once it is tested again. It is also known as a "W" pattern. It generates a buy signal. This is what a typical double bottom pattern looks like.

ENSCO INTL Daily Chart

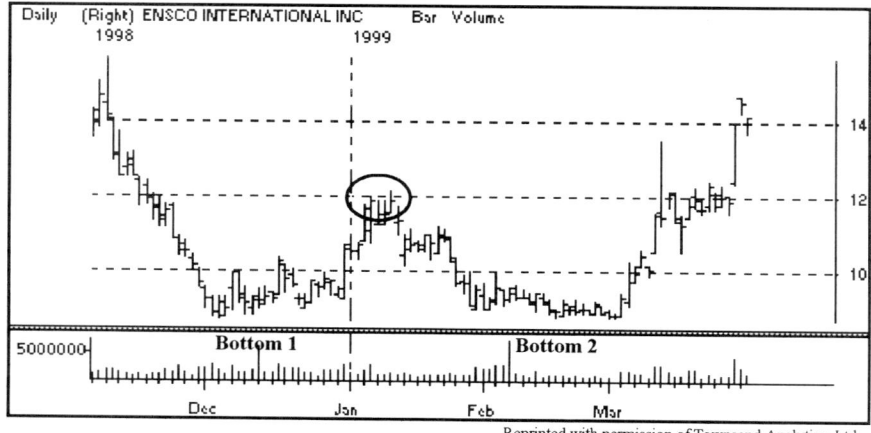

Reprinted with permission of Townsend Analytics, Ltd.

Can you see the "W"? If you connect all the bars together and draw a line it will be similar to the alphabet letter "W". The way to play this pattern is to buy the stock at the support levels, in this case at 8 3/4 or so and hold it. A test of the 12 level (marked by the circle) is the next price target, if support holds at 8 3/4 successfully. A breakout over 12 is considered very bullish, indeed the stock went as high as 15 once it broke out. The chart below shows another example of a double bottom pattern.

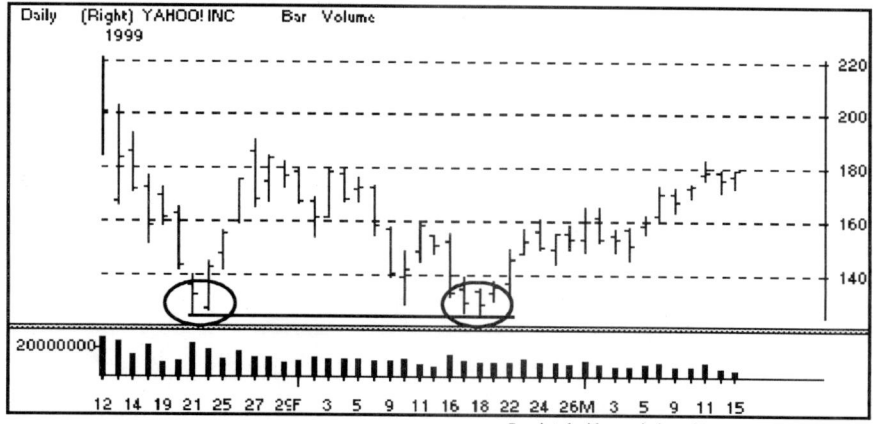

Reprinted with permission of Townsend Analytics, Ltd.

Yahoo is a very volatile stock, it declined sharply from 225 to 124 and turned around there. It rallied all the way to 190 and then turned around and went back down to 124. The 124 level held again and Yahoo rose again and eventually traded at 180. So Yahoo double bottomed at 124.

Double Top

This pattern is when resistance holds once it is tested again. It generates a sell signal. This is what a typical double top pattern looks like.

Pairgain Technology Daily Chart

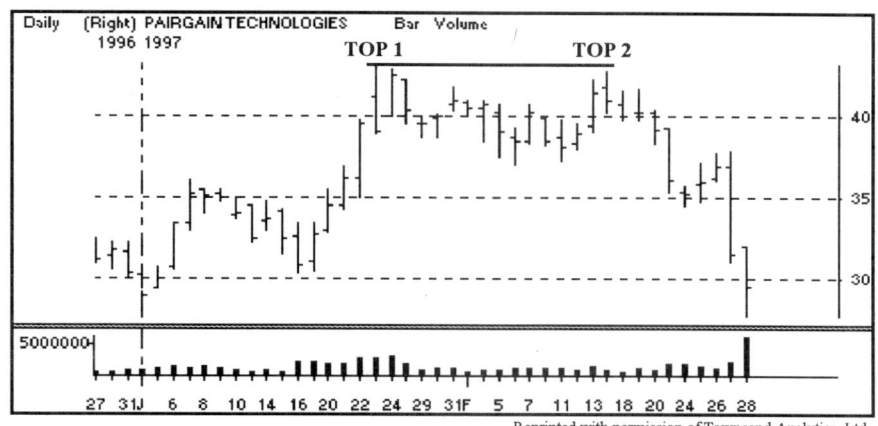

Reprinted with permission of Townsend Analytics, Ltd.

Pairgain Technology made a high at 43 1/4. It then pulled back in price and consolidated for 3 weeks before attempting to take the old resistance level (high) out. However, the attempt was unsuccessful as resistance was strong at that price level. The stock topped out and declined sharply from that point. In fact, it went all the way down to $6 a share.

Cisco Systems Daily Chart

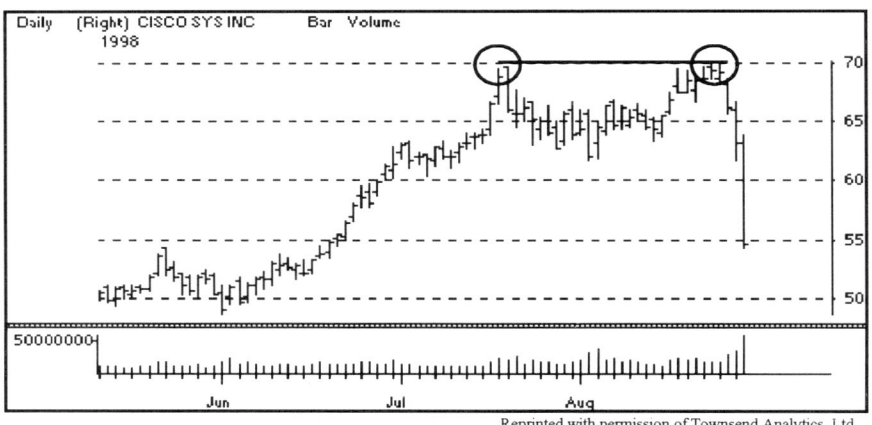

Reprinted with permission of Townsend Analytics, Ltd.

Cisco Systems double topped at 70 and declined sharply just like Pairgain technology did in the previous example. In both cases, resistance held the stock for the second time at or around the previous resistance level. This suggested that investors' expectations were for the stock to decline in price. This is the reason that the resistance level could not be successfully penetrated, once it was tested for the second time. It is also possible to have a triple top pattern which works the same way. If resistance is not successfully penetrated, once tested for the third time, the stock will decline in price, which will generate a sell signal.

Head and Shoulders

This is a bearish pattern that is easy to spot. This pattern is considered as a reversal pattern in an uptrending stocks. Trading on this pattern is also more reliable in uptrending stocks. It is a combination of three tops. The example below will illustrate a typical head and shoulders pattern.

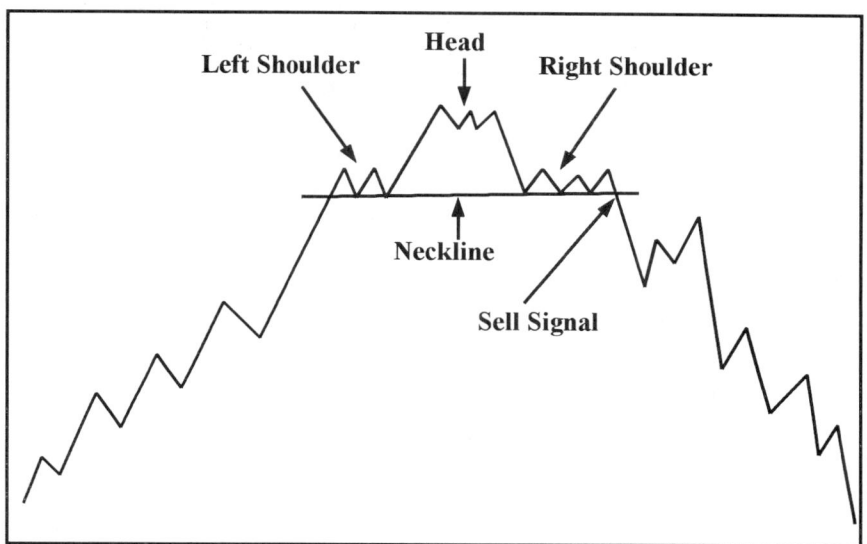

The logic behind this pattern is that investors were buying the stock pushing it all the way up to the tops of the left shoulder. The stock then comes down in price to the neckline and rallies back up to a higher high (the head area). The stock then pulls back to the neckline again. Some buyers step in and push the stock price higher, this will be the top of the right shoulder. However, sellers then push the stock price back down to the neckline. Once the stock price goes below the neckline a sell signal is generated. The characteristics of volume in this pattern are important. The heaviest volume occurs in the formation of the left shoulder. The volume decreases in the formation of the head, and decreases even more in the formation of the right shoulder. Once the neckline is penetrated, volume increases as the stock starts its decline.

Reverse Head and Shoulders

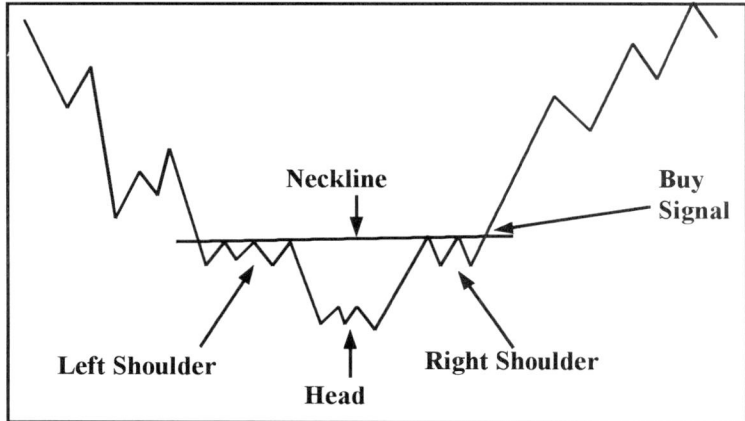

The head and shoulders pattern can also be inverted. It can be found in downtrending stocks and it will generate a buy signal once the neckline is penetrated. This breakout should come on increased volume. This can signal the reversal of the downtrend and a new uptrend can start.

Saucer (cup) and a Handle

This is one of the most popular patterns for a long position. The cup and a handle is looked at as a correction (cup) followed by a consolidation (handle). The buy point is when a breakout from the handle occurs. Here are some examples of a cup and handle patterns.

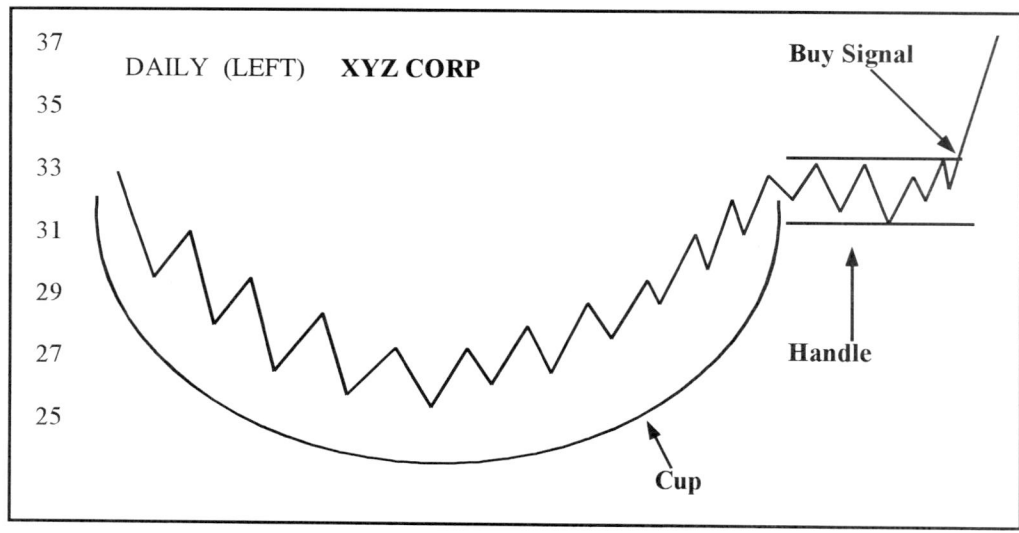

Cup and a Handle Pattern Example 2

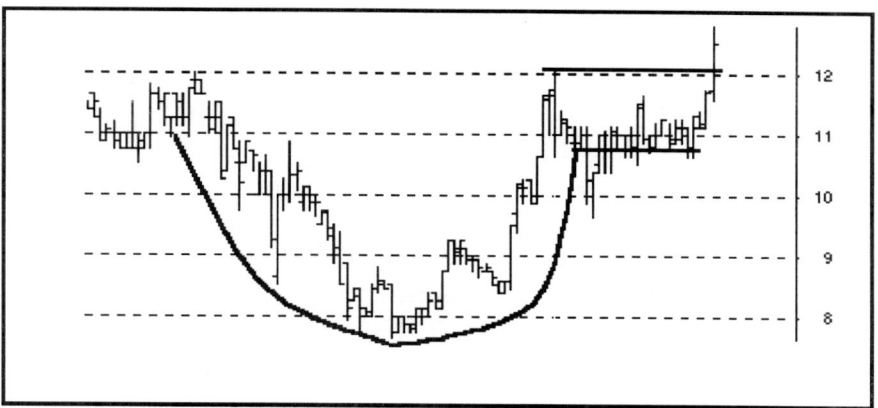

A buy signal is generated once the price goes over the previous tops of the handle, at 12 1/4.

Result of Example 2

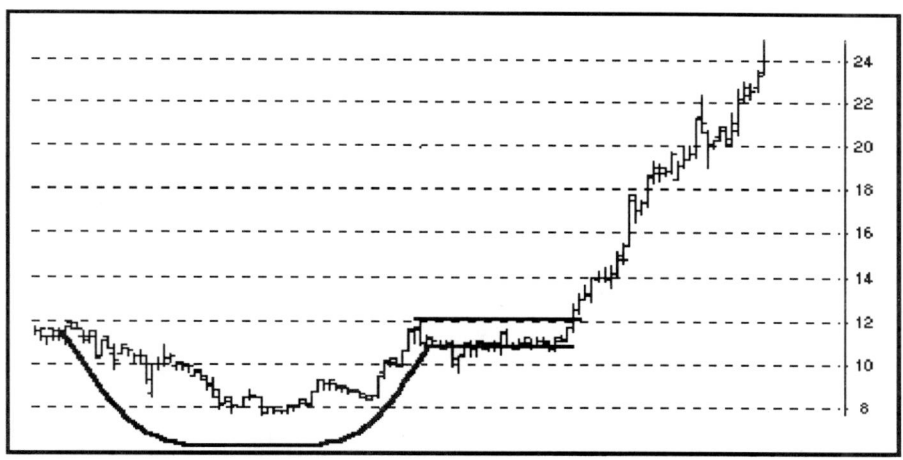

The stock more than doubled in price in a short period of time.

Trading in a Channel

When a stock trades in a pattern in which drawing straight lines under the bottoms and over the tops result in two parallel lines, the area in between the lines is called a channel. There are three types of channel trading: Horizontal Trading Channel, Declining Channel and Rising Channel. In all three cases, we buy when a stock hits the bottom range of the channel and we sell when the stock hits the top range of the channel. We will reverse positions when a stock breaks out of its channel. Let's look at a Horizontal Trading Channel first. We draw three parallel lines. The first over the bottoms, the second over the tops and the third at the midpoint between the two line. This line shows us more clearly in which range of the channel the stock is currently trading. Once the stock hits the bottom line, or close to it, we buy it. We sell it when it hits the top line, or close to it.

Horizontal Trading Channel

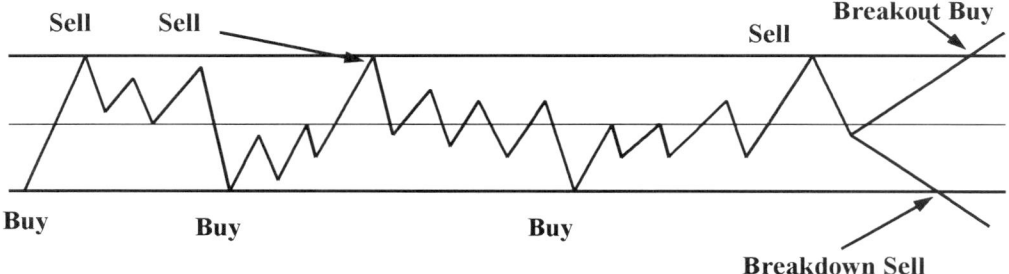

Declining Channel

We trade this pattern the same way. We short sell at the top line and we cover our short on the bottom line. If a breakout occurs, then we will buy the stock. If it breaks down we will short.

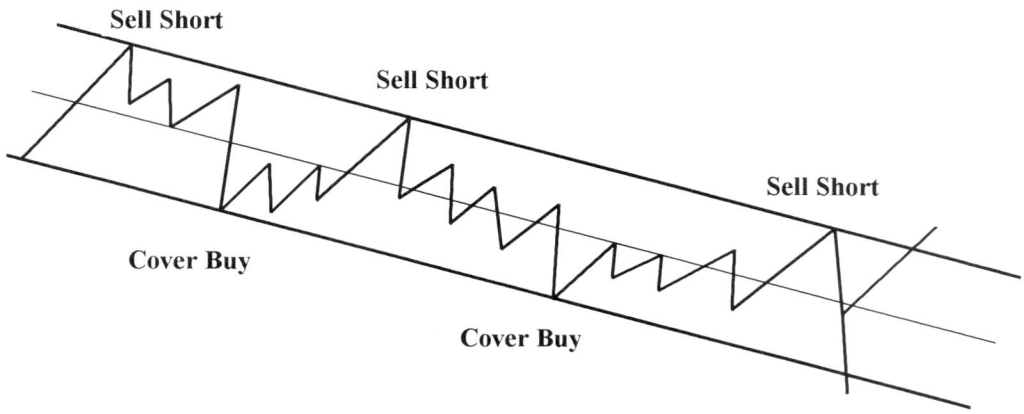

Rising Channel

We trade this pattern the same way. We buy at the bottom line and we sell at the top line. If a breakout occurs, then we will buy the stock. If it breaks down, we will short it.

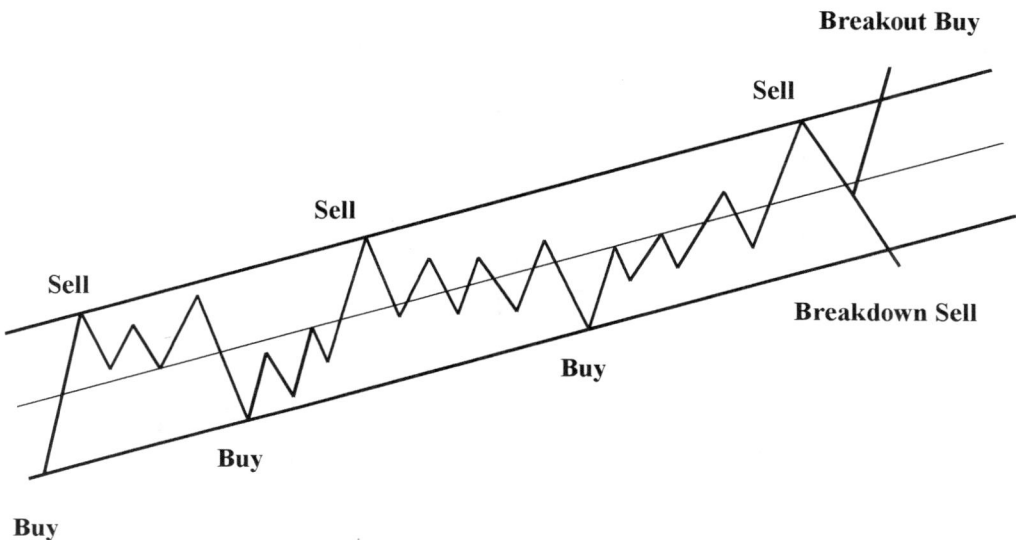

Rising Channel Play Example 1.

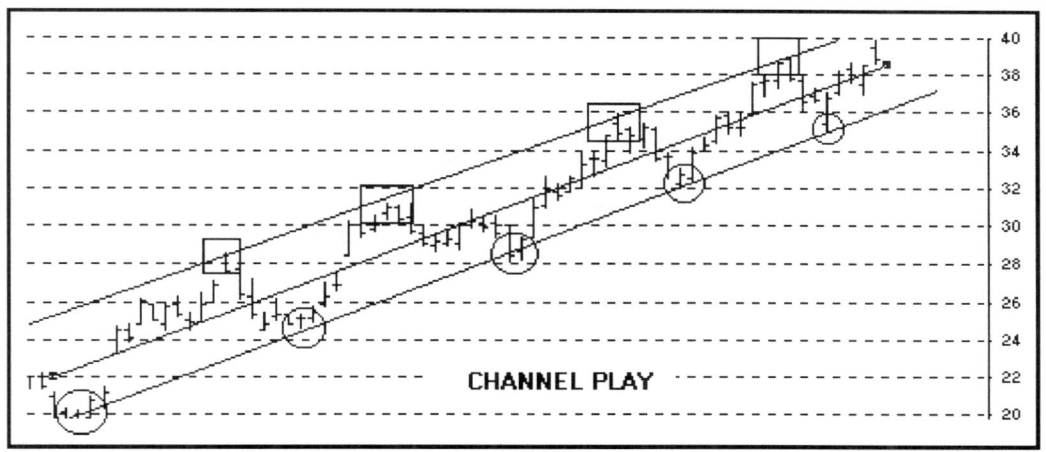

Reprinted with permission of Townsend Analytics, Ltd.

Buy points are represented by the circles and sell points are represented by the squares.

Rising Channel Play Example 2.

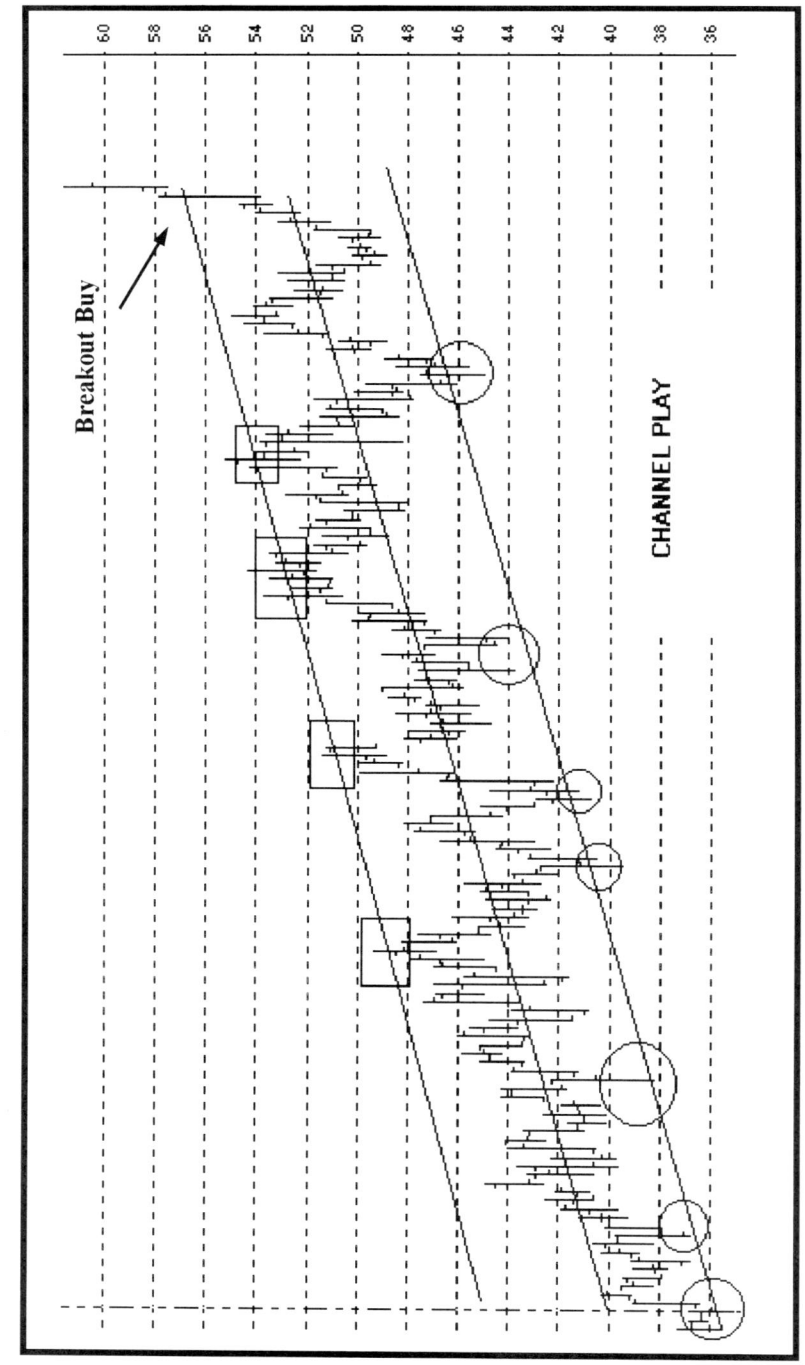

This example shows another rising channel. Buy at the circles, sell at the squares.

Horizontal Trading Channel Example 1.

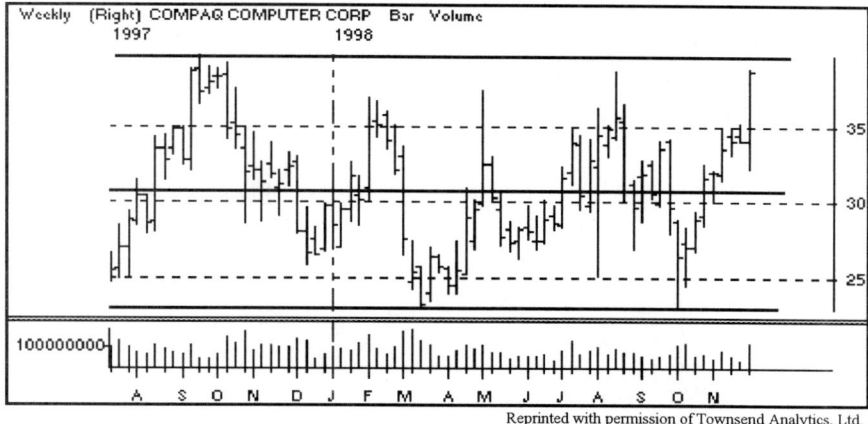

Compaq Computer in a 73-week-long channel in the chart above.

Horizontal Trading Channel Example 2.

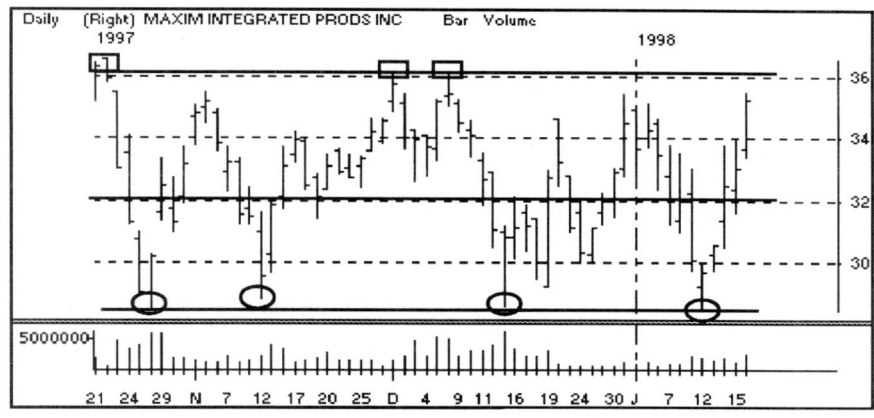

Maxim was in a 12 week extra volatile channel between 28 and 36. The circles represent the buy point and squares the sell point. However, in hindsight, buying anywhere under 30 (6 opportunities) and selling over 34 (6 opportunities) would have put a couple of coins in your pocket.

Continuation Patterns

These are the bread and butter patterns for short term trading. They normally represent short term consolidation or indecision between the bulls and bears before a stock resumes its movement continuing in the direction of its trend. These patterns are called triangles, wedges, flags, and pennants. These patterns can be found on bar charts that cover long period of time or very short period of time, such as a one-day, one-minute chart. These patterns are traded the same way, regardless if you analyze one-month bars on a 20-year chart, or 5-minute bars on a 5-day chart.

Symmetrical Triangle in an Uptrend

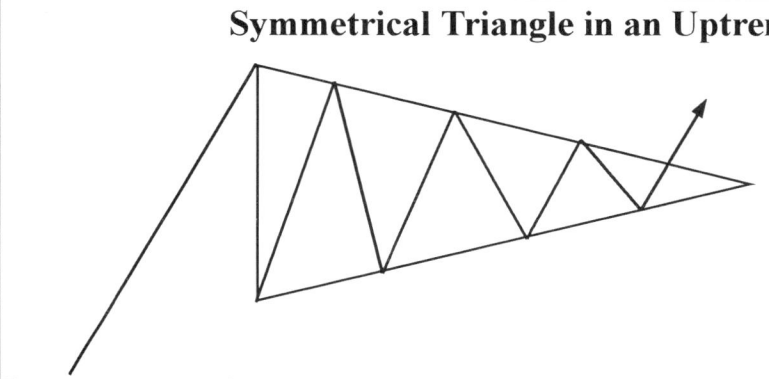

In an uptrending stock, if a penetration through the top resistance line of the triangle occurs then it suggests a continuation of the existing trend, hence it is a bullish (buy) signal.

Symmetrical Triangle in a Downtrend

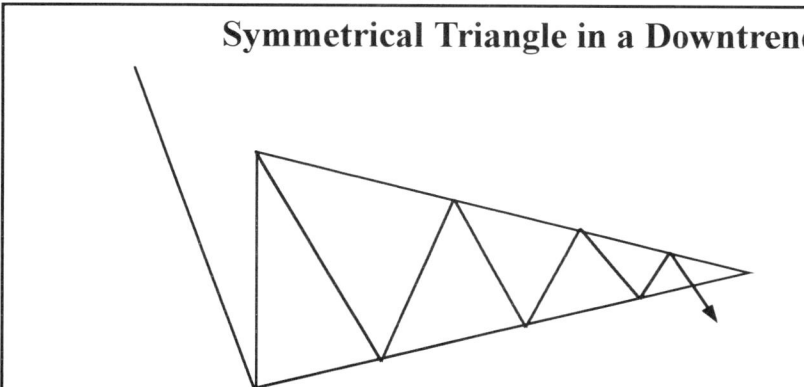

In a downtrending stock, if a penetration through the bottom support line of the triangle occurs then it suggests a continuation of the existing trend, hence it is a bearish (sell) signal.

The logic behind these patterns is that the stock is in an indecision phase. The bottoms are rising as investors are willing to pay more for the stock yet the tops are declining as investors are not too enthusiastic about holding the stock and are selling it. The trading price range of the stock narrows, this typically occurs on low volume. Once there is a change in the forces of supply and demand a breakout from the triangle pattern can occur. This will normally happen with increase in volume. Once a successful breakout takes place, a continuation of the trend will resume.

Right Angle Triangles

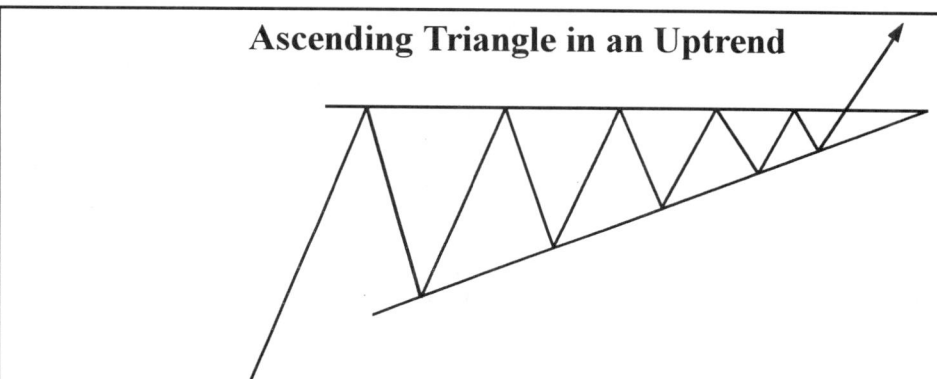

Ascending Triangle in an Uptrend

In an uptrending stock, if a penetration through the top resistance line of the Ascending Triangle occurs then it suggests a continuation of the existing trend, hence it is a bullish (buy) signal.

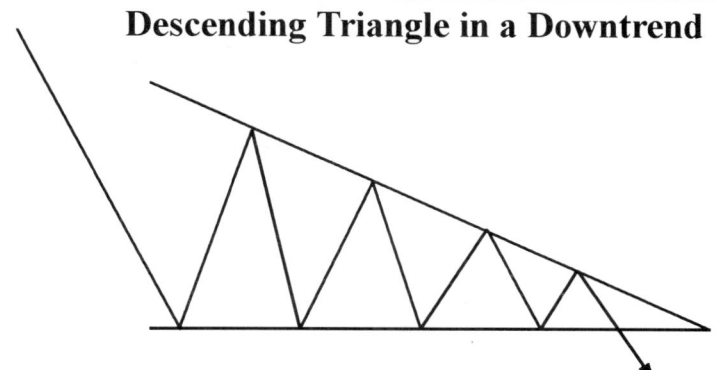

Descending Triangle in a Downtrend

In a downtrending stock, if a penetration through the bottom support line of the Descending Triangle occurs then it suggests a continuation of the existing trend, hence it is a bearish (sell) signal.

Please note that volume is normally lower in the formation time of a continuation pattern and should increase when the breakout occurs. This is true for triangles, flags and wedges.

Flags

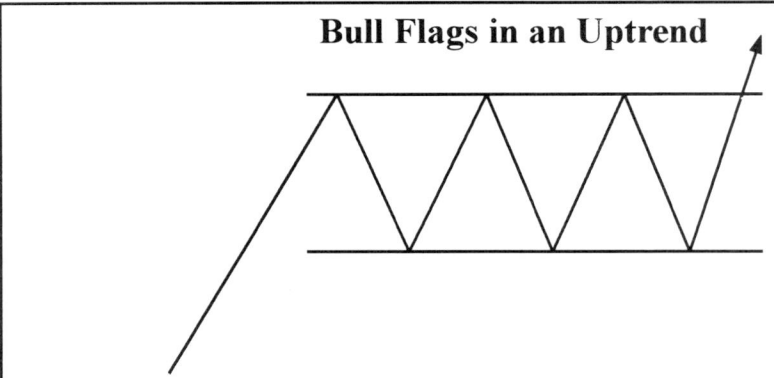

In an uptrending stock, if a penetration through the top resistance line of the Flag occurs then it suggests a continuation of the existing trend, hence it is a bullish (buy) signal.

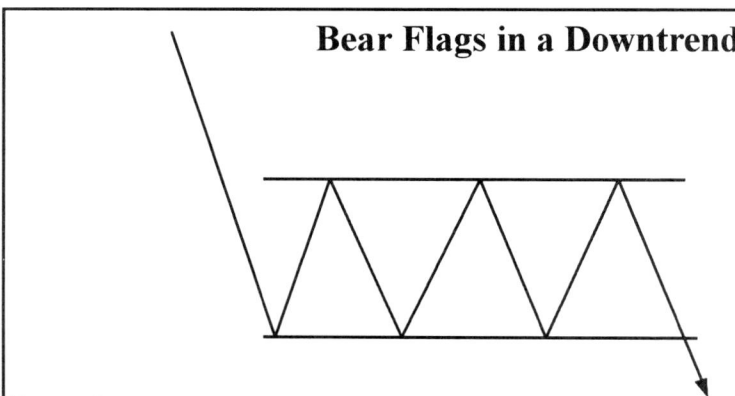

In a downtrending stock, if a penetration through the bottom support line of the Flag occurs then it suggests a continuation of the existing trend, hence it is a bearish (sell) signal.

Wedges

Wedges are actually an exception as they are reversal patterns. They represent short term indecision or consolidation period, between the bulls and the bears, before a stock reverses its movement starting a new trend.

Falling Wedge in a Downtrend

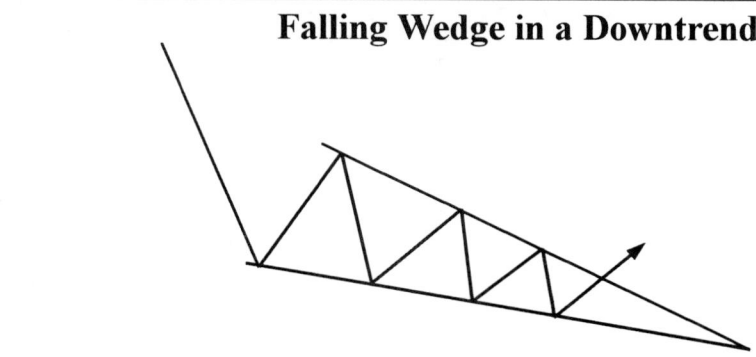

In a downtrending stock, if a penetration through the top resistance line of the Falling Wedge occurs then it suggests a reversal of the existing trend, hence it is a bullish (buy) signal.

Rising Wedges in an Uptrend

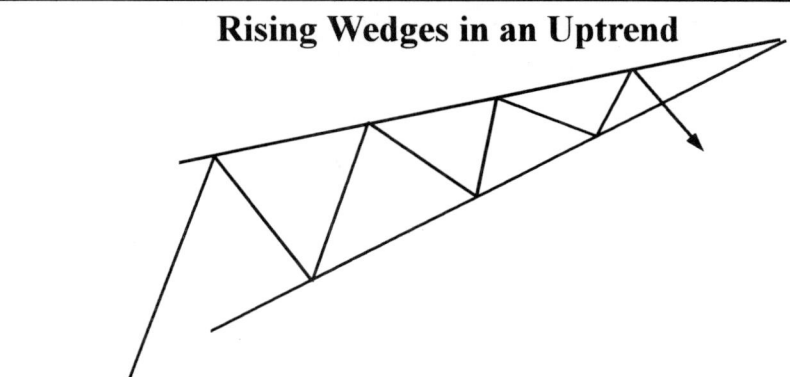

In an uptrending stock, if a penetration through the bottom support line of the Rising wedge occurs then it suggests a reversal of the existing trend, hence it is a bearish (sell) signal.

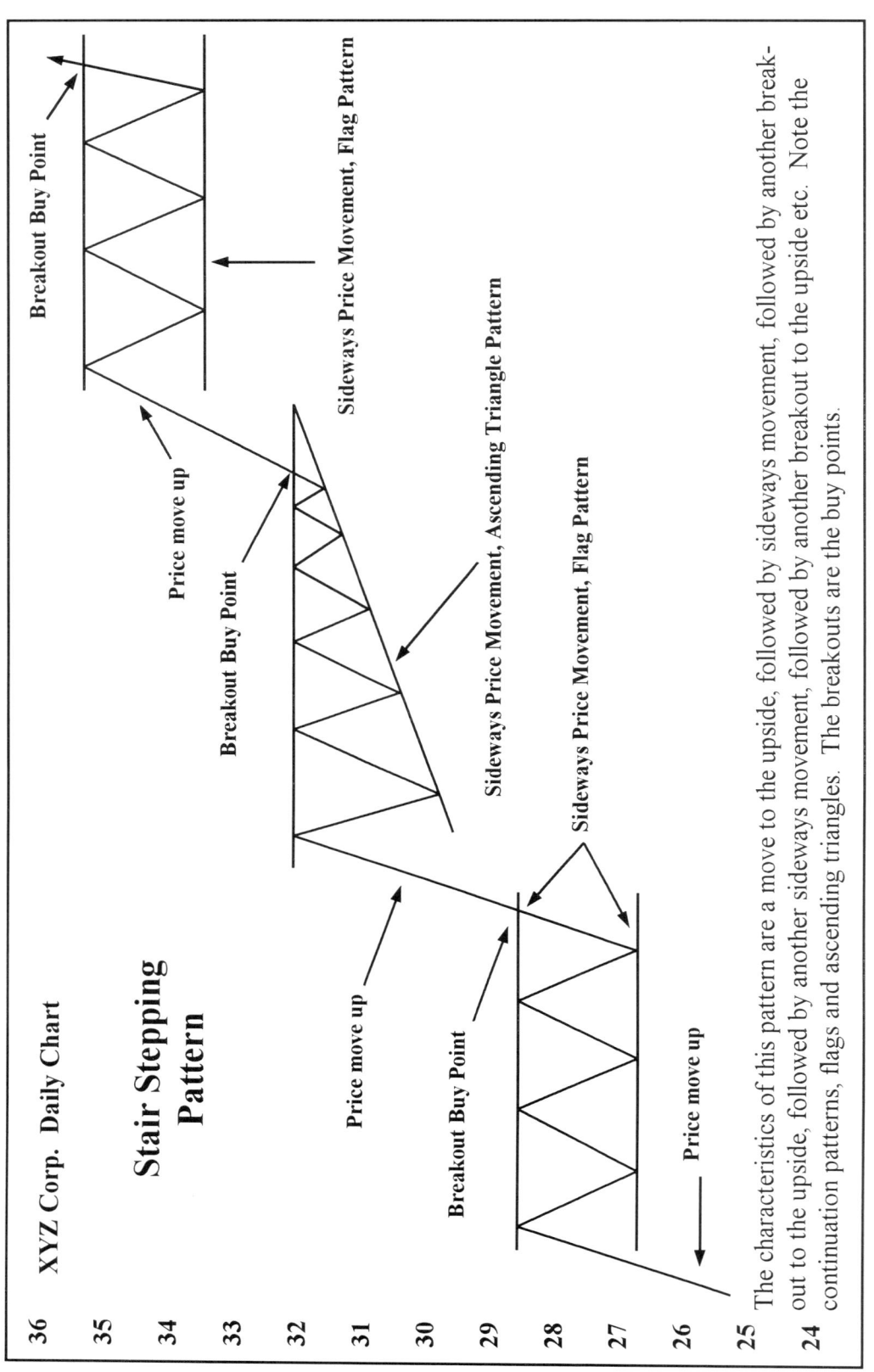

RSI

I use three technical indicators when I look at a chart of a security: Volume, MA, and RSI. I like to keep things simple, so I gave up on applying any other technical indicators to a chart. I use volume to determine the reliability of price movements. I use MA to determine long term and short term trends and as support and resistance levels. I use RSI (Relative Strength Index) to determine if a stock is overbought or oversold. This indicator is not to be used alone. It is a momentum indicator which measures a stock's price performance relative to its past performance. RSI just like MA can have different time periods. You can use a 10-day, 14-day, 21-day, or any number of days RSI (just like 10-day MA, 20-day MA, etc.) RSI has a range of numbers between 0-100. A sell signal is generated when the RSI crosses over 80. A buy signal is generated when the RSI crosses under 20 (some analysts use 30 and 70, rather than 20 and 80.) However, when I analyze a chart using RSI, I only use RSI as an overbought, oversold indicator. I do not sell my position because the RSI went over 80, and I do not cover short positions because the RSI went under 20. Other things have to occur for me to close my positions.

This is how I use RSI: If a stock is looking good for a long position, but its RSI is over 80, I will not buy it. If a stock is looking good for a short position, but its RSI is under 20, I will not short. This is the only reason I use RSI. In short, I do not buy stocks which have RSI greater than 80. I do not short stocks with RSI under 20. If I have an open position and RSI was at these levels, I will only close my position based on the actual price movement at the time, regardless of what the RSI is. I have seen stocks that had RSI of 100 and 0, in the past.

This is how RSI is calculated: RSI equals the average of the closing prices of the up days divided by the average of the closing prices of the down days. The specified time frame determines the volatility of the indicator. For instance, a nine-day time period under study will be more volatile than a 21-day time span. I normally run three RSI lines on the chart, 10-day RSI, 14-day RSI and 21-day RSI. You have to experiment with this indicator and see which time period works best for you. Let's look at the chart on the following page.

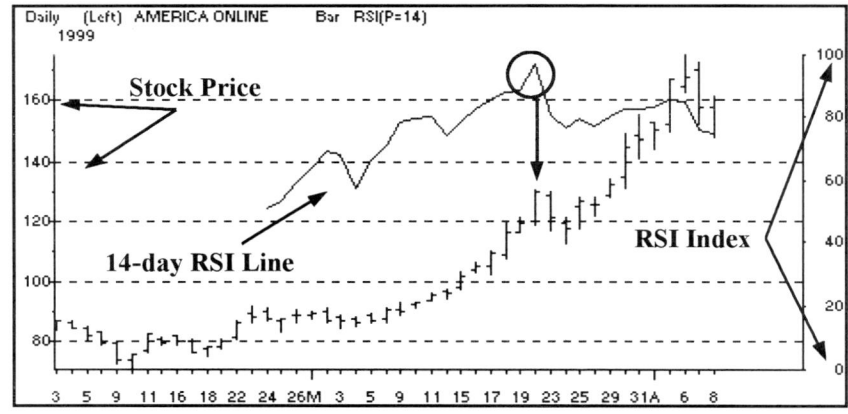

Reprinted with permission of Townsend Analytics, Ltd.

In this chart the 14-day RSI is displayed over the price chart. The RSI range of 0-100 is on the right and the stock prices are on the left. Note: the section marked by the circle is when AOL's RSI crossed over 85. The RSI actually hit 96. The stock price declined from 130 to 110 in the next two days. It also climbed up from there all the way to 175 1/2 in the next nine days. The overbought signal was valid, however, a stock like AOL can trade at over 80 RSI without a problem. This is why you need to look at past performance or you will leave money on the table.

Intraday Charts

Intraday charts illustrate the price activity of a stock during the trading day. It is a great tool for daytrading and short-term trading. You can run a 1-minute intraday chart over one day or a even a 60-minute chart over 10 days. The same rules apply; support and resistance, trends, continuation patterns, breakouts, etc. Let's look at a case study featuring intraday charts and see how they can help us in finding trading opportunities.

CNET 4-Day 10-Minute Bar Chart

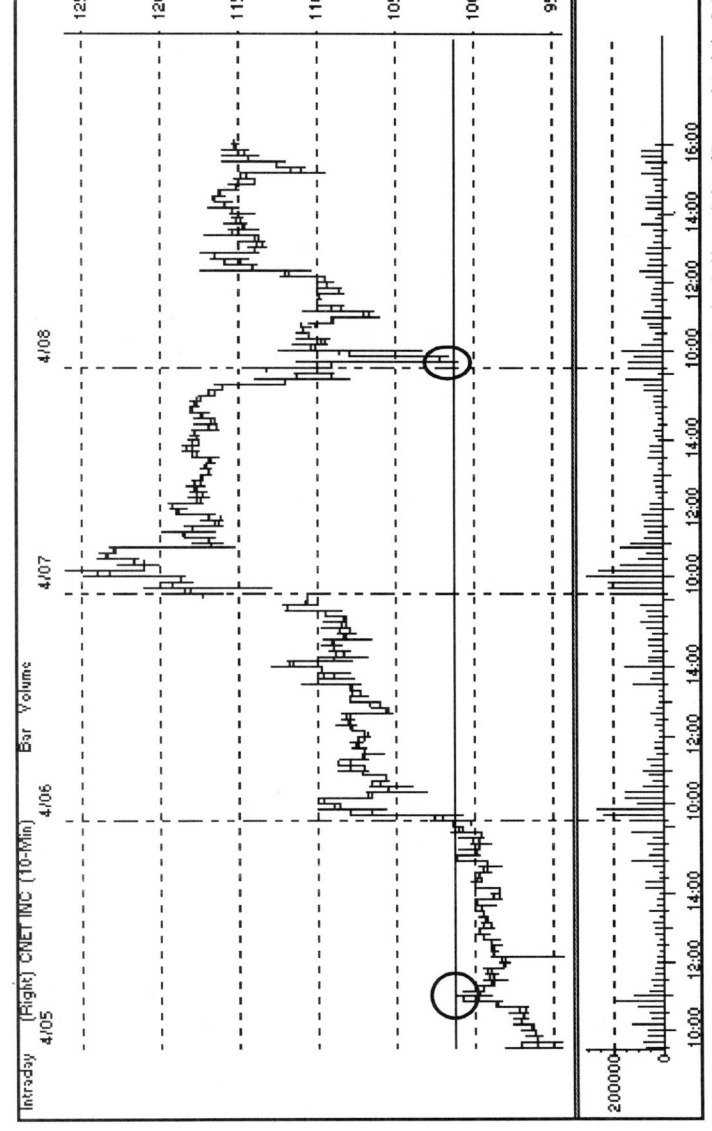

On 4/8/99 CNET was selling off hard in the morning. We knew a bounce would come at some point and we wanted to find out where support was present. We brought up a 4 day 10 minute chart and we found support at 101 1/4. CNET indeed bounced at 101 and went all the way up to 117 1/2, the same day.

We can take a closer look at CNET action that day. Here is a 5 minute intraday chart showing the action.

CNET 5-Minute Bar Chart

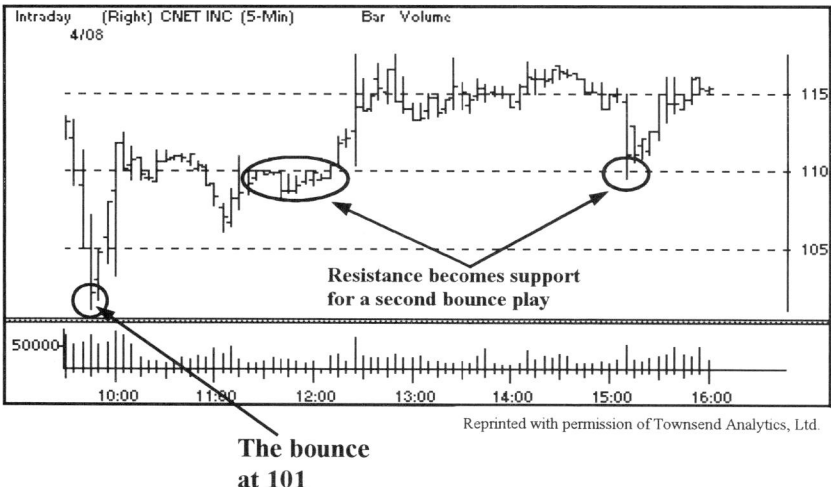

CNET went back to 112 1/2 in 15 minutes. If we entered a trade to buy CNET at 101 1/4 on ISLD, we could have made 11+ points in 15 minutes. Later in the day, CNET went down to 109 3/4 and bounced back up to 117. This was another good potential trade for 6+ points.

Technical Analysis Summary

Technical analysis is used to analyze price movement over a period of time. The important elements of technical analysis are the trend, support and resistance. These reflect the supply and demand for a security. A technical trader waits for a certain technical setup before he enters a trade. We have featured a variety of technical setups which you should become familiar with. If I could add my two cents here, I would recommend to keep things simple. In other words, look to trade simple technical patterns such as support, resistance and breakouts. If you master these patterns, you will never have to study any complex technical indicators looking for more confirmation. In fact, these simple patterns make most of my successful tradings.

Section Three

Introduction to Level II

Charts used in this section are provided by RealTick™ III and are used with the express written permission of Townsend Analytics, Ltd. RealTick™ III is a trademark and copyright of Townsend Analytics, Ltd.

Introduction to Level II Quote

Level II Quote is a quotation system for NASDAQ stocks which displays bids and offers by Market Makers in a particular stock. You can see exactly which Market Maker, in that stock, is bidding for shares or offering shares for sale. You can see at which price he is interested in buying or selling, and how many shares he is interested in buying or selling at that price. The example below will show a Level II Quote screen.

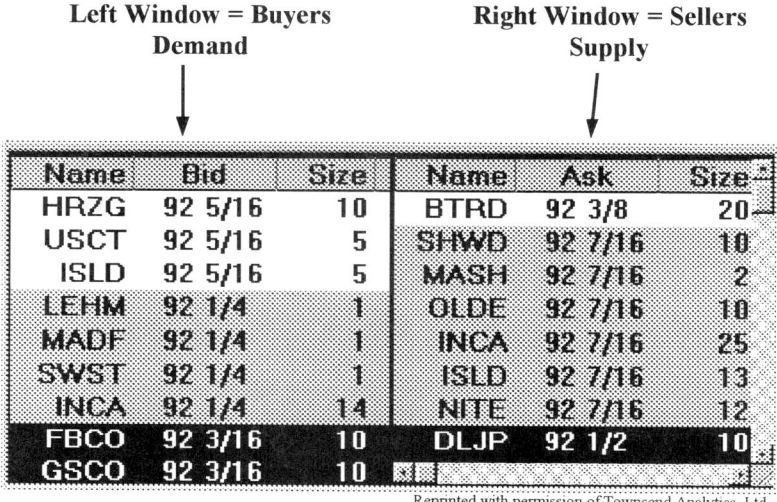

Reprinted with permission of Townsend Analytics, Ltd.

This is what a basic Level II Quote window looks like. It is divided into two windows: a left window and a right window. Each window has three columns in it. The window on the left side is the Bid window. All Market Makers listed in that window are bidding for the stock. The window on the right is the Ask window. All the Market Makers in that window are offering stock for sale. The way I look at it is the left window represents buyers, and the right window represents sellers.

Let's look at the left window (the buyers window first). Reading the columns from left to right we have Name, Bid and Size.

Name: The name is a 4 letter code which represents a Market Maker in that security. The name stands for the identity of the Market Maker. It is important to know who that Market Maker is. We will cover the importance of identifying the Market Makers later in this book.

Bid: This is the price that the Market Maker is willing to buy the stock for. See if you can find MADF on the Bid side and see how much he is willing to pay for the stock.

Size: This number indicates how many shares the Market Maker is willing to buy at that price. The Size is quoted in 100 share lots. So a Size of 5 will be 5 X 100 = 500, a Size of 12 is 12 X 100 = 1200 shares. Let's look at MADF again. He is the fifth Market Maker from the top down. He is bidding 92 1/4 (to answer the previous question) for 100 shares (Size of 1 X 100). INCA is bidding 92 1/4 for 1400 shares. FBCO is bidding 92 3/16 for 1000 shares.

Ask: The right window works the same way, but instead of bidding, Market Makers are offering shares for sale at the price listed in the Ask column. The Size is how many shares they offer.

You might have noticed that there were different color ranges in both the Bid and Ask windows. These colors will vary depending on how the quotation software is set up. The use of colors in a Level II screen is nothing more than a visual aid. It helps us identify how many Market Makers and/or ECNs are at each price level. The use of the different color ranges eases the process of identifying how many buyers or sellers are stacked at each price level. In our example, there are three color ranges: white, gray and black.

Bid Color Ranges

Name	Bid	Size	Name	Ask	Size
HRZG	92 5/16	10	BTRD	92 3/8	20
USCT	92 5/16	5	SHWD	92 7/16	10
ISLD	92 5/16	5	MASH	92 7/16	2
LEHM	92 1/4	1	OLDE	92 7/16	10
MADF	92 1/4	1	INCA	92 7/16	25
SWST	92 1/4	1	ISLD	92 7/16	13
INCA	92 1/4	14	NITE	92 7/16	12
FBCO	92 3/16	10	DLJP	92 1/2	10
GSCO	92 3/16	10			

Offer Color Ranges

Reprinted with permission of Townsend Analytics, Ltd.

If we look at the left window you can see that there are three color ranges: white, gray and black. The best Bid is in the white color range (white background) and has 3 bidders in it. HRZG, USCT and ISLD. They are all bidding 92 5/16 for the stock. This is the only thing they have in common and that's why they are in the first range of color, the white range, which represents the best Bid. Note that the best Bid will always be displayed at the top of the Level II Quote window, no matter what the background color is, as it is sorted in a descending order from the best Bid to the worst Bid, top to bottom. The second best Bid (outside of the current market) is displayed in the gray shaded area and the third best Bid (outside of the current market) is displayed in the black shaded area.

The color ranges on the Ask side are the same. The best offer is displayed in the white color zone, the second best offer (outside of the current market) is displayed in the gray shaded area and the third best offer (outside of the current market) is displayed in the black shaded area. Note that the best Ask will always be displayed at the top of the Level II Quote window, no matter what the background color is, as it is sorted in an ascending order from the best offer to the worst offer.

Let's look at the quote screen again and assume that BTRD, who is offering 2000 shares for sale at 92 3/8, sold his 2000 shares and has left the best offer. It is hard to see without a visual aid, but the gray background area of the offer side will change to white background instantaneously, as soon as BTRD leaves the offer. At the same time, the black background area will change to gray and the best offer will go up to 92 7/16. We will look at some examples of what the Level II screen will look like when Market Makers leave the best Bid or best Ask later on in this book, but first we need to learn more about the anatomy of a Level II screen.

The Level II Quote window has two parts to it. The actual Level II Quote window displaying bids, offers and sizes, as illustrated in the previous two examples, and a multiquote window displaying additional data. There are different multiquote windows that can accompany a Level II Quote window which can be customized by the user. We will study both a basic multiquote window and a customized multiquote window, which I use on a daily basis, and show how the data can be used.

Multiquote Window

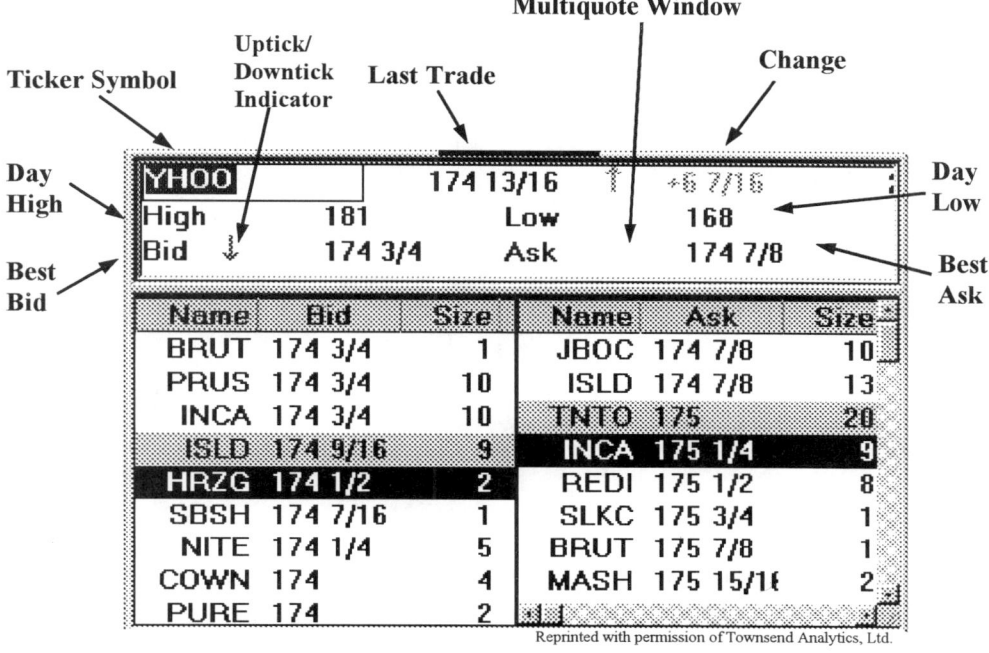

Ticker Symbol: The four letter code NASDAQ uses to identify a stock.

Last Trade: The last price the stock traded at.

Change: The price change from the previous day's closing price.

Day Low: The lowest price the stock traded at, today.

Day High: The highest price the stock traded at, today.

Uptick/Downtick indicator: An arrow indicating if the best Bid has upticked or downticked from the previous best Bid. An arrow pointing down indicates a downtick and an arrow pointing up indicates an uptick.

Best Bid: Indicates the best Bid, the inside Bid. This is useful when a Market Maker is stuck in your Level II screen, or if your Level II Quote lags, this may happen at times, so keep an eye to make sure the best Bid on your multiquote screen matches the best Bid on your Level II screen and the same for the Ask.

Best Ask: Indicates the best offer price, the inside offer.

This is a custom multiquote window that I use. It has additional valuable information. I use it with Townsend Analytics' Real tick III software.

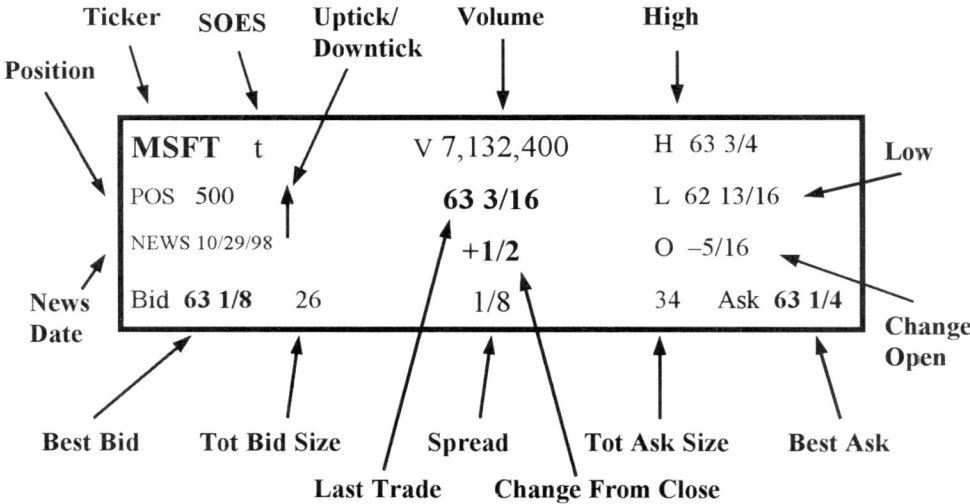

This multiquote window has 16 different data fields, twice as many as the previous one. Here are the definitions of the other eight fields not explained in the previous section.

SOES: The letter "t" indicates that a SOES order can be used with this security. If the letter "t" is not present then you cannot use SOES orders to buy or sell that security. You will have to use other execution vehicles to buy or sell.

Volume: The total number of shares traded so far today.

Change Open: The change in the stock price from the first trade of the day, the opening trade.

Spread: Calculates the difference between the best Ask and the best Bid.

News Date: Indicates the latest news date on the stock.

Position: Shows your open position, long or short in the stock.

Total Bid Size: The total number of shares on the best Bid, in 100 share lots.

Total Ask Size: The total number of shares on the best Ask, in 100 share lots.

What Does Level II Quote Tell Us?

There are some advantages to using Level II Quotes, especially for intraday and short term trading. The first advantage is the ability to see what is going on beyond the inside market. I refer to it as the depth the Bid or the Ask show. This is also referred to as the strength of the Bid or Ask, or the overall interest to buy or sell a stock by the Market Makers.

	MSFT		92 1/4	↑	+2 5/8		
	High	92 1/2	Low		90 1/4		
	Bid ↑	92 3/16	Ask		92 1/4		
Two color range.	**Name**	**Bid**	**Size**	**Name**	**Ask**	**Size**	One color range.
	HRZG	92 3/16	10	MWSE	92 1/4	10	
	FBCO	92 3/16	10	BRUT	92 1/4	1	
9 +	INCA	92 3/16	20	BTRD	92 1/4	1	
Market	GSCO	92 3/16	10	INCA	92 1/4	6	8
Makers	MASH	92 3/16	10	MASH	92 1/4	6	Market
want to	ISLD	92 3/16	10	NITE	92 1/4	10	Makers
buy at	MSCO	92 1/8	10	ISLD	92 1/4	4	want to
92 1/8-	SWST	92 1/8	1	PERT	92 1/4	10	sell at
92 3/16	MLCO	92 1/8	10				92 1/4

Reprinted with permission of Townsend Analytics, Ltd.

This example shows Microsoft stock. Let's look at the Level II Quote window. The first thing I see is that there are only two color ranges on the Bid and one color range on the Ask. I have my Level II window sized up so I can see eight Market Makers on the offer, and nine on the Bid, immediately, without scrolling down further. Knowing this, let's see what we can learn from this scenario at a quick glance.

1. The Inside Market is 92 3/16 X 92 1/4. A spread of 1/16 (a teenie).

2. The offer is showing **strength** (weakness for the security,) as there are eight Market Makers, right this second, who are **interested** in selling at 92 1/4. I call this **depth** on the offer, as it will take a lot of buying for the offering price to rise significantly.

3. The Bid is showing **strength** as well, as there are nine Market Makers who are **interested** in buying MSFT within 1/8 of a point from the best offer. There is **depth** on the Bid side as well.

Depth: I use the word depth, because I look at a Level II window from top to bottom. In general, if the eight Market Makers in my Level II screen on the Bid side, or the Ask side, are within 1/4 of a point difference from the best offer to the worst offer or best Bid to worst Bid, then there is depth on that side. In other words, if it will take at least eight Market Makers to drop out from either the Bid side or the Ask size and the stock will only move 1/4 of a point, then it indicates that there is depth on that side (Bid or Ask side). The Size also matters, but I first want to know how many different parties (Market Makers) are showing their interest to buy or sell a security. Once I have determined that, I look at the total size they are interested in buying or selling. In this case, the best Bid has six interested MMs with 70 total size. The best offer has eight interested MMs with 48 total size. The next thing to determine is who is buying versus who is selling.

Here is another example of a Level II Quote screen. Now that we know more about depth, we can further analyze a given situation. Before we continue, I want to mention one more thing about the color ranges in a Level II screen. The first three color ranges from top to bottom represent the best Bid/Ask, the second best Bid/Ask and the third best Bid/Ask. If there is more than one Market Maker present in the same color range level, then he is bidding/offering at the exact same price a fellow Market Maker is, who is in the same color range as he is. However, there is also the 4th color range (white) following the first three color ranges, from top to bottom. This color range includes all the other Bids/Asks, which can range in price. This means that a Market Maker can Bid $1 and be in the same color range as a Market Maker who Bids $91, in this case. So keep that in mind. In some cases, it is important to know who is at the 4th color range and at what price, especially for stocks who show no great depth. Let's see what we can tell about CNET, at a quick glance. I chose CNET because it trades at about the same price as MSFT and has an average daily volume of 2.5 million shares.

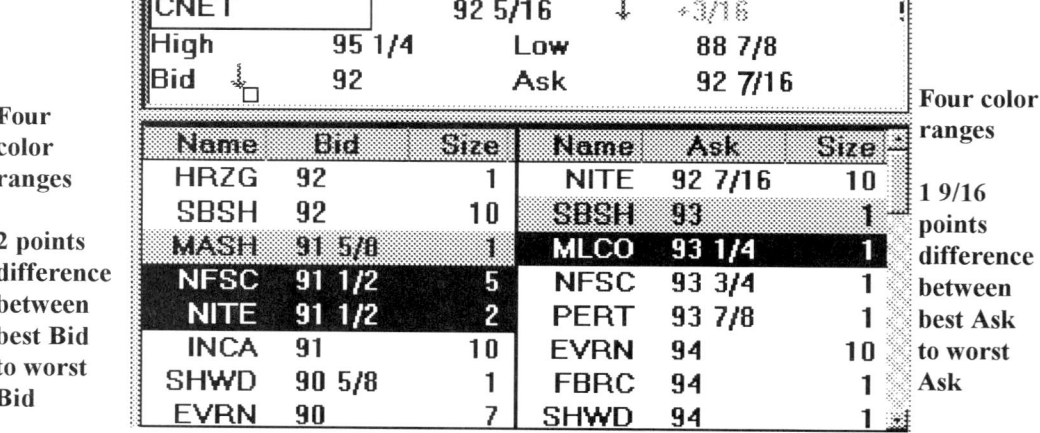

Reprinted with permission of Townsend Analytics, Ltd.

1. The Inside Market is 92 X 92 7/16. A spread of 7/16.

2. There are four color ranges on both the Bid and Ask side.

3. The Ask side is not showing strength or depth. There is not much interest from the Market Makers to sell the stock.

4. The Bid side is not showing strength or depth. There is not much interest from the Market Makers to buy the stock.

5. If we look at the worst Bid and worst Ask, there is a 4 point spread, whereas MSFT, in the previous example had an 1/8 spread between the worst Bid and worst Ask.

6. If some moderate selling is to take place, and the Market Makers in the first three color ranges on the Bid side were to leave, the best Bid will fall 1 point from 92 to 91. The total amount of shares Market Makers are interested in buying in the first three color ranges is 1900 shares.

7. If some moderate buying is to take place, and the Market Makers in the first three color ranges on the offer side were to leave, the best offer will increase by 1 5/16 from 92 7/16 to 93 3/4. The total amount of shares Market Makers are interested in selling in the first three color ranges is 1200 shares.

8. The total number of shares on the Bid side for all eight Market Makers is 3700 shares, and the difference between the best Bid to the worst Bid is 2 points. So if the top seven Market Makers were to leave the Bid, the best Bid will fall 2 points from 92 to 90.

9. The total number of shares on the Ask side for all eight Market Makers is 2600 shares, and the difference between the best Ask to the worst Ask is 1 9/16. So if the top seven Market Makers were to leave the offer, the best Ask will rise 1 9/16 from 92 7/16 to 94.

Both examples we looked at were different yet similar. The main difference was that MSFT showed us depth, both on the Ask and the Bid side. Where CNET showed no depth on either the Bid or Ask side. The stocks were similar in the price they were trading at, around 92, but more importantly, neither one of them was showing an edge in making a decision to buy or sell. Based on the Level II Quote screen alone, we cannot see an edge that will help us in making a decision to buy or sell the stock. We would have to take other factors into consideration in cases such as these two.

The next example shows a snap-shot of Yahoo Level II Quote window.

	YHOO		174 7/16	↑ +6 1/16	
	High	181	Low	168	
	Bid ↓	174 1/4	Ask	174 7/16	

	Name	Bid	Size	Name	Ask	Size	
Three color ranges	ISLD	174 1/4	3	ISLD	174 7/16	3	Four color ranges
	INCA	174 1/8	3	INCA	174 5/8	9	
	SBSH	174 1/8	3	TNTO	174 3/4	8	
1/4 difference between best Bid to worst Bid	COWN	174	4	SBSH	175	1	1 1/16 difference between best Ask to worst Ask
	PURE	174	2	PERT	175 1/8	1	
	REDI	174	2	AGIS	175 5/16	2	
	MLCO	174	10	REDI	175 1/2	8	
	PERT	174	1	MASH	175 1/2	5	
	BRUT	174	4				

Reprinted with permission of Townsend Analytics, Ltd.

This is where a Level II Quote window can be helpful in showing which side of the equation, bulls versus bears, buyers versus sellers, supply versus demand, is showing more strength.

1. The Inside Market is 174 1/4 X 174 7/16. A spread of 3/16.

2. There are three color ranges on the Bid side and four color ranges on the Ask side.

3. The Ask side is not showing strength or depth. There is not much interest from Market Makers to sell the stock.

4. The Bid side is showing more depth than the offer side. This is sign of strength as there is interest from Market Makers to buy the stock.

5. If we look at the worst Bid and worst Ask there is a 1 1/2 point spread.

6. If some moderate selling is to take place, and the top seven Market Makers in the first three color ranges on the Bid side were to leave, the best Bid will fall 1/4 point from 174 1/4 to 174. The total amount of shares Market Makers are interest in buying in the first three color ranges is 2800 shares.

7. If some moderate buying is to take place, and the top seven Market Makers on the offer side were to leave, the best offer will increase by 1 1/16 from 174 7/16 to 175 1/2. The total amount of shares Market Makers are interest in selling in the first three color ranges is 2000 shares.

8. The total number of shares on the Bid side for all eight Market Makers is 3200 shares, and the difference between the best Bid to the worst Bid is 1/4 point.

9. The total number of shares on the Ask side for all eight Market Makers is 3700 shares, and the difference between the best Ask to the worst Ask is 1 1/16.

Based on the information we get from the Level II Quote alone, it seems that buying Yahoo makes more sense than selling it. We will look at this scenario later in one of our case studies examples.

We have looked at the anatomy of the Level II Quote and multiquote windows. We learned how to sort and analyze the data in these windows. We have featured different scenarios which showed depth or the lack of it. We have talked about the importance of the number in the Size column and showed how color ranges work. If at this point you did not get a good grasp of it, then I suggest you read these sections over again. It also takes time and practice to learn how to read a Level II Quote screen, especially in real time, when it changes rapidly. The thing I recommend is to practice reading Level II Quotes of less active stocks and move on to more active stocks as you feel your skills have improved. I am not saying to trade less active stocks, but just to analyze their Level II Quote screens as it will not change as rapidly as the ones of more active stocks will. With time, this will become second nature to you.

The Big Market Makers

It is extremely important to know who is buying or selling a particular stock. Some Market Makers are bigger players than other Market Makers and their presence on the Bid or Ask makes all the difference in the world, especially, for intraday and short-term trading. I think that the most valuable element in following the Level II Quote window is that I can track the activities of the big influential Market Makers. I have scored big profits with this analysis in the past and avoided bigger losses as well. The following is a list of the most active, influential, well-capitalized Market Makers.

Code	Firm Name
GSCO	GOLDMAN, SACHS & CO.
MLCO	MERRILL LYNCH, PIERCE, FENNER & SMITH INC.
MSCO	MORGAN STANLEY & CO., INCORPORATED
BEST	BEAR, STEARNS & CO. INC.
FBCO	CREDIT SUISSE FIRST BOSTON CORPORATION
PWJC	PAINEWEBBER INCORPORATED
MASH	MAYER & SCHWEITZER, INC.
NITE	KNIGHT SECURITIES, INC.
SBSH	SALOMON SMITH BARNEY INC.
SLKC	SPEAR LEEDS & KELLOGG CAPITAL MARKETS
HRZG	HERZOG, HEINE, GEDULD, INC.
LEHM	LEHMAN BROTHERS INC.
DLJP	DONALDSON, LUFKIN & JENRETTE SECURITIES CORPORATION
JPMS	J. P. MORGAN SECURITIES INC.
WARR	WARBURG DILLON READ LLC

This list contains, in my opinion and experience, the 15 most active Market Makers in the NASDAQ stock market. Get to know their code names as they will appear on a Level II Quote screen. Keep in mind that there are over 650 market participants making a market in a certain stock, so each stock can be unique as who is the active Market Maker is in that security.

Who is the AX?

The AX is the leading Market Maker. Remember, there are over 650 Market Makers in different securities, who make their money from trading profits. This causes competition which is good for the general investor. In theory, the competition among traders and trading firms is what narrows down the spread between the Bid and the Ask, which gives the buyer or seller a better "deal" on the fill price. This competition also brings in another element that is important to understand. They all want to be on the right side of the coin! In many cases, a stock can be controlled by a leading Market Maker, who is well capitalized, as he can sell or buy a very big number of shares. He can stand in the face of a rally and support a stock in panic selling situations. I have seen each one of the listed Market Makers kill a strong momentum in a stock or hold a stock up in the face of massive selling. Once the other big firms saw his actions they joined him in selling or buying, because they all want to be on the right side of the fence. The important thing is to learn how to locate the leading Market Maker, the AX, and avoid getting caught on the other side of the fence. The AX will normally spend more time on one side of the inside market, best Bid or best Ask than on the other side of the inside market. They will appear to do both selling and buying, but the key thing is to pay attention to how much they are buying versus selling. When you look at a Level II Quote screen for a while, you will be able to see and follow the movement of Market Makers. Pay attention to who is spending time where. Using Time & Sales Print Report will help in pointing out the AX. The easiest way to spot an AX is when he is sitting on the best offer or Bid with a size of 1000 shares, yet the print report shows several 1000 shares block going by at his price, and he does not leave his position on the inside Bid or offer. I have seen situations where 100,000 shares or more traded at that price and the Market Maker never left the inside Bid or offer. Pay attention to who is the active leading Market Maker and which side he is on.

Time & Sales Print Report

Time and sales is a transaction print report in which the time, the number of shares, and execution price are printed. Here is a snap-shot of Time & Sales Report for Yahoo Inc.

Date	Time	Price	Volume
4/1/99	14:58	175 1/4	200
4/1/99	14:58	175 5/16	100
4/1/99	14:58	175 1/4	100
4/1/99	14:58	175 1/4	100
4/1/99	14:58	175 5/16	100
4/1/99	14:58	175 1/4	300
4/1/99	14:58		
4/1/99	14:58		
4/1/99	14:58	175 1/4	200
4/1/99	14:58	175 1/4	200
4/1/99	14:58	175 1/4	200
4/1/99	14:59	175 3/16	300
4/1/99	14:59	175 3/16	500
4/1/99	14:59	175 1/8	1000
4/1/99	14:59	175	1000

Reprinted with permission of Townsend Analytics, Ltd.

There are four columns in this Time & Sales Print Report. Let's look at them from left to right.

Date: The date the trade took place.

Time: The time the transaction was reported.

Price: The price the trade was executed at.

Volume: The number of shares that were traded in the transaction.

Using Time and Sales with Level II

The Time and Sales report is an important tool for intraday and short-term trading. It shows the actual trades that are taking place and at what price. It helps in determining momentum for a stock and helps in identifying an AX. It is easy to see waves of buyers and sellers and the overall dynamics of the trades as they go by in front of your eyes. I use a **ticker** as a part of my Level II Quote window, which is similar to Time & Sales. The ticker does not show the time for every transaction, but it does show the number of shares and execution prices, as trades take place. The trades appearing on the ticker are in color, red or green on a black background. When there is a lot of buying, you see mostly green prints on the ticker, and when there is a lot of selling you see mostly red prints on the ticker. So, if you see a sea of green on your ticker and the stock is not going up, there is a serious seller out there. If you see a sea of red and the stock is not going down then there is a serious buyer out there. This is when you can find out who the AX is.

For example, let's say that DLJP is on the best offer for MSFT at 92 1/4. He is the only one there. When you look at the ticker, you see a sea of green prints flying by, yet DLJP is not changing his best offer price. In many cases, you will see trades start going at higher prices like 92 5/16, 92 3/8, yet DLJP is still on the best offer at 92 1/4. Before you know it, the world will join him on the offer to sell. The stock will tick down in price, and that sea of green will turn into a sea of red. In other cases, DLJP might tick up his best offer to 92 5/16, then to 92 3/8 etc. He is still a seller, but he is letting the stock go up somewhat. As soon as the Bid ticks down though, he may tick down the offer, and a sea of red prints will follow. In general, daytraders do not go against the AX. The most well known AX is GSCO. With the popularity of daytrading, and the amount of daytraders who follow GSCO, it gets even harder to make a buck if you are on the other side of the fence. However, you must beware of Market Makers' tricks and head fakes, which we will explore later.

Here is an example of an AX standing in the path of a stock as he is a strong seller. The AX is COWN.

WPNE		6 1/16		+2 1/8	
High	6 7/8	Low		3 15/16	
Bid	6 1/32	Ask		6 1/16	

Name	Bid	Size	Name	Ask	Size
HRZG	6 1/32	11	COWN	6 1/16	1
SHWD	6	4	TNTO	6 1/8	13
ISLD	6	10	SHWD	6 1/8	2
NITE	5 7/8	5	USCT	6 1/8	1
SLKC	5 7/8	1	ISLD	6 1/8	7
MASH	5 13/16	10	WDCO	6 1/4	10
USCT	5 13/16	1	MASH	6 1/4	1
COWN	5 5/8	1	NITE	6 1/4	6
WDCO	5 1/2	10	HRZG	6 1/4	11
BRUT	5 3/8	4			

Date	Time	Price	Volume
4/7/99	13:12		
4/7/99	13:12	6 1/16	1000
4/7/99	13:12		
4/7/99	13:12		
4/7/99	13:12	6 1/16	1000
4/7/99	13:12	6 1/16	100
4/7/99	13:12	6 1/16	1000
4/7/99	13:12		
4/7/99	13:12		
4/7/99	13:12	6 1/16	1000
4/7/99	13:12	6 1/16	100
4/7/99	13:12	6 1/16	2000
4/7/99	13:12		
4/7/99	13:12		
4/7/99	13:12		
4/7/99	13:12	6 1/16	100

Reprinted with permission of Townsend Analytics, Ltd.

White Pine Software (WPNE) had a nice day. It was up 50% on big volume. There were many buyers for the stock, and one very strong AX. Look at COWN sitting at the best offer showing 100 shares at 6 1/16. Look at the Time and Sales, it is all green, all trades are going at 6 1/16, actually 6300 shares. COWN is lying to us about the size of 100. Let's see what happens next.

WPNE		6 1/16		+2 1/8	
High	6 7/8	Low		3 15/16	
Bid	6 1/16	Ask		6 1/8	

Name	Bid	Size	Name	Ask	Size
NITE	6 1/16	5	COWN	6 1/8	10
HRZG	6 1/32	11	HRZG	6 1/4	11
ISLD	6 1/32	10	MASH	6 1/4	14
MASH	6	50	TNTO	6 1/4	10
SHWD	6	4	ISLD	6 1/4	14
SLKC	5 7/8	1	NITE	6 1/4	6
USCT	5 13/16	1	SHWD	6 1/4	5
COWN	5 11/16	1	USCT	6 3/8	1
WDCO	5 5/8	10	WDCO	6 3/8	10
BRUT	5 3/8	4			

Date	Time	Price	Volume
4/7/99	13:13		
4/7/99	13:13		
4/7/99	13:13	6 1/8	400
4/7/99	13:13	6 1/8	900
4/7/99	13:13	6 1/8	2000
4/7/99	13:13		
4/7/99	13:13		
4/7/99	13:13	6 1/8	100
4/7/99	13:13	6 1/16	100
4/7/99	13:13	6 1/8	100
4/7/99	13:13	6 1/16	100
4/7/99	13:13		
4/7/99	13:13		
4/7/99	13:13	6 1/8	100
4/7/99	13:13		
4/7/99	13:13		
4/7/99	13:13	6 1/16	800

Reprinted with permission of Townsend Analytics, Ltd.

At this stage COWN finally ticked up, he is showing a size of 1000, he is the only one on the best Ask at 6 1/8 but look at Time and Sales, 3600 shares went at 6 1/8 so far.

WPNE		6 1/8	↑ +2 3/16	
High	6 7/8	Low	3 15/16	
Bid ↑	6 1/16	Ask	6 3/16	

Name	Bid	Size	Name	Ask	Size
NITE	6 1/16	5	USCT	6 3/16	1
HRZG	6 1/32	11	COWN	6 3/16	10
ISLD	6 1/32	10	HRZG	6 1/4	11
MASH	6	50	MASH	6 1/4	14
SHWD	6	4	TNTO	6 1/4	10
SLKC	5 7/8	1	ISLD	6 1/4	14
COWN	5 3/4	10	NITE	6 1/4	6
WDCO	5 5/8	10	SHWD	6 1/4	5
USCT	5 5/8	1	WDCO	6 3/8	10
BRUT	5 3/8	4			

		---- WHITE PINE SOFT		
Date	Time	Price	Volume	
4/7/99	13:13			
4/7/99	13:13	6 1/16	800	
4/7/99	13:13	6 1/8	1000	
4/7/99	13:13	6 1/8	200	
4/7/99	13:13	6 1/8	100	
4/7/99	13:14	6 1/8	2000	
4/7/99	13:14	6 1/8	2000	
4/7/99	13:14			
4/7/99	13:14			
4/7/99	13:14	6 1/8	800	
4/7/99	13:14	6 1/8	1000	
4/7/99	13:14	6 1/8	300	
4/7/99	13:14	6 1/8	600	
4/7/99	13:14	6 1/8	200	
4/7/99	13:14	6 1/8	3000	
4/7/99	13:14			
4/7/99	13:14			

Reprinted with permission of Townsend Analytics, Ltd.

COWN ticks up again. Look at all the trades that went by at 6 1/8. Remember, he was the only seller. As you can see, 12,000 shares went by at 6 1/8. At this point, you should know that the upside potential for WPNE is very limited, because COWN is a serious seller, who has plenty of shares to sell.

WPNE		6 1/8	↑ +2 3/16	
High	6 7/8	Low	3 15/16	
Bid ↓	6 1/16	Ask	6 1/8	

Name	Bid	Size	Name	Ask	Size
NITE	6 1/16	5	COWN	6 1/8	1
HRZG	6 1/32	11	ISLD	6 1/8	10
MASH	6 1/32	10	USCT	6 3/16	1
SHWD	6	4	TNTO	6 3/16	20
ISLD	6	5	NITE	6 1/4	6
SLKC	5 7/8	1	HRZG	6 1/4	11
COWN	5 11/16	1	SHWD	6 1/4	5
WDCO	5 5/8	10	MASH	6 1/4	14
USCT	5 5/8	1	WDCO	6 3/8	10
BRUT	5 3/8	4			

		---- WHITE PINE SOFT		
Date	Time	Price	Volume	
4/7/99	13:15			
4/7/99	13:15	6 3/16	200	
4/7/99	13:15			
4/7/99	13:15			
4/7/99	13:15	6 1/16	1000	
4/7/99	13:15			
4/7/99	13:15			
4/7/99	13:15	6 3/16	1300	
4/7/99	13:15	6 1/16	500	
4/7/99	13:15			
4/7/99	13:15			
4/7/99	13:15	6 1/16	400	
4/7/99	13:15			
4/7/99	13:15			
4/7/99	13:15	6 1/8	100	
4/7/99	13:15			
4/7/99	13:15			

Reprinted with permission of Townsend Analytics, Ltd.

ISLD came in between the Bid and the Ask at 6 1/8. COWN immediately ticked down to be on the best offer. The AX likes to be on the best Ask or best Bid position. In this case, COWN positions himself on the best Ask as he is a serious seller. As soon as another MM or ECN downticks, COWN or any other Ax will tick down as well and join them.

WPNE		6 1/32	↓	+2 3/32	
High	6 7/8	Low		3 15/16	
Bid ↓	6 1/32	Ask		6 1/16	

Name	Bid	Size	Name	Ask	Size
HRZG	6 1/32	9	ISLD	6 1/16	1
NITE	6	10	COWN	6 1/16	1
MASH	6	10	WDCO	6 1/8	10
ISLD	6	5	USCT	6 1/8	10
SHWD	5 31/32	3	SHWD	6 7/32	1
SLKC	5 15/16	1	NITE	6 1/4	6
USCT	5 5/8	1	MASH	6 1/4	14
COWN	5 5/8	1	HRZG	6 1/4	11
BRUT	5 3/8	4	TNTO	6 1/4	10
WDCO	5 3/8	10			

----WHITE PINE SOFT			
Date	Time	Price	Volume
4/7/99	13:15		
4/7/99	13:15		
4/7/99	13:15		
4/7/99	13:15	6 1/32	1000
4/7/99	13:15		
4/7/99	13:15		
4/7/99	13:15	6 1/8	800
4/7/99	13:15	6 1/32	200
4/7/99	13:15		
4/7/99	13:15		
4/7/99	13:15		
4/7/99	13:15		
4/7/99	13:15		
4/7/99	13:16		
4/7/99	13:16		

Reprinted with permission of Townsend Analytics, Ltd.

ISLD ticks down to 6 1/16, COWN joins them immediately. Daytraders will rush to get out at this point.

WPNE		6	↓	+2 1/16	
High	6 7/8	Low		3 15/16	
Bid ↓	5 31/32	Ask		6	

Name	Bid	Size	Name	Ask	Size
SHWD	5 31/32	3	TNTO	6	20
NITE	5 7/8	5	ISLD	6 1/32	10
HRZG	5 13/16	5	COWN	6 1/16	1
SLKC	5 13/16	1	WDCO	6 1/8	10
MASH	5 3/4	1	USCT	6 1/8	1
ISLD	5 21/32	13	SHWD	6 7/32	1
COWN	5 5/8	1	HRZG	6 1/4	11
USCT	5 5/8	1	MASH	6 1/4	14
BRUT	5 3/8	4	NITE	6 1/4	6
WDCO	5 3/8	10			

----WHITE PINE SOFT			
Date	Time	Price	Volume
4/7/99	13:16		
4/7/99	13:16		
4/7/99	13:16	6	500
4/7/99	13:16	6	1000
4/7/99	13:16	6	100
4/7/99	13:16	6	3000
4/7/99	13:16		
4/7/99	13:16		
4/7/99	13:16		
4/7/99	13:16		
4/7/99	13:16		
4/7/99	13:16		
4/7/99	13:16		
4/7/99	13:16		
4/7/99	13:16	6	1000

Reprinted with permission of Townsend Analytics, Ltd.

Note all the prints at 6 on time and sales. These are not orders to buy, those are daytraders bailing out. TNTO is at the best offer at 6 now. Those are daytraders who entered sell orders on ARCA trying to get out on the Bid when it was 6.

WPNE		6	↓	+2 1/16			WHITE PINE SOFT		
High	6 7/8	Low		3 15/16		Date	Time	Price	Volume
Bid ↓	5 7/8	Ask		6		4/7/99	13:16	6	500
						4/7/99	13:16	6	1000
Name	Bid	Size	Name	Ask	Size	4/7/99	13:16	6	100
MASH	5 7/8	10	TNTO	6	20	4/7/99	13:16	6	3000
SHWD	5 27/32	5	USCT	6	10	4/7/99	13:16		
HRZG	5 13/16	5	COWN	6	1	4/7/99	13:16		
SLKC	5 13/16	1	ISLD	6 1/32	10	4/7/99	13:16		
NITE	5 13/16	5	WDCO	6 1/8	10	4/7/99	13:16		
ISLD	5 21/32	13	SHWD	6 7/32	1	4/7/99	13:16		
USCT	5 5/8	1	HRZG	6 1/4	11	4/7/99	13:16		
COWN	5 9/16	1	MASH	6 1/4	14	4/7/99	13:16	6	1000
BRUT	5 3/8	4	NITE	6 1/4	6	4/7/99	13:16		
WDCO	5 3/8	10				4/7/99	13:16		

Reprinted with permission of Townsend Analytics, Ltd.

COWN joins the best offer again. Note that the time is 13:16. No trades took place since the last example as you can see on the Time and Sales report.

WPNE		5 15/16	↓	+2			WHITE PINE SOFT		
High	6 7/8	Low		3 15/16		Date	Time	Price	Volume
Bid ↓	5 15/16	Ask		6		4/7/99	13:24		
						4/7/99	13:24		
Name	Bid	Size	Name	Ask	Size	4/7/99	13:24	6	1000
SLKC	5 15/16	1	COWN	6	1	4/7/99	13:24	6	100
HRZG	5 7/8	3	ISLD	6 1/16	36	4/7/99	13:24	6 1/16	100
NITE	5 7/8	10	SHWD	6 1/8	1	4/7/99	13:24	6	1000
WDCO	5 3/4	10	USCT	6 3/16	1	4/7/99	13:24	6	10000
MASH	5 3/4	1	HRZG	6 1/4	63	4/7/99	13:24		
SHWD	5 11/16	5	NITE	6 1/4	6	4/7/99	13:24		
USCT	5 5/8	1	TNTO	6 1/4	20	4/7/99	13:25	5 15/16	900
COWN	5 5/8	1	MASH	6 1/4	14	4/7/99	13:25	6	300
ISLD	5 5/8	10	REDI	6 1/2	10	4/7/99	13:25	6	500
BRUT	5 3/8	4				4/7/99	13:25		
						4/7/99	13:25		
						4/7/99	13:25	5 15/16	500

Reprinted with permission of Townsend Analytics, Ltd.

8 minutes go by, COWN is still on the best offer, alone, showing a size of 100 shares. Look at the trades on Time and Sales Report. 12,900 shares traded at 6. SLKC is the best Bid at 5 15/16.

WPNE			5 15/16 ↓	+2	
High	6 7/8		Low	3 15/16	
Bid ↓	5 7/8		Ask	5 15/16	

Name	Bid	Size	Name	Ask	Size
HRZG	5 7/8	3	COWN	5 15/16	1
NITE	5 7/8	20	TNTO	6	20
WDCO	5 3/4	10	ISLD	6 1/16	36
SLKC	5 3/4	1	SHWD	6 1/8	1
MASH	5 3/4	1	USCT	6 3/16	1
SHWD	5 11/16	5	HRZG	6 1/4	63
USCT	5 5/8	1	NITE	6 1/4	6
ISLD	5 5/8	10	MASH	6 1/4	14
COWN	5 9/16	1	REDI	6 1/2	10
BRUT	5 3/8	4			

----WHITE PINE SOFT			
Date	Time	Price	Volume
4/7/99	13:25	6	300
4/7/99	13:25	6	500
4/7/99	13:25		
4/7/99	13:25		
4/7/99	13:25	5 15/16	500
4/7/99	13:25		
4/7/99	13:25		
4/7/99	13:25		
4/7/99	13:25		
4/7/99	13:25		
4/7/99	13:25		
4/7/99	13:25		
4/7/99	13:25		
4/7/99	13:25		
4/7/99	13:25		

Reprinted with permission of Townsend Analytics, Ltd.

No trades took place, TNTO came in with 2000 at 6, the last 500 shares traded at 5 15/16 took the best Bid of SLKC, at 5 15/16 out, as seen in the previous example. COWN sees the opening and ticks down to sell at 5 15/16. He does not want to share his spot with TNTO.

WPNE			6 ↑	+2 1/16	
High	6 7/8		Low	3 15/16	
Bid ↓	5 7/8		Ask	6	

Name	Bid	Size	Name	Ask	Size
NITE	5 7/8	6	TNTO	6	20
COWN	5 13/16	1	HRZG	6	6
SLKC	5 3/4	1	ISLD	6 1/16	6
MASH	5 3/4	1	SHWD	6 1/8	1
SHWD	5 11/16	5	USCT	6 3/16	1
WDCO	5 11/16	10	COWN	6 3/16	1
ISLD	5 11/16	10	MASH	6 1/4	14
USCT	5 5/8	1	NITE	6 1/4	6
HRZG	5 5/8	7	WDCO	6 7/16	10
BRUT	5 3/8	4			

----WHITE PINE SOFT			
Date	Time	Price	Volume
4/7/99	13:25		
4/7/99	13:25		
4/7/99	13:25	5 7/8	300
4/7/99	13:25	5 7/8	700
4/7/99	13:25		
4/7/99	13:25		
4/7/99	13:25	5 7/8	300
4/7/99	13:25		
4/7/99	13:25		
4/7/99	13:25	5 7/8	700
4/7/99	13:25	6	500
4/7/99	13:25	5 15/16	500
4/7/99	13:25	5 15/16	100
4/7/99	13:26		
4/7/99	13:26		
4/7/99	13:26	6	400

Reprinted with permission of Townsend Analytics, Ltd.

This is my favorite part: COWN throws in a little head fake as he leaves the best offer at 5 15/16, and goes on the Bid, not the best Bid, but the second best Bid at 5 13/16. He is trying to tell people who are watching, "I am done selling. I want to buy." Should we believe him?

WPNE		5 13/16	↓	↑1 7/8	
High	6 7/8		Low		3 15/16
Bid ↓	5 13/16		Ask		6

Name	Bid	Size	Name	Ask	Size
NITE	5 13/16	5	NITE	6	20
SLKC	5 3/4	1	COWN	6	80
MASH	5 3/4	1	HRZG	6	12
ISLD	5 3/4	2	ISLD	6	10
SHWD	5 11/16	5	MASH	6 1/16	10
WDCO	5 11/16	10	SHWD	6 1/8	1
USCT	5 5/8	1	USCT	6 3/16	1
HRZG	5 5/8	7	TNTO	6 1/4	20
BRUT	5 3/8	4	WDCO	6 7/16	10
COWN	5 3/8	20			

WHITE PINE SOFT			
Date	Time	Price	Volume
4/7/99	13:29		
4/7/99	13:29		
4/7/99	13:29		
4/7/99	13:29		
4/7/99	13:29		
4/7/99	13:29		
4/7/99	13:30		
4/7/99	13:30		
4/7/99	13:31	5 13/16	1800
4/7/99	13:31		
4/7/99	13:31		
4/7/99	13:32	5 13/16	100
4/7/99	13:32	5 13/16	400
4/7/99	13:32		
4/7/99	13:32		
4/7/99	13:32	5 13/16	400

Reprinted with permission of Townsend Analytics, Ltd.

Of course, we should have not believed him. As soon as the Bid ticked down to 5 13/16, COWN tripped over his long liar nose and left the Bid. He also popped up on the best Ask showing size of 8000 for sale. Needless to say, COWN just killed the momentum in the stock. This is why it is so important to identify the AX.

The Dynamics of Level II Quote Window

When a stock is moving fast, only a handful of experienced traders will care which MM is at what price. Instead, traders watch the action on the screen. They watch how fast the levels change as the buying or selling frenzy goes on. Is the action pausing? Is it time for reversal? The movements on the screen along with the prints on the ticker show them the momentum.

CNET		92 5/16	↓	↑3/16	
High	95 1/4		Low		88 7/8
Bid ↓	92		Ask		92 5/16

Name	Bid	Size	Name	Ask	Size
HRZG	92	1	NITE	92 7/16	10
SBSH	92	10	SBSH	93	1
MASH	91 5/8	1	MLCO	93 1/4	1
NFSC	91 1/2	5	NFSC	93 3/4	1
NITE	91 1/2	2	PERT	93 7/8	1
INCA	91	10	EVRN	94	10
SHWD	90 5/8	1	FBRC	94	1
EVRN	90	7	SHWD	94	1

Reprinted with permission of Townsend Analytics, Ltd.

When a stock goes up in price, the movement on the screen is counter clockwise. It looks as the Bids are falling out from the bottom of the screen and the Ask side spits out the best offer. The best Bids will be pushed down in this action and be replaced with higher numbers. The best offer will be pushed out of the top and be replaced by a higher number.

CNET			92 5/16 ↓	+3/16	
High		95 1/4	Low	88 7/8	
Bid ↓		92	Ask	92 5/16	

Name	Bid	Size	Name	Ask	Size
HRZG	92	1	NITE	92 7/16	10
SBSH	92	10	SBSH	93	1
MASH	91 5/8	1	MLCO	93 1/4	1
NFSC	91 1/2	5	NFSC	93 3/4	1
NITE	91 1/2	2	PERT	93 7/8	1
INCA	91	10	EVRN	94	10
SHWD	90 5/8	1	FBRC	94	1
EVRN	90	7	SHWD	94	1

Reprinted with permission of Townsend Analytics, Ltd.

When a stock goes down in price, the movement on the screen is clockwise. It looks as the offers are falling out from the bottom of the screen and the Bid side spits out the best Bid. The best offer will be pushed down in this action and be replaced with lower numbers. The best Bid will be pushed out of the top and be replaced by a lower number.

Section Four

Advanced Order Execution Systems

Charts used in this section are provided by RealTick™ III and are used with the express written permission of Townsend Analytics, Ltd. RealTick™ III is a trademark and copyright of Townsend Analytics, Ltd.

NASDAQ Order Execution Systems

The following execution systems are not offered by traditional online discount brokers. They are offered by daytrading firms such as the Day Trading Company, in Irvine, CA. These order execution systems provide a very liberal way to route your order. In fact, you can be in total control in purchasing or selling a stock, because you choose the actual route for your order. You can buy a stock from a particular Market Maker or ECN by preferencing your order. You can trade between the Bid and Ask, you can even make a market as you Bid for stock, or offer stock at the inside market via an ECN. There are major advantages in using these order execution vehicles, but you must learn them very well before you attempt to use them. After all, you control the faith of getting in or out of a stock with your mouse click. You must know which way is the best and fastest way to enter or exit a position to be able to enjoy the advantages this system offers, otherwise, it will become a disadvantage.

SOES

SOES, Small Order Execution System, is an automated trading system that lets SOES participants enter and execute orders in active SOES-authorized NASDAQ securities. The stocks are separated into tiers of 200, 500 and 1,000 shares, depending on the trading characteristics of the stock. SOES participation is mandatory for Market Makers in the Nasdaq National Market. You may enter a SOES market order and/or marketable SOES limit orders. SOES does not permit all or none, fill or kill, good till cancel and good till date, type of orders. SOES orders are executed against Market Makers at the inside quote in rotation. Once a SOES order has been entered, SOES follows these steps to execute the order:

1. Identifies the Market Maker quoting the best price and who is first in line for SOES executions.
2. Executes the order.
3. Delivers trade report to the order-entry firm and the executing Market Maker.

The Market Makers displayed quote size reduces after each SOES execution. Market Makers can elect to update quotes automatically or manually after their displayed quote size is reduced to zero. Market Makers accept SOES executions up to the size of their displayed quote.

There are a few important things you need to know about SOES.

1. SOES was considered one of the fastest ways to get in or out of a stock. Orders used to be executed almost instantaneously. If you wanted to buy a stock that was going up in price in a fast moving market, it would have been an ideal execution vehicle to use, or if a stock was falling down hard and you needed to get out fast, SOES, again, was an ideal execution system to use. However, with the growing numbers of traders with access to SOES, Market Makers started suffering huge losses. Think about it this way, if a Market Maker was showing a Bid for INTC at X dollars and his size is 1000 shares, he has to honor 1000 shares for a SOES order. Now, let's say GSCO ticked down on the offer and 100 daytraders saw it and acted on it sending a SOES market sell order for 1000 shares, each. The poor Market Maker on the Bid would have gotten killed having to buy 100,000 shares of INTC (100 X 1000) from daytraders. Recent changes in SOES policy is giving a Market Maker the opportunity to back off from his Bid or offer once he is hit by a SOES order. He actually has time "to think about it" and refresh his quote without having to be exposed to excessive selling pressure.

2. All SOES orders are executed in the inside market, hence, you cannot enjoy price improvements. Orders to buy will get executed at the best Ask and orders to sell will be executed at the best Bid, even if the spread is 4 points.

3. You may use SOES to short sell a stock. It must be on an uptick, of course.

4. The 5 minute rule: This rule applies to all SOES orders. Once you have entered a SOES order for a stock, to buy or sell, and got filled, you must wait 5 minutes before you can enter another SOES order for that same stock, on the same side (buy or sell). For example, if you want to buy 2000 shares of PAIR, for which the SOES tier is 1000 shares, you can enter a SOES order to buy 1000 shares, but you have to wait 5 minutes before you can enter another SOES **buy** order for PAIR. However, if you wanted to buy a different stock via SOES or sell the 1000 shares of PAIR you just bought via SOES, you could do that anytime. There is no time restriction there. The time restriction only applies to placing an additional SOES order, in the same stock, on the **same** side (Bid or Ask), once you have executed an order via SOES in that stock.

5. With the growing popularity of ECNs, it is very common to see them at the inside market, which affects the efficiency of SOES orders, as you cannot SOES an ECN. This causes a big problem. All SOES orders must be exe-

cuted at the inside market. However, if an ECN represents the best Bid all by itself, and you wanted to sell using a SOES order, you cannot get a fill until a Market Maker joins the ECN on the best Bid, or the ECN leaves the best Bid and a Market Maker who is not in the process of filling a SOES order is at the best Bid.

ECN →

AMZN			171	↓	-1 3/16	
High		180 1/8	Low		167 1/2	
Bid ↓		170 15/16	Ask		171	

Name	Bid	Size	Name	Ask	Size
INCA	170 15/16	2	SWST	171	1
MASH	170 5/8	2	INCA	171 1/4	2
NITE	170 1/2	5	SLKC	171 3/8	1
PERT	170 1/2	10	HRZG	171 1/2	4
SBSH	170	1	MASH	171 1/2	3
SHWD	170	5	FBCO	171 3/4	1
FBCO	169 3/4	1	SHWD	171 15/16	5
NFSC	169 5/8	10	PERT	172	1

_{Reprinted with permission of Townsend Analytics, Ltd.}

Let's look at the above Level II Quote window. On the Bid side, you see INCA with 200 shares @170 15/16 followed by MASH with 200 shares @ 170 5/8, followed by NITE and PERT. Now, let's say that we were long 200 shares of AMZN. The stock was going down, and we wanted to sell. If we placed a sell SOES in this case, it would not get filled because INCA, which is an ECN represents the best Bid. Your order would become executable only if there is a Market Maker at the inside Bid. Here is the other problem. If INCA's Bid is taken out, then we will have MASH at 170 5/8 as the best Bid. Since he is the only Market Maker there, we have to pray that he is not in the process of filling another SOES order. If he is, then we have to wait for a Market Maker who is eligible for a SOES order and who is not in the process of filling another SOES order to be present at the inside Bid, before we could sell our stock. If there is a strong selling pressure, it would be almost guaranteed that we would get filled when the stock starts moving back up after it took a huge dive. The order will be executed one or two ticks away from the bottom. Sound familiar? Here is more information about what happens when an ECN represents the best Bid or offer: "Effective Monday, February 23, 1998, SOES orders will no longer be immediately returned when an ECN is alone at the inside (i.e., there are no Market Makers at the inside quote), in an NNM security. Now, SOES orders will be held in queue until executable for a specified period of time, initially set at 90 seconds. This "hold time" will give the market three options: 1) allow the ECN to move away, creating a new inside; 2) give the Market Makers time to adjust their quotes to create a new inside; or 3) allow the Market Maker to join the ECN at their price. If one of these events happens prior to the end of the ninety seconds, the order will either execute or be rejected if it is no longer executable. If none of these conditions occur, however, the order will time out at the end of the 90 seconds and be returned to the entering firm."

SOES can be used successfully with some stocks and in certain scenarios. However, as time goes on, I don't use SOES as often, because it is not as efficient as it used to be.

SelectNet

SelectNet offers traders the ability to automate the negotiation and execution of trades. Orders of any size up to 6 digits can be traded on SelectNet. SelectNet allows you to deal with all Market Makers or one individual Market Maker. Your order can be broadcasted to all Market Makers or preferenced to a specific Market Maker. Let's look at these type of order entries in more detail.

Broadcasting your order on SelectNet: When you enter a limit buy or sell order via SelectNet, you are broadcasting your order to all Market Makers (unless you preference the order.) The advantage in using an order like that is when there is a big spread. For instance, if XYZ stock's inside market is 85 3/8 X 85 7/8 then there is 1/2 point spread. You can buy at the best offer, 85 7/8, or you can electronically, try and negotiate a better price using SelectNet. If you were willing to pay 85 9/16 for the stock, then you can enter a SelectNet buy order at 85 9/16. Your order will be broadcasted to all Market Makers and if there was a Market Maker who was interested in selling at 85 9/16, you might get a fill. So, you can use SelectNet to trade in between the spread. You can also enter terms such as, all or none. Your order remains open until you cancel it, or the trading day ends.

SelectNet Preference Orders: SelectNet allows order-entry firms and Market Makers to direct orders to specified Market Makers, including ECNs. If a SelectNet order is directed to a specific Market Maker and is at the Market Maker's current Bid or offer, at the time the order was received, the Market Maker is subject to the Firm Quote Rule and has liability for its quoted price up to his displayed size. A Market Maker may respond to a preference order which is delivered to his trading terminal by:
1. Accepting the order.
2. Price improving the order.

3. Declining the order.
4. Countering or accepting a portion of the order.
5. Allowing the order to expire or time out.

Ten-Second Minimum Life of Preferenced SelectNet Orders: The SEC has approved a Nasdaq proposal to require a minimum life on preferenced SelectNet orders. Effectively immediately, Nasdaq will require a 10 second minimum life on preferenced SelectNet orders to Market Makers or ECNs. The 10 second period is measured by Nasdaq's clock. It is a violation of NASD conduct rules to cancel or attempt to cancel a preferenced SelectNet order prior to the expiration of this 10 second period. What this is saying is that the Market Maker has 10 seconds to look at your order and make a decision before you can even attempt to cancel it. You may use conditional terms, such as all-or-none, when you SelectNet preference a Market Maker other than an ECN.

Prohibition on Sending Conditional SelectNet Orders to ECNs: The SEC also approved a Nasdaq proposal that prohibits NASD members from placing any special conditions on SelectNet orders directed to ECNs. Those conditions include all-or-none orders, minimum-size orders, and non-negotiable orders.

You may enter orders which are out of the inside market via SelectNet Preference. This is a big advantage. You may Ask, why is it advantageous to sell a stock below the best Bid or buy a stock higher than the best offer? Aren't we supposed to buy low and sell high? Let's look at the same example used in the SOES section.

AMZN		171	↓	-1 3/16	
High	180 1/8	Low		167 1/2	
Bid ↓	170 15/16	Ask		171	

Name	Bid	Size	Name	Ask	Size
INCA	170 15/16	2	SWST	171	1
MASH	170 5/8	2	INCA	171 1/4	2
NITE	170 1/2	5	SLKC	171 3/8	1
PERT	170 1/2	10	HRZG	171 1/2	4
SBSH	170	1	MASH	171 1/2	3
SHWD	170	5	FBCO	171 3/4	1
FBCO	169 3/4	1	SHWD	171 15/16	5
NFSC	169 5/8	10	PERT	172	1

_{Reprinted with permission of Townsend Analytics, Ltd.}

The scenario was that we were long 200 AMZN and the stock was sliding down quickly. On the Bid side, you see INCA with 200 shares @170 15/16, followed by MASH with 200 shares @ 170 5/8, followed by NITE with 500 shares @ 170 1/2 and PERT with 1000 shares @ 170 1/2 . Remember, if we placed a sell SOES in this case, it will not get filled because INCA, which is an ECN represents the best Bid. Our order will become executable only if there is a Market Maker at the inside Bid. Here is the other problem: If INCA's Bid was taken out, then we will have MASH at 170 5/8 as the best Bid. Since he is the only Market Maker there, we have to pray that he is not in the process of filling another SOES order. If he is, then we have to wait for a Market Maker, who is eligible for a SOES order, who is not in the process of filling another SOES order, to be present at the inside Bid, before we could sell our stock.

In this situation, we could either SelectNet Preference MASH @ 170 5/8, NITE @ 170 1/2 or PERT @ 170 1/2. If the stock is moving down fast, I would not even bother trying to SelectNet INCA at the best Bid. I would go straight to PERT or NITE with a Preference order. I have seen a $100 stock drop 60 points in 14 minutes. If you did not use a SelectNet Preference, priced below the best Bid, you would have never been able to get out. Time and Sales report shows you the prints as they go by, and when they are all below the best Bid, you know that the stock is free falling. SOES will never get you out in this situation, not until the stock ticks back up. And forget about trying to sell between the spread, that won't work either. In this certain situation, we have to sell below the inside market, or buy at a higher price than the inside market. Such are the laws of supply and demand.

ECNs

ECN, Electronic Communications Network, matches orders from buyers and sellers together and executes them against each other. ECNs allow subscribing members to post Bids and offers for a stock. Non subscribers may not post Bids and offers on an ECN, but they may enter an order to buy or sell from an ECN subscriber who is posting a Bid or an offer for a stock, on that ECN, via a SelectNet Preference order. ECN subscribers are similar to Market Makers as they are able to post Bids and offers. The best Bid and best offer currently on an ECN are posted on a Level II Quote screen, however, unless you have access to the ECN book of orders, you cannot see if there are more sellers or buyers at a higher or lower price at any given time. The ECNs are growing in popularity and often represent the best Bid or offer for a security during the trading day. They are also becoming very liquid as the number of transactions and total number of shares traded on the ECNs are growing rapidly. The following are the code names and ECN names in the Nasdaq stock market, today.

Code	Firm Name
INCA	INSTINET CORPORATION
ISLD	ISLAND ECN
BTRD	B-TRADE SERVICES LLC
REDI	SPEAR, LEEDS & KELLOGG/Redi ECN
ATTN	ATTAIN-ECN
ARCA	TERRA NOVA TRADING, L.L.C.
STRK	STRIKE TECHNOLOGIES, L.L.C.
BRUT	THE BRASS UTILITY, L.L.C.
NTRD	PIM GLOBAL EQUITIES - ECN

The way an ECN executes orders is actually very simple. Let's say I have access to the Island ECN and I wanted to buy 500 shares of XYZ at 65 1/8. Once my order was entered, the ECN will look for a match. If there is an order to sell on the ECN book at 65 1/8 or lower, I will get a fill. If there is no matching order on the offer side then my order will be placed on the ECN book. It is also possible to get a partial fill, if someone is willing to sell 100 shares at 65 1/8, I will get a fill for 100 shares, and the balance of my order, 400 shares, will be placed on the ECN book.

I will be using the Island ECN exclusively in all of the following examples for the simple reason that the ISLD ECN is the most accessible ECN out there, and direct access to the ISLD is offered by more daytrading firms than any other ECN.

The Island book shows all open limit orders to buy and sell a stock. Let's look at an example featuring Yahoo stock. The next table shows the open orders on the ISLD ECN book.

	Bid Side	Ask Side
Total 1000 @ 176 1/16	600 @ 176 1/16	100 @ 176 1/4
	400 @ 176 1/16	100 @ 176 1/2
	400 @ 176	200 @ 176 3/4
	100 @ 176	400 @ 176 15/16

The book simply shows the number of shares a buyer or a seller is interested in and at what price. This is what this scenario will look like on a Level II Quote window.

YHOO		176	↓	-7 5/8
High	181	Low		168
Bid	176 1/16	Ask		176 1/8

Name	Bid	Size	Name	Ask	Size
ISLD	176 1/16	10	NITE	176 1/8	1
TNTO	176	4	BRUT	176 1/4	2
INCA	175 3/4	3	ISLD	176 1/4	1
REDI	175 3/4	6	MLCO	176 3/8	10
SLKC	175 11/16	1	TNTO	176 7/16	3
MASH	175 1/2	8	MASH	176 5/8	1
MLCO	175 1/8	10	SBSH	176 7/8	1
NITE	175 1/8	5	HMQT	177	10
HRZG	175	1			

Reprinted with permission of Townsend Analytics, Ltd.

Only the best Bid and best Ask are shown in the Level II Quote window. 1000 shares at 176 1/16 Bid and 100 shares at 176 1/4 offer. Although, there are two different orders to buy at 176 1/16, one for 400 shares and the other for 600, they will be totaled together on a Level II screen as they show the total amount of shares available at the best Bid or offering price on the ISLD book. The ISLD book, however, will show all the different orders by themselves.

Let's look at what happens next as the stock is trading.

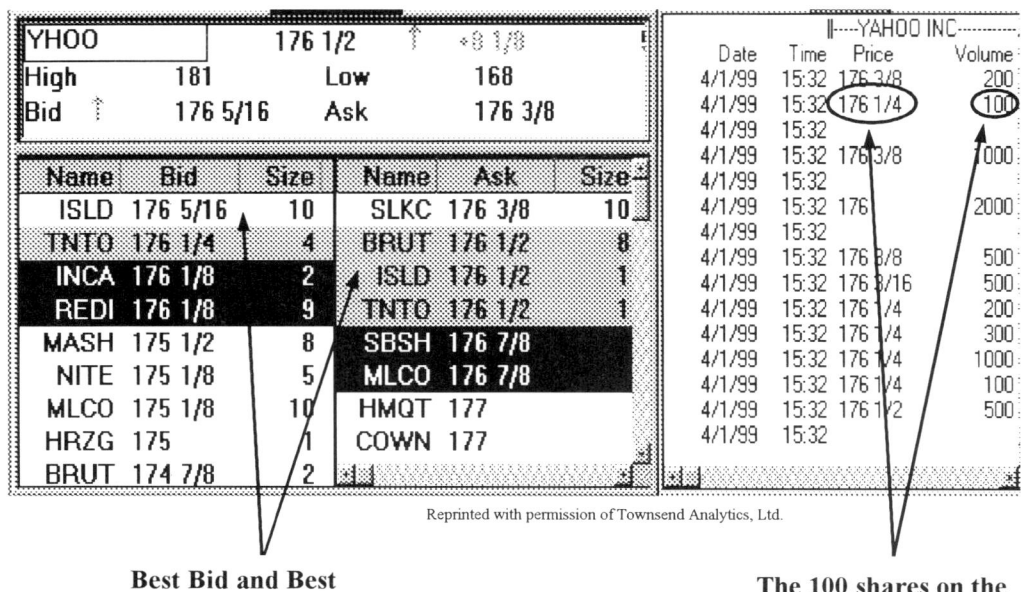

Reprinted with permission of Townsend Analytics, Ltd.

Best Bid and Best Ask have changed

The 100 shares on the offer were taken out

Buyers came in and Yahoo stock traded up. You can see the 100 shares offered on ISLD go by on the Time & Sale Report. New Bidders came in at higher prices, so the stock has ticked up, both on the Bid and the Ask side. We can look at the ISLD book again to see where these buyers and sellers are.

	Bid Side	Ask Side	
(1)	300 @ 176 5/16	100 @ 176 1/2	(4)
	700 @ 176 5/16	200 @ 176 3/4	(5)
(2)	400 @ 176 1/4	756 @ 176 3/4	(6)
(3)	600 @ 176 1/16	400 @ 176 15/16	(7)

1. Two new orders to buy Yahoo at 176 5/16 were entered, the total of 1000 shares is shown in the Level II Quote window, as it is the best Bid on ISLD.

2. Another new order to buy 400 shares at 176 1/4 was entered.

3. These are the same 600 shares that were the best Bid on ISLD shown in the previous snap-shot. They were a part of the total 1000 shares shown in

the Level II Quote window.

4. Once the 100 shares at 176 1/4, shown in the previous snap-shot, were taken out (traded), the next best offer, 100 shares at 176 1/2, has moved up and became the best offer. You can see it in the Level II Quote window snap-shot above.

5. These are the same 200 shares that were offered for sale in the previous snap-shot.

6. A new seller stepped in with 756 shares for sale. You can place orders for an odd-lot number of shares on ISLD. On a Level II screen it will only show as 700, should it become the best offer.

7. These are the same shares that were offered at 176 15/16 in the previous snap-shot.

The size displayed is always the actual size that is on the book. This means that if you see the ISLD on the best Bid or offer with 100 shares, that is all that is available at that price, unless new orders are being entered in. Whereas, when a Market Maker displays a size of 100 shares on the best Bid or offer, the Market Maker might be interested in buying or selling 25,000 shares, or more at that price, but they are not showing their real hand. ECNs always show their real hand, in size, once at the best Bid or offer. This leaves an open door for Market Makers to fake us out, which we will explore later.

Playing Market Maker

By using the ISLD ECN, we can play Market Maker. The ISLD ECN is very liquid in the actively traded stocks. This gives us an opportunity to participate in the market like a Market Maker. It might not be proper to compare it to a Market Maker, but I feel that if my Bid for a stock represents the inside market, (best Bid for a stock), and it is broadcasted on a Level II (and Level I) Quote screen, as the best Bid, then I am making a market in the stock. Here is an example, let's say that XYZ inside market quote is 85 1/8 X 85 3/4. If I enter an order to buy XYZ on ISLD at 85 3/16 then the quote will change to 85 3/16 X 85 3/4. I am now representing the best Bid, and if any order to sell at the market comes in from subscribing online trading firms such as Datek, I will get a fill at 85 3/16. I can then turn around and offer the stock at 85 11/16, which will be the best offer, and if a market order to buy the stock comes in from a subscribing firm like Datek, I will be filled again. Nice, I just made 1/2 a point profit by playing a Market Maker. Of course, this is all easier said than done, but the fact remains that ISLD offers us the opportunity to Bid or offer a stock at the best Bid or best offer. The beauty of it is that our order is broadcast to everyone. Everybody who has access to Level II Quotes or level I quotes will see it. Trading on ISLD is very efficient and can save you a lot of points in the long run. Probably 90% of my NASDAQ trades are executed on ISLD ECN.

More ISLD Stuff

1. Since ISLD allows for odd-lot orders to be placed on the book, you may get a lot of partial fills. I remember trying to buy 1000 shares of HCOM @ 8 5/8 and getting a fill of 2 shares, twice. This is the only draw back, and normally, you get at least 100 shares. In the more active stocks you can get your entire ordered filled fairly quickly (it may be a combination of partial fills).

2. You may buy or sell stock on ISLD outside of the inside market. Example, XYZ is going up in price very fast. You want to buy the stock, and the current inside market is 85 1/2 X 85 9/16. However, you know that everyone else is trying to buy as the momentum is so strong. At this time, you see that there are 500 shares on ISLD being offered at 85 7/8. You can enter an order to buy at 85 7/8 and hit that seller on ISLD. In a fast moving market, sometimes going out of market like that is very profitable.

3. Because you can trade outside of the market on ISLD you need to be careful when you enter an order. Sometimes things just move too fast in front of your eyes, and you can make mistakes. I heard a story of a fellow who bought 2000 shares of a hot IPO on their first day of trading. The stock was at 104 best Bid as it fell from 115. He decided to enter a sell order out of market on ISLD, as he was panicking. He was planning on entering the number 100, but instead he entered 10. A pop up warning window was telling him that he was selling below the market, he clicked OK, knowing that 100 was lower than 104. This poor, unlucky guy sold his 2000 shares in 27 different partial fills all the way down to $37. There were no buyers on ISLD at decent prices, but he did not know. He thought that he would pick up all the buyers over 100, he picked up all the buyers over 37 instead. Needless to say, he lost a lot of money. Remember this, always make sure you check your order thoroughly before you click the buy/sell button.

4. **You may not lock or cross a market!** This is actually very important. You cannot enter an order on ISLD to buy or sell a stock that would lock or cross the market. This is how you lock or cross a market when you use ISLD.

Name	Bid	Size	Name	Ask	Size
INCA	177 15/16	3	MASH	178	21
ISLD	177 7/8	4	BRUT	178 1/16	4
TNTO	177 13/16	3	INCA	178 1/16	10
MASH	177 3/4	2	TNTO	178 3/16	4
BEST	177 5/8	1	MLCO	178 3/8	10
FBCO	177 5/8	1	HRZG	178 3/8	1
HRZG	177 9/16	1	HRCO	178 1/2	1
SLKC	177 9/16	1	REDI	178 1/2	2
AGIS	177 5/16	1			

YHOO 178 ↑ +9 5/8
High 181 Low 168
Bid ↑ 177 15/16 Ask 178

Reprinted with permission of Townsend Analytics, Ltd.

Yahoo's inside market is 177 15/16 X 178. Let's say I wanted to buy the stock at 178 as it was going up. If I enter a buy order on ISLD at 178, I would be crossing the market! This is why. Remember when we enter an order to buy a stock on ISLD, ISLD is looking to match the order with a seller. If a seller is not there, then it places your order on the book, and your Bid is visible to the world. In this case, you entered an order to buy YHOO at 178 on ISLD. ISLD is searching for a seller but can't find one at 178 or better (look at the Level II screen, only MASH is selling at 178), it will now attempt to post your order as a Bid at 178. However, since the best offer is 178, your Bid will cross the market as it will be 178 X 178. This is against the rules implemented by Nasdaq, so the order will kick back to you saying that it was "killed by the exchange for reason: would lock or cross market." This is why it is important to remember how to use all execution vehicles. Here is another example of what can happen when entering orders on ISLD.

YHOO		177 7/32	↓	-8 27/32
High	181	Low		168
Bid ↑	177 1/16	Ask		177 1/4

Name	Bid	Size	Name	Ask	Size
ISLD	177 1/16	10	BRUT	177 1/4	1
PRUS	177 1/16	10	INCA	177 1/4	5
MLCO	177	2	ISLD	177 1/4	7
TNTO	176 15/16	1	COWN	177 3/8	10
REDI	176 13/16	9	TNTO	177 7/16	2
FBCO	176 1/2	1	PERT	177 1/2	1
BRUT	176 1/2	2	HRCO	177 1/2	1
HRZG	176 1/4	1	REDI	177 1/2	1
AGIS	176 3/16	1			

← 700 shares @ 177 1/4

Reprinted with permission of Townsend Analytics, Ltd.

In this case, let's assume that we wanted to buy 1000 shares of YHOO on ISLD at the offer price of 177 1/4. We enter the order and get a fill of 700 shares and the rest of the order gets killed. The reason is that there were only 700 shares offered on ISLD which were matched against our order, the remaining 300 shares, would cross the market at 177 1/4, so the exchange kicks back the remainder of the unfilled order.

However, the most frustrating situation occurs when you see the 700 shares offered by ISLD on the Ask and you want to buy 500 shares. You enter and order to buy, but someone else got to those shares a fraction of a second before you did. Your order kicks back telling you that the exchange killed it for the reason it will lock or cross the market. But you feel cheated because you saw those 700 shares right there on the best Ask, where did they go ... Well, either someone else got them or the order was cancelled by the offering party, just before you hit him with your buy order. Can you feel the frustration now? Can you imagine your frustration when you see the stock is up 35 points from that entry you got "cheated" on, in a matter of 2 hours? You will have to learn to live with it! It is a part of the game.

ARCA

This is another execution system that was put together by Terra Nova Trading and Townsend Analytics. Recently, Goldman Sachs and E*Trade Group bought about 25% ownership each in this execution system. The increase in the popularity of daytrading is obviously evident with this latest investment of these two powerhouses in ARCA. ARCA is a unique order execution system as it is not an ECN or a primary Nasdaq execution system, but a set of formulas which makes a decision in how to route an order. ARCA works like this:

When you enter an order to buy or sell a stock with ARCA, the first thing ARCA will do is look for an ECN at your specified price. If it finds an ECN that meets your price it will SelectNet preference your order to that ECN. If there is no ECN found at the specified price it will determine which one of the Market Makers at the inside market is the most active in the stock, based on their data. Once it determines who that Market Maker is, it will SelectNet preference that Market Maker. ARCA will leave the SelectNet preference order open for a maximum of 30 seconds. If the order is rejected or expired, ARCA will preference the second most active Market Maker and repeat the preference process until the order gets filled or cancelled by you. Orders on ARCA will remain open (live) unless you cancel. You may not place odd-lot orders on ARCA, all orders must be in multiples of 100 shares. You can also use ARCA to trade in between the spread. You can bid or offer a stock. ARCA uses ARCA ECN and if it is unable to find a match for your order, it will place it on ARCA ECN. This is a really nice feature.

There are advantages to using ARCA as it does all the thinking for you, but there are also disadvantages. Due to the popularity of daytrading more and more orders come in on the ARCA system. In fast moving markets, up or down, demand and supply are pretty much one-sided. There are a lot of buyers or a lot of sellers. If there are 100 daytraders who want to sell 1000 shares of XYZ Corp at the exact same time using ARCA, the efficiency of the system will be its enemy. Who would ARCA preference all those shares to? Who wants to wait 30 seconds in a blood-bath scenario before being able to cancel an order? But, it can also work in your favor, as it is really hard to know how to route your orders in this situation, especially, when you are about to take a big loss.

ARCA is a good execution vehicle, especially for beginners who want to Bid and offer stock like a Market Maker. It is very simple as it does all the thinking for you. However, I do not recommend trading a fast moving market situation using ARCA, it is too slow for these scenarios.

Market Makers Tricks

It would be a perfect stock market if the sizes shown on a Level II Quote window were the truth, the only truth, and nothing but the truth. However, I am afraid it isn't so. Market Makers are artists, or as my buddy refers to them, actors. They are experts in the art of deception. If you have not, yet, been caught in a situation, where you thought you had the upper hand, only to find out that you were totally fooled by a Market Maker, you must have not been trading with a Level II Quote screen. We have discussed the presence of an AX, the leading Market Maker, and how important it is to know who it is. Once you recognized who the active Market Maker is, you can run into some problems when he starts pulling tricks out of his hat. Before we continue, it is important to understand that Market Makers are out there to make money from a markup, buying a stock low and selling it slightly higher, or short selling a stock and covering at a slightly lower price. It is impossible to try and second guess why a Market Maker is a buyer or a seller. They can have an order sitting on their table, they might want to take a short-term position, long or short. They can be just scalping a stock making fractional gains, or who knows what they are doing. If a Market Maker has an order to sell 200,000 shares from a big institution sitting on his desk, then he will sell some at price X and buy some at price A, sell some more at price Z buy some at price B etc. He will average out a certain sell price and be net −200,000 shares at the end of the day and fill that order. Normally, a Market Maker will not take one side only and make it so obvious that he has "some" shares for sale. He will be bouncing back and forth from the Bid to the Ask, he will use INCA and other methods to deceive the traders. The important thing to remember is that Market Makers can fool you, and there is no golden rules on how to avoid it.

Example 1: There are 10 different MMs on the best Bid with 1000 shares size each. There is only one MM on the best Ask showing a size of 1000 shares. The ticker is showing many trades at the Ask price and the stock is not ticking up, what is going on? The Market Maker on the best offer has "some" shares to unload. He recognizes this golden opportunity to sell his inventory in the face of a strong rally. He will remain alone at the best offer, and he will unload as many shares as he can at that price.

Example 2: Consider that example 1 just took place 1/2 an hour ago. At this time, you see that same Market Maker who was doing all the selling sitting on the best Bid. In addition, you see the ECNs joining him on the best Bid and the sizes on the best offer are diminishing leaving only INCA and ISLD on the offer with 2000 shares each. In this case, many traders will rush in as they see the AX is buying, trying to take the ISLD and INCA best offer out. The ticker is all green. Daytraders in this case will even go out of market to buy the stock. But something interesting is happening. The sizes on ISLD and INCA keep on coming back, they are taken out and coming back, the ticker is all green, finally ISLD and INCA are gone and guess what, the AX is switching over from best Bid to best offer. Ouch that hurts, it was the AX offering all the shares on the ECNs, but no one knew it was him. He looked like a buyer on the best Bid.

Example 3. An AX is selling a stock hard and he is the only one on the offer. He switches sides to the best Bid, and this creates even a bigger buying frenzy. In the meantime, he is selling on INCA and ISLD as the stock moves up 3/8. He keeps on ticking up his Bid looking like a serious buyer, but since every one else is buying, there are no sellers really, so he is not buying a lot of shares, in the meantime he is unloading on INCA, ISLD and SelectNet. That MM can run the price up and then kill the momentum as he switches sides over to the best offer. The stock can fall down 1/2 a point really quickly where he will sit on INCA, ISLD or SelectNet and cover some short positions for a good quick profit.

I never base my trading decision on which MM is buying or selling. In general, I try and stay out of an AX's way. However, if I see something I like, and I wanted to be in that stock, the MM tricks will be the last thing that will make me change my mind. The important thing to know is which MM is an overall buyer and who is a seller, so if you need to enter a SelectNet Preference order to enter or exit a position, you can immediately preference that MM.

Which Execution System Should I Use?

This is the one million dollar question. Things change rapidly in the stock market and what is true today will not be true in a few months, but I will do my best in giving a general idea using different scenarios as to which execution system I would use. Before I continue, if you noticed, the section about SOES orders was written in past tense, "SOES was considered one of the fastest ways to get in or out of a stock." It **WAS.** Keep that in mind, as what I write in present tense could become past tense sooner than we know.

The stock market has become extremely volatile. The new wave of online trading and interest in Internet stocks has changed the face of trading. A stock can go up or down as much as 10-35 points in matter of minutes. This is when you must know how to get in or out **FAST.**

First let's look at Bidding or offering a stock. As I previously mentioned, I use the ISLD ECN about 90% of the time to execute NASDAQ trades. The reason is that ISLD is very liquid since it is used by numerous subscribing firms who give their customers direct access to the ECN. This is done electronically and confirmations for filled orders and cancellations are instantaneous.

AMZN		171	↓	–1 3/16
High	180 1/8	Low		167 1/2
Bid ↓	170 15/16	Ask		171

Name	Bid	Size	Name	Ask	Size
INCA	170 15/16	2	SWST	171	1
MASH	170 5/8	2	INCA	171 1/4	2
NITE	170 1/2	5	SLKC	171 3/8	1
PERT	170 1/2	10	HRZG	171 1/2	4
SBSH	170	1	MASH	171 1/2	3
SHWD	170	5	FBCO	171 3/4	1
FBCO	169 3/4	1	SHWD	171 15/16	5
NFSC	169 5/8	10	PERT	172	1

Reprinted with permission of Townsend Analytics, Ltd.

Let's look at the Level II quote screen above for AMZN. The inside market for AMZN is 170 15/16 X 171. If I wanted to buy AMZN at or below the best Bid price (170 15/16 or lower), I will enter a limit order to buy AMZN at the desired price using the ISLD ECN. I will be bidding for AMZN in this case. In other words, **if you want to bid for a stock at or below the inside market, route your order using ISLD.**

If I wanted to sell AMZN at the best offer or at a higher price (171 or higher), I will enter a limit order to sell AMZN at the desired price using the ISLD ECN. I will be offering the stock in this case. In other words, **if you want to offer a stock at the best offer or at a higher price, route your order using ISLD.**

If you want to buy at the best offer and ISLD is present at that price level route your order using ISLD.

If you want to sell at the best Bid and ISLD is present at that price level route you order using ISLD.

In the case you want to buy or sell at the inside market and ISLD is not present at that price level, you may use ARCA, SelectNet or SelectNet Preference.

If a stock is moving up fast and you want to get in you should:

1. Enter a buy on ISLD up to three levels above the best offer. This may cross or lock a market. If it does just keep clicking "buy ISLD." You might get lucky and a sell order will hit just as you place a buy order.

2. SelectNet Preference MM up to three color levels above the best offer.

3. Enter a buy on ARCA up to three color levels above the best offer.

4. **Wait for a price pull-back!** Buy it when it comes down and turns around to go up again.

If a stock is tanking hard, and you need to get out!

1. Take out the Best ISLD Bid (out of market).

2. SelectNet Preference up to five color levels below best Bid.

3. **Do not use SOES.**

4. **Do not use Arca.**

In less volatile stocks, you may not need to go more than 1-2 color ranges out of market, but in crazy volatile stocks, you can even miss it five color ranges below best Bid. You must know the stock you are trading!

Section Five

Trading for a Living

Charts used in this section are provided by RealTick™ III and are used with the express written permission of Townsend Analytics, Ltd. RealTick™ III is a trademark and copyright of Townsend Analytics, Ltd.

Trading for a Living

This is a full-time job! In fact, it is more than a full-time job. **Short-term trading consists of three key elements: Research, Strategy and Execution.** The first element, research, is done after the market closes and before the market opens. You scan for potential winners, look at charts, analyze market data, etc. Once you have found a potential trade, you go into the next phase which is trading strategy. In this phase, you plan out your trade. Once you have completed the strategy for your trade you move on to execution. Execution is done during market hours in which you simply execute your trading plans (strategy).

Research

Most of the research I do takes place at night, after the market closes. I follow hundreds of stocks and scan for new stocks, on a daily basis. I have learned to glance at a chart of a stock in a couple of seconds and determine if there is something I like. This does take some practice, but when you do it for a while it becomes routine. Once I finish reviewing charts of the stocks I follow on a daily basis, I run a scan for stocks which have traded 30% over their average daily volume. This can be done at this website, *http://www.iqc.com/research/customscan.asp* I check the following fields before I run the scan:

1. Stock Price between 5-1000
2. Volume between 500,000 and 100,000,000
3. Volume 30% higher

You can set the exchange, industry, prices and volume anyway you like them. The key criteria of this scan is the volume change in the last trading session. This is important, because most of the breakouts, pattern confirmations, etc. take place on higher than average volume. Once I have the results in front of me, I only look at stocks that have moved up or down, in price, 5/8 of a point, or more. I then enter each stock into my study page. My study page consists of a multiquote window linked to three charts. When I enter a symbol into the multiquote window, it updates all three charts, at once. These charts include:

1. 120-Day Daily Bar Chart with the following technical indicators, 50-day MA, 20-day MA, 10-day MA, 14-day RSI, 10-day RSI and volume. (This chart takes about 70% of my screen)

2. 350-Day Daily Bar Chart with the following technical indicators, 200-day MA and 50-day MA

3. 5-minute Intraday Bar Chart with Volume.

I use the intraday chart to make sure the volume for the stock, that day, did not come in a span of 20 minutes or so, like a few blocks by institutions. Remember, I am looking for stocks which are moving on higher than average daily volume. I want to see that the interest in the stock was there for a good part of the trading day, unless it was at the last hour, which will be studied differently. Every stock that I like from the looks of the chart, I enter into a list which I call the Candidate List. I then turn to *briefing.com* to see if any of the candidates are due to report earnings or scheduled for a stock split. I need to see if a stock is going up in anticipation of some news, earnings, stock split, etc. I do not normally like to hold stocks into earnings release as it represents added risk. I also stay away from Biotech stocks which are moving in anticipation of FDA approval etc., as these will sell off, more often than not, on the news regardless if the news is good or not. When I finish analyzing what is moving these stocks, I narrow it down to a Final List. I then bring up a chart for each one of these stocks and write out a trading strategy.

Please note, although I stated above that research is done after the market closes and before the market opens, you can also do research during market hours. In fact, you can run real-time scans and find potential trades, I will talk about real-time scans later.

Trading Strategy

This is the most important element for successful trading. Every trade you enter should have a strategy behind it. This strategy must include an entry price, a target price, a stop loss price and a time frame. You must also calculate the risk/reward ratio before you enter a trade. This can be done by dividing the full potential profit at the target price by the maximum amount of money you are willing to lose. I like to trade on a 5 to 1 ratio, but will take position in a 3 to 1 ratio as well.

Here is an example:

XYZ is trading at 91 1/4. By the look of the chart, I think it can go to 96 over the next 2 weeks, There is good support at 90, but stronger support at 89. This is how I create my trading strategy. If I buy right now my entry price will be 91 1/4, my selling price target is 96. If I sold at 96 then I will make 4 3/4 points. I know there is support at 90, if it breaks below 90 I will sell at 89 3/4. My stop loss is 1 1/2 points. The risk reward ratio is 4.75/1.5=3.16. It is over 3, so I will consider it a moderate risk reward ratio, and will execute a trade.

I use a Trading Strategy Table to make all these entries, so it is easier to keep track of. I am including this table so you can copy it, if you wish.

Explanations of the Fields in the Trading Strategy Table: I have filled in the fields using the data from the last example of XYZ stock. I have made up numbers for resistance level and earnings date as they were not used in the example. The rest of the data should match the entries in the respective fields.

Stock Symbol: XYZ
In this field, enter the ticker symbol for the stock.

Current Price: 91 1/4
In this field, enter the last price the stock traded at. If you do the research at night, it should be the closing price from the previous trading day.

Target Price : 96
In this field, enter the price you think the stock will go to.

Time Frame: 2 Weeks
In this field, enter the amount of time you think the stock can reach the target price. Keep in mind that when you are in a position, there is the time cost (opportunity cost) as your money is tied up in a position and can be allocated elsewhere.

Entry Point : 91 1/4
In this field, enter the price you want to enter the position at. It can be higher or lower than the current price, depending if you are looking to buy a dip or a breakout, etc.

Stop Loss: 89 3/4
In this field, enter the maximum you are willing to lose. If the stock goes in the other direction, at what price must you get out to limit your losses to the maximum you have allowed?

Risk/Reward: 3.16
In this field, enter the result from the calculation of the risk/reward ratio.

Trading Strategy Table

Stock Symbol	Current Price	Target Price	Time Frame	Entry Point	Stop Loss	Risk/ Reward	Support Level	Resistance Level	Earnings Date	Desired Position

Support Level: 90
In this field, enter the support levels as you see them on the chart.

Resistance Level: 96 7/8
In this field, enter the resistance levels as you see them on the chart.

Earnings Date: 6/26
In this field, enter the scheduled date for the next earnings release.

Position Desired: Long
In this field, enter long or short.

Once we have filled in the data and established a trading strategy, all that is left is to execute it!

Execution

This is the fun part. You have worked so hard to find candidates for your next trade. You have developed a trading plan for each one of the candidates. Now, all that is left to do is execute your trading plan. The way I look at it, is as if I am a soldier who has to follow orders in a battle. My superiors have worked hard to research the situation, they have sent their findings to the experts who developed the war plan, I now have to follow. If I disobey my orders, I would be charged and tried in military court. Sounds harsh, doesn't it? The execution part of the business is the disciplinary one. You must possess these essential disciplinary skills in order to execute your strategy as planned. You have to think of yourself as three different people who do three different jobs. The first is research, the second is strategy and the third is execution. Discipline is the key to executing trades. Of the three key elements of trading, no one element is more important than the others. One can be more fun than the others, but all three are essential.

Trade Records

It is important to keep trade records for every trade you make. These can be analyzed later to determine which type of plays are more successful than others, and which stocks, industries or types of plays you should avoid completely. I have created a special form to help me keep track of all my trades and their performance. Let's use the data from the previous example and say that I bought XYZ at 91 1/8 and sold it 6 days later at 94 5/16.

Original Strategy

Stock Symbol	Current Price	Target Price	Time Frame	Entry Point	Stop Loss	Risk/Reward
XYZ	91 1/4	96	2 Weeks	91 1/4	89 3/4	3.16

Actual Executed Trade

Stock Symbol	Position Taken	Share Number	Entry Price	Exit Price	Time Held	Profit/Loss
XYZ	LONG	500	91 1/8	94 5/16	6 DAYS	+1593.75

Notes:

XYZ's quote was 91 X 91 5/16. I entered an order to buy on ISLD at 91 1/8 and got a fill. The stock went as low as 90 11/16 and never went lower. I stayed in the position for 6 days. My target price was 96, but the stock seemed to have peaked at 95 1/4 on the 4th day of the trade. I trailed my stop loss and placed it 3/4 away from the high of 95 1/4 to protect profits. The stock sold off and I took best ISLD out at 94 5/16, best bid was 94 7/16 at the time, but I wanted a sure fill so I took out the best ISLD.

Trade Records

Original Strategy

Stock Symbol	Current Price	Target Price	Time Frame	Entry Point	Stop Loss	Risk/ Reward

Actual Executed Trade

Stock Symbol	Position Taken	Share Number	Entry Price	Exit Price	Time Held	Profit/ Loss

Notes

_____

_____

_____

_____

_____

_____

_____

_____

Ego

It is important to understand that ego plays a major role in trading stocks. It probably represents the best and worst quality a trader can have. I am not an expert on the definition of ego in trading, but I know of one thing that is found in abundance, and that is losing because your ego does not allow you to close a losing position quickly. I have mentioned before that you have to think of yourself as three different people who have three different jobs. Wait, don't call the "white jacket people" on me yet. The big problem, in this business, is that you can be, and will be, wrong in finding the "good" candidates and in developing trading strategies. What arises from that is the fact that you have to admit you were wrong when you take a realized loss. If you have a big loss sitting in your portfolio, that is not realized, then it is because you have not yet admitted that you were wrong. In short-term trading, as a business, we have to admit that we are wrong on a daily basis and cut our losses short. I would rather have one winner that reaches my price target make up for three losers, than have three winners making up for one loser. In short, lose your ego when you take losses. The bottom line is the important thing! As long as you turn a profit, you are doing well.

Money Management

It is important to understand the difference between investing and trading for a living. When we invest money, we look to make a certain return on the investment which is normally measured by percent. When we trade for a living, we try to create income, which is measured by dollars and cents. I have found that you need to keep the two separate! You should have an investment account, for long-term growth, pension, etc., and a short-term trading account which will be traded for the purpose of generating income. **Your short-term trading account should never have more money in it than the total amount of money you are willing to lose!** No one is willing to lose money. What I mean by willing to lose is an amount of money you do not need to live on, pay bills etc., and if it was lost, you will not be left naked without a dime to call your mother on Christmas eve. I have found that most short term traders are comfortable with either $50,000, $75,000 or $100,000 accounts plus margin, which gives them a buying power of twice the principle amount. In all of the following examples, I will use a $50,000 account plus margin, which will be $100,000 buying power (you must have a margin account in order to short sell).

If I had a $50,000 short term account, this is how I would manage it. First, I would divide the buying power (50,000 x 2 = 100,000 on margin) into four (which gives me $25,000). This is as much as I will put into one position. Next, I take the $25,000 and divide it into two. I like to get into a position in two stages (especially in real volatile stocks), so I will use $12,500 in the first stage and another $12,500 in the second stage (if stock price is $5, I might even buy in three stages). If I wanted to hold a stock overnight, It cannot be tie up more than 15% of my buying power. There is an additional risk to holding a position overnight.

Once I establish a new position, I follow it closely. If it does not do what I thought it would do, I will close it immediately. I always set stop loss orders (they vary with volatility etc. but normally at 7/8 loss from my entry point). Next, if the stock is going in the anticipated direction what do I do? I use trailing stops. As the stock moves up, I increase (decrease in a short position) the limit on the stop (again depending on volatility, etc.) I will make it tighter and tighter, as the stock gets closer to the price target, until I get stopped out.

Example: On 4/21/98 HCOM was moving up nicely in the morning to $10.00 a share, then it came back to $8.625 and traded in that range most of the day. I placed a Stop buy order for 1000 shares at 10 1/8. The stock hit 10 1/8 (intra day high) and I got a fill. I bought another 700 shares at 10 3/8, and another 700 shares at 10 5/8. The stock went completely vertical at this point. It hit 14 in the next 5 minutes of trading, and I started placing my stop loss orders, 1 point behind, so when the stock hit 15, I placed my stop at 14. When the stock hit 16, I placed my stop at 15. When It hit 18, I placed my stop at 17. The stock went as high as 18 1/4 and took a nose dive. I got stopped out at 16 1/2 (this is how fast it dropped all the way to 10 3/8 in a few minutes). I managed a very nice profit in this trade by exercising trailing stop-loss strategy. You may choose to practice mental stop-loss strategy or electronically set them up. Some brokers offer stop loss orders and some don't. If you have general questions about stop loss orders, consult your broker as each broker may have a different policy in regards to accepting these type of orders. The next question is, what do I do with the profits? I hope all we ever have to worry about is what to do with the profits :-).

Please note, this money management example is very aggressive and may not be appropriate for everyone. Although $25,000 sounds like a lot of money, it does not buy that many shares. For instance, $25,000 would not even buy 100 shares of EBAY, at one point of time. Keep in mind that short-term trading is very risky. Capital allocation, in many cases, has to be very aggressive.

The Sweeping Philosophy

It is actually very simple. At the end of each week, I call my broker and order a check! I keep my short-term trading account at the principle of $50,000, everything over that amount is swept out of the account. If I made $100 or $40,000 that week, it does not matter, I will order a check for that amount. I use that money to pay my bills, take my wife out to dinner, travel, or buy my baby new shoes. If I have made more money than I planned on spending, I will allocate it to longer term investments, most of which will be applied to stock index funds, or spiders (SPY or QQQ on the American stock exchange.) This system allows me to enjoy the fruits of my work and invest for long term growth. If I have a losing week, I do not add money back into the account. I will work with the same capital until I get back over $50,000 and draw checks again. This will prevent me from losing a lot if I hit a slump.

Winning Streaks

These are wonderful and dangerous at the same time. The positive effect is of course the fact that you are making money. The danger is that every streak comes to an end. You must exercise the same trading strategy throughout your winning streak. Do not think that you are God and can't do anything wrong. At the same time, do not get gun-shy and start trading smaller shares because you are afraid to lose. You must keep trading the same size shares as you have been. Do not raise your bets and do not lower them. Stay at your comfort level. The mistakes most often made by traders in big winning streaks is either that they increase their stakes and expose themselves to a big beating which will be more devastating mentally than financially, or reduce their stakes which will have the same effect. For example, let's say that I have been running hot making profitable trades over a period of eight weeks. I normally trade 800 shares of stock in the price range of 25-40. I see this stock, XYZ, at $50 a share, and think it has the potential to be a winner. Let's look at a few scenarios.

A. You just cashed out of a big winning position in which you made $20,000, so you decide to buy 100 shares **for fun**. The stock goes down to 49, you say to yourself, I am only down $100, I can afford it and you stay in. The stock goes down to 48 1/2, you say to yourself, I can't be wrong on this thing and you buy 1000 shares at that price. Stock goes down to 48, you say to yourself, I know I am right on this one, and you buy another 1000 shares. Make a long story short, you are losing money and you spit out the shares you bought at $44. Did you have fun? Your fun trade just cost you $9,100. But it is not the lost money that will hurt you, it is the psychological effects that come with it.

B. Since you are running so hot, you decide to buy 2000 shares right off the bat at 50. We know the stock went down as we said before, in any case, it does not matter where you got out, as it will be with a loss, on what is more than double your normal position. That will be psychologically devastating as well.

You can paint these two examples any color you want, the basic idea remains the same. You have changed your comfort level of trading by changing the normal number of shares you trade. You did it because you have enjoyed a winning streak. This will normally be a turning point, which could toss you straight into a brutal losing streak. This streak of losing trades will be, more often than not, a direct result of the mental damage your last trade did to you. Psychology is present in each and every trade you do. Don't you forget that.

Losing Streaks

These are no fun! We all want to avoid a losing streak. Unfortunately, they do pop in every once in a while. I have explained the importance of sticking to your comfort level of trading. However, if you get off track and change the way you normally trade (successfully trade), and suffer monetary losses in the process, then you must take an immediate break and regroup! This can save you a lot of money and more importantly, aggravation.

If you lose 30% of your capital, take a break and regroup. Once you have done that, go back to trading, do not add money back into your account, work with the $35,000 you have left. Your goal is not to bring the account back to $50,000, but to get back on track and make profitable trades. This is very important. Many losing streaks continue because of mental problems and loss of discipline. These problems arise from the simple fact that you want to make back what you have just lost. This problem is closely associated to gambling as. A few years ago, I remember sitting at a roulette table in Las Vegas. They have these electronic boards which display the last 15 or 20 numbers that hit. This guy walked up to the table and placed a $100 gaming token on Red. He turned to me and said, "Look, five Black numbers came out in a row. I am sure it is going to be a Red number this time." I smiled at him and thought to myself, as a stock trader, you should never go against the trend, but I did not say anything. The dealer rolled the ball and a Black number came out. The guy lost his bet, but he was convinced that it was time that a Red number will come out. After all, how can he be wrong? It is mathematically impossible... He placed a $200 bet on Red, and another Black number came out. This is when he "lost it", he lost his mental state of mind and could not think rationally. He kept betting on Red, doubling down his bet (100, 200, 400, 800, 1600 etc.,) and I swear the entire display board was Black. He got completely cleaned out and left the table in disbelief. I also left the table in disbelief shortly after he did. I never saw a Red number come out. However, my disbelief had nothing to do with the fact that the display board was showing all Black numbers. It was the fact, I just saw a guy completely lose it. I decided to use this example because it is similar to losing streaks in stock trading. It has to do with two things:

1. Losing your mental state of mind. Arguably, I think that guy on the table was temporarily insane (I always loved this phrase, because I don't know too many people who can keep cool all the time).
2. Raising the stakes to try and make all that you have lost back.

The hardest thing to do is adjust back to the value of what one unit means. If you make an average of $300 a trade and now you had three trades in a row in which you made $5,000 each, the next time you will have a $350 open position profit, it will not look as attractive as it did before. Why? Because the expectation level has changed. The same works in a losing streak. If you have just lost $5,000, three time in a row, an open position profit of $400 will not look attractive either. This is very hard to do, but it is a must. Never judge an open position by dollars and cents. When it is time to get out, get out! You need to make small profitable trades to build your confidence back up. Stick to your comfort level and hopefully you will get out of your losing streak quickly.

If you lose 50% of your capital, take a break again. Go over all your trading records and see why you are losing. It can be a variety of reasons, but you must be doing something wrong. It can be as simple as reading the market wrong. You must find the elements which are causing you the losses. Once you have found some answers, reevaluate your strategies. Many experts recommend paper trading again at this point. I disagree with it because paper trading, if done successfully at this point, will not build your confidence back up. It will hurt you more in the sense that you will be upset you did not have real money in the trade, which will harm your mental state of mind. You have to trade out of a losing streak, you can't paper trade out of it. You may consider trading fewer shares at this point, but you must keep the same trading strategy you would have if you were trading a full position. If you lose 50% of your capital, you will need to make 100% on your capital to get back to the initial principle. If you had 50K and lost 25K, you will need to double the 25K to get back to 50K. If you have managed to get back on track and have more than a handful of successful trades, you may add money to your account (up to 40K total). So, if you were able to get from 25K to 32K, you may add 8K to your account. Every week you sweep out all profits and leave the account at 40K until you paid off the loan amount (the money you have added). Now, you can build the account back up to 50K and sweep profits out from that point on. If at anytime, you lost all your account or the good part of it, but was able to trade successfully and are in the green overall, you may start over with another principle amount. If you did not show success and you lost all, or most, of your capital, consider looking for another line of work. This is not for you. Don't argue with it and don't throw good money after bad money. Let's face it, some of us are not going to make it in this business, just like in any other business.

Note, if you want to increase your capital, you may sweep out 50% of profits and leave the other 50% in the account until you have reached the capital level you are seeking. You must sweep at least 50% of profits in order to learn the discipline part of the business. Once you have reached the desired level of capital, you need to sweep 100% of profits out of your account. I can write many horror stories of once very successful traders, I personally know, who failed to sweep money out of their accounts because of GREED. Needless to say, they lost everything. Their message to you is to master the money management segment of this book, and do not let GREED get the best of you. Sweep the profits out!

You Don't Have to Trade Everyday

Remember that you can always take a day/week/month off if the market does not look right to you. You don't have to trade just so you feel that you are working. I take many "breaks" when things don't look right to me. In fact, numerous times I will do all my research, get up at 5:00 AM and be ready to execute my game plan, only to find out that what I was planning on doing was not doable, for whatever reason, i.e. missed an entry, big gap up/down, bad vibes, etc. When these conditions present themselves, I will call the local golf course, get an early tee time, and leave the trading desk. I do that, because I know that if I stayed around when I am in the wrong mental state of mind, I could make costly mistakes. I'd rather hit a white ball and get frustrated beyond belief scoring in triple digits than stick around when things don't feel right. The beauty of the stock market is that there are always new opportunities to make a trade. I regard this last statement as an essential element for my successful trading. It works well for me, and my wife is fine with it. This may not work for everyone, but I do believe that if you are not in the right mental state of mind, you better not trade. Golfing during market hours is against work ethics, but I look at it as a part of my job! And needless to say, I take my job very seriously. I hope that sharing this with you will improve your trading habits and not the other way around (four days of golf, and only one day of trading). Remember that when things don't look right, you can just walk away. If there is something you like to do (like a hobby), you might as well enjoy that and regroup for the next battle.

Dealing With Pressure

Everyone deals with pressure in his or her own unique way. There is no golden rule. The stock market does add more pressure to your life, and it is no secret, it is harder to operate under pressure. Many traders think that you should write down goals in terms of how much money you are going to make and how you are going to make it. I completely disagree with that theory. I think that using a methodology like that will only add more stress and place you under pressure to perform. Sometimes good opportunities just do not represent themselves. In fact, I cannot tell you if I am going to make $5,000 tomorrow or lose $5,000. This is why I cannot have daily goals, or even annual goals. The only goal I have is to be ahead of the game and execute more profitable trades than losing trades as opportunities represent themselves. I do not force trades, so I can make some goal. I think that you should have fun with trading, other than put yourself under pressure to perform. Relax and enjoy your job.

Supervising Your Trades

All trades should be supervised in the same manner! This is very difficult to do because of the psychological ties you have with your last trade or trades. In fact, you will find out that the process of decision making, while you are in a trade, will be directly related to the outcome of your last trade, whether it was a winner or a loser. You will make different judgement calls in winning streaks than you would in losing streaks. You must remember to follow the same guidelines when you have an open position and look at the facts, the trade is presenting you with, at the same manner. Do not make trading decisions which are derived from other activities, such as a fight with your spouse, child or neighbor. Keep your focus on the facts. Let the stock and only the stock tell you what to do. Try to remain objective at all times. Remember, you are not married to the stock. You can close your position at any time. Stick to your trading strategy. You should only reevaluate a trade if a stock tells you to. This means that you should look for new developments which you did not account for in your original trading strategy. You may need to change your game plan. However, you should never reevaluate a trade and make trading decisions caused by changes not directly related to the stock.

Finding Stocks to Trade

We have talked about research before the market opens and mentioned that research can be done during market hours as well. You can find new candidates running a real-time scan or looking at the winners, losers and most actives. However, you still have to develop a trading strategy for each candidate. During market hours, it has to be done quickly. I recommend not to jump into a stock just because you see it moving that second. You always have to know why you are taking a position in a stock. This is true for both short-term position trading and intraday trading. I find that running real-time scans using a program such as First Alert is very helpful.

Real-Time Scan Formulas

I have developed formulas and filters to scan the entire stock market for stocks which meet certain criteria. At this time, I know you can run them using First Alert. I don't know of any other program that you can use these filters with, however, you can research that. **These formulas are copyrighted and may not be used without the express written authorization of Tony Oz**. Vendors may not sell these formulas as a part of their service. If you are interested in using these formulas for personal use, please contact Tony Oz to get permission.

Basic Volume Alert Scan

Formula:
1. AvgVol20>250,000
2. Volume>AvgVol20 %Q X 1.5
3. NetChange>=5/8
4. Price>10
5. Price<100
6. AvgVol20<3,000,000

This scan filters the entire market looking for $10-$100 stocks that are moving up or down on higher than 1.5 times 20-day average daily volume. I use this screen to see which stocks are moving. I try to detect the stocks early enough in the day for potential intraday trades or even swing trades. The big bonus is when I find a stock that breaks up or down on high volume for the first day. I look for a minimal change of 5/8. I try to omit stocks that trade more than 3,000,000 on a daily basis, because I am looking for the "new" kid on the block. I also try to stay away from stocks that trade less than 250,000 shares a day to ensure some liquidity. The %Q means that the change in average daily volume is prorated for the entire day. Let's say a stock trades 650K a day. If we use 1.5 X AvgVol20 alone then the stock will not hit the results screen until it traded 975K. The %Q calculates it on a minute basis.

Once a stock shows up on the scan as it meets the scan's criteria, you should look at a daily chart to see where the stock is. Consider all the technical patterns you know and see if you have a potential candidate for a trade. Plan out a trade strategy and execute it. The next example illustrates a stock which showed up in our scan and was attractive.

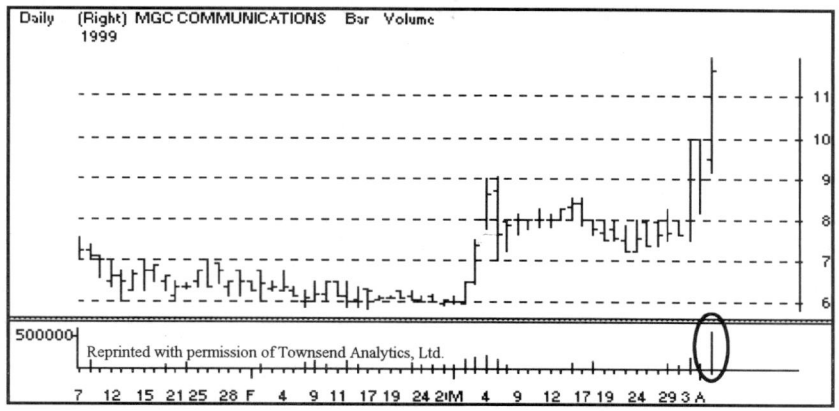

This example illustrates a first day of a move on volume. Note the relative long volume bar on the chart, you can see a corrective phase prior to this move on volume. This is an attractive scenario. It is the FIRST DAY OF THE MOVE, more likely than not, more will follow.

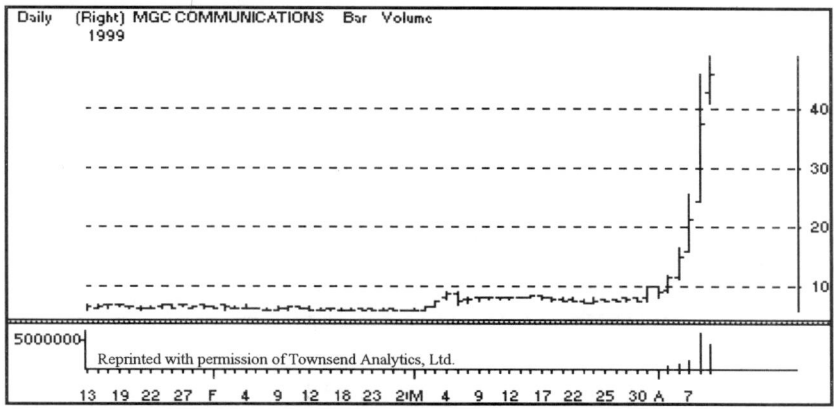

This is what the stock did in the next four days. It went from 10 1/2, where we spotted it on our scan to 49. Not too bad ...

2-Month High Scan

1. AvgVol20>250K
2. Vol>AvgVol20%Q X 1.25
3. Ask>60 day high
4. Last>$12
5. 14 day RSI>50
6. Open< previous close X 1.07

This scan filters the entire market looking for $12+ stocks that are making a 2 month high on higher than 1.25 times 20-day average daily volume. We are trying to eliminate stocks which gapped up by more than 7%. Let's look at following charts to illustrate this scan.

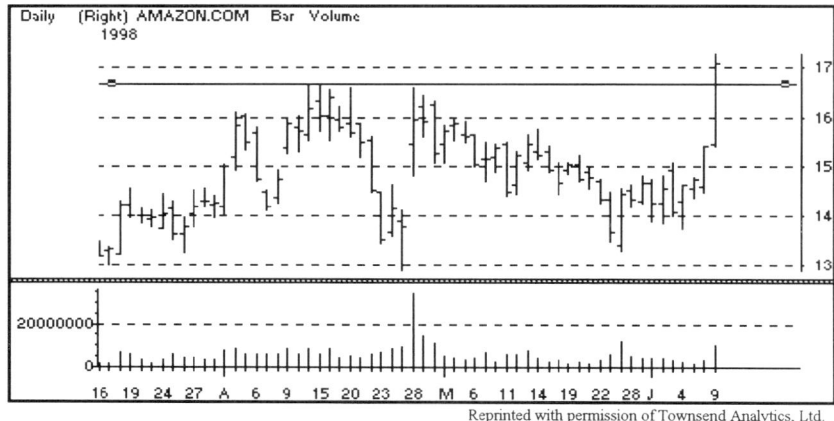

Reprinted with permission of Townsend Analytics, Ltd.

In this case AMZN made a 2-month high, breaking out through resistance levels. A long position was to be taken in this case. Note the volume bar is relatively longer than all but one of the last 20 volume bars.

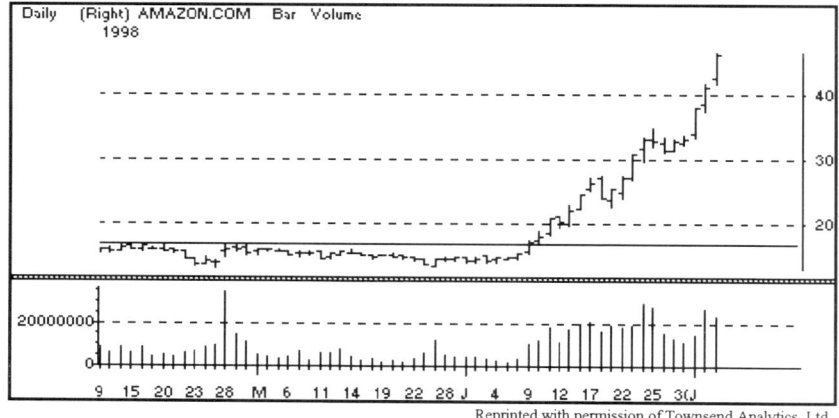

Reprinted with permission of Townsend Analytics, Ltd.

This is what AMZN did in the 18 days following the breakout, up 178%.

This is another example of a 2-month high that showed up on the scan. In this case, the stock is not breaking out of resistance and has enjoyed a big run. This is when we do not buy the stock! You need to remember that not all stocks showing up in the scan are a good buy. Evaluate risk/reward ratio. Look for stock breaking through resistance for the first time in 2 months.

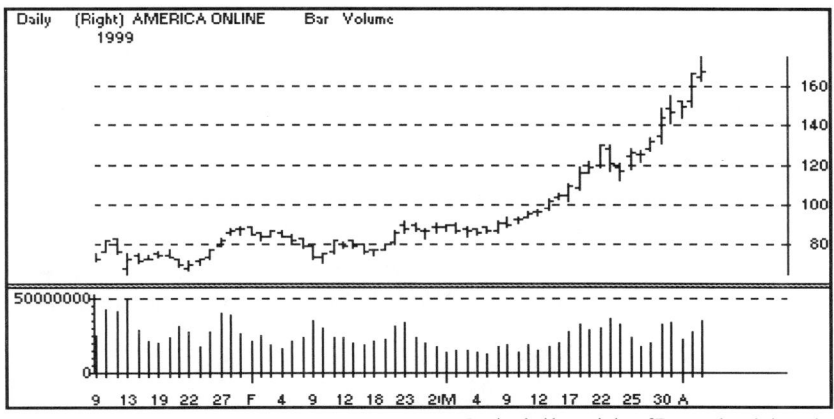

Reprinted with permission of Townsend Analytics, Ltd.

2-Month Low Scan

Formula:

1. AvgVol20>250K
2. Vol>AvgVol20%Q X 1.25
3. Bid<60 day low
4. Last>$8
5. 14 day RSI<50
6. Open> previous close X 0.93

This scan filters the entire market looking for $8+ stocks that are making a 2-month low on higher than 1.25 times 20-day average daily volume. We are trying to eliminate stocks which gapped down by more than 7%.

Let's look at following charts to illustrate this scan.

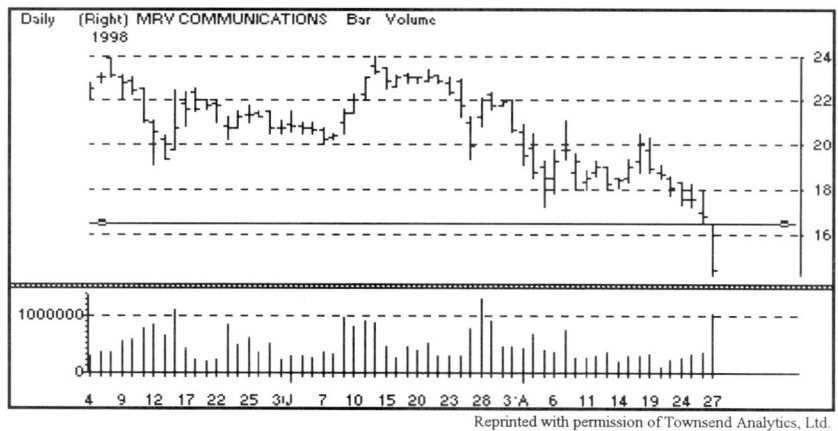

MRVC broke down to a 2-month low on more than 1.25 times average volume. A continuation followed as the stock crashed down the next three days (a huge gap down came in the following day it showed up in the scan).

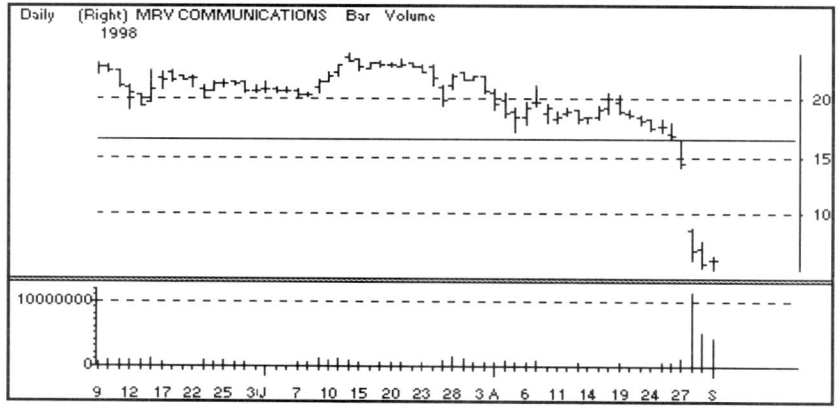

Short Swing Trade Scan

Formula:

1. AvgVol20>500K
2. Vol>AvgVol20%Q X 1.25
3. NetChange<=-5/8
4. Last>8
5. Last<=RangeBottom10%

This filter looks for stocks over $8 with average daily volume in excess of 500,000 which are on pace to trade more than 1.25 times average daily volume. We are adding the 85% rule here by the range. (If a stock closes at the bottom 10% of its trading range it has an 85% chance to make a lower low the next day.) Stocks which meet this criteria and have a good solid chart will be considered as a short position for 2-10 days.

The MRVC example used previously will also suit this filter.

Long Swing 1

Formula:

1. AvgVol20>500K
2. Vol>AvgVol20%Q X 1.25
3. NetChange>=5/8
4. Last>5
5. Last>=RangeTop10%

RangeTop10% is calculated as so: High-[(high-low)x0.1]

This filter looks for stocks over $5 with average daily volume in excess of 500,000 which are on pace to trade more than 1.25 times average daily volume.. We are adding the 85% rule here by the range. (If a stock closes at the top 10% of its trading range it has an 85% chance to make a higher high the next day.) Stocks which meet this criteria and have a good solid chart will be considered as a long position for 2-10 days.

Refer to the AMZN example we used before as an example for this scan.

Long Swing 2

Formula:

1. AvgVol20>450K
2. Vol>AvgVol20%Q X 1.25
3. NetChange>=5/8
4. Last>=20
5. Last<=80
6. Last>=RangeTop17%
7. Open <= previous close + 3/4
8. 14 day RSI<82

This screen is similar to long swing 1. We put a price of $20-$80 a share and we changed the range to the top 17% from top 10% (this is done because if a stock has a trading range of 1 point and closes 1/8 off the high it will not show on the scan, because it is at the top 12.5% of the trading range. Since 1/8 could be the spread between the bid and ask, we changed the filter to top 17%). We also eliminated all stocks that gapped up by more than 3/4. We have also added RSI <82 as we do not want overbought securities.

The Tony Oz Power Screen

This is the one I like to use a lot for a long position.

Formula:

1. AvgVol20>250K
2. Vol>AvgVol20%Q X 1.5
3. NetChange>=5/8
4. Last>=20
5. Last<=200
6. Last>=RangeTop17%
7. Open <= previous close + 2
8. 14 day RSI<80
9. Ask>60 day high
10. Open <= Previous close x 1.04

We are looking for a stock which is making a 2-month high, RSI lower than 80. We eliminate 4% and 2 points + gap ups. We like the last trade to be at the top 17% of the trading range. We like this price movement to take place on 1.5 times average daily volume. Minimum average volume is set at 250,000. As always, the chart must look good.

Learning Curve

Just like anything else in life, trading for a living takes practice and experience. You will only get better if you are willing to learn from your own success and failure. This learning process is not cheap. You have to pay to play, and you have to lose in order to learn from losses. Do not fool yourself thinking that you can beat the market right off the get go. You must be willing to experience pain, yet, remain focused and look at it as a learning experience. If you think college was expensive, wait until you taste the tuition of the stock market. In fact, over time, it makes college tuition look cheap. The only thing I would recommend is that you keep a positive attitude. Do not be afraid to lose, and do not expect anything. Do not expect to make a fortune in the stock market in the first week, month or year. They say good things come to those who wait. Be patient and keep learning. Study everything you do, and each and every decision you make. You must accept the fact that the stock market is not a get rich quick vehicle. You have an opportunity to **learn** how to become a successful trader. Make the best out of it.

Paper Trading

This is a way to practice stock trading. The only thing is that you do not actually execute a trade in the stock market, but you do it on paper. This is a great way to learn how to trade cheaply. However, this method lacks one of the most important elements of trading which is the actual risk and the emotions tied up to that risk. People operate differently when they have their own money on the line. There is difference in pressure and emotions caused by that pressure. However, I recommend you paper trade first, before you risk any money. See if you can trade on paper successfully first. Then, you can start real trading. There is a good website to practice paper trading: *www.marketplayer.com*. You can engage in simulated trading there and compete in their stock picking contests.

Chat Rooms

It is very rare that a chat room will contribute to successful trading. I think they are distracting and full of bad information. It is lonely out there and chat rooms represent a great social meeting place. However, many "traders" post fake paper trades to boost their ego. The biggest drawback I think a chat room has is that it makes you sell your positions too early as you see a member posts "out BGEN + 3/4." Now, you have a good gain too, and you want to post that you have made some money, so you sell your position to tell all your chat buddies "out BGEN +7/8" and you watch BGEN go up another 4 points from there. Chat rooms are creating a competitive environment which can really hurt your bottom line. I know, because I used to be in a chat room. It also prevents you from finding new trades on your own as you are too busy communicating with other traders. I like the idea of getting together with 3-4 traders who share the same trading strategies as you do and communicating either on a telephone via conference calling, using a headset, or a private chat room using AOL Instant Messenger, which is better than following a big public chat room. I was contacted once by someone who wanted me to do a subscriber-based chat room in which I would do real-time stock picks. That could have been something really big, a big money maker. However, I just don't believe in it. Successful stock traders make their own stock picks, trading plans and executions. I do think however that subscribing to an advisory website, such as *bestreturns.com* can be useful as they run a market scan and post potential trades. They narrow down your research time as they provide you with a final list of stocks that looked attractive to them. You should never trade these stock picks blindly though. You still have to do your own research and see that you can create a trading plan for these potential picks. Once you researched it further, and these stocks met your own criteria, you may proceed and trade them on your own terms.

Please note, I do not think that all chat rooms are bad. There are some decent ones out there. Unfortunately, I can not recommend any of them, because they could turn around and become the last place on earth both you and I would want to be in by the time this book is printed. However, if you can sort the good ones from the bad ones, a chat room can become a valuable educational tool. However, you will need to leave it eventually.

Secrets to Successful Trading... What Does It Take?

Fun: You must enjoy what you do. You need to have fun trading stocks. If you don't have fun trading and miss a few heart beats here and there, you will make yourself sick. Put away all the stress and pressure which arise from having to pay the bills. When you are financially stressed out you will hurt your bottom line. Do not compete with yourself or other traders as it will only add pressure to your job. Enjoy what you do, the rest will come together for you. Trading under pressure and extra stress is not fun, this will influence your trading decision making process in a negative way.

Confidence: You need to have confidence in yourself. You must trust your ability to make trading decisions and have confidence in your trading system and methodology.

Discipline: You must be disciplined. You need to execute your game plan according to your trading strategy. Stick to your trading system and methodology. Do not force trades and get out when you are supposed to get out.

Patience: Wait for the right set-up. Do not get in trades because you are lacking the patience to wait for the right set-up! Wait, wait, wait, be patient! I am sure you have heard this cliché before, "good things happen to those who wait." It is true. Once you have entered a trade, you need to give the trade the time to develop. Have patience, and do not close positions unless your trading strategy tells you to. Patience will many times improve buying points and selling points.

Money Management: Stick to and obey your money management strategy. This includes capital preservation, ordering paychecks, making long term investment contributions, etc. Keep firm rules with regards to money management.

Taking the Blame: Forget your ego. When you are wrong, you are wrong! Admit it at once and close the position. Do not try and justify your losses. Do not blame them on poor order execution by your broker, or system failure. Say, "I was wrong, I learned my lesson" and move on to your next trade. You can't call stocks with 100% success ratio, remember that. Limit your losses when you are wrong, by confessing to them and taking immediate action.

Attitude: Keep a positive attitude at all times. Every day is a new day, regardless if you are experiencing a long winning streak or a long losing streak. Keep the same attitude, follow the same rules, regardless if you are enjoying big success, or suffering big losses.

Make Your Own Trades: All your trades should be based on your own research. Do not buy a stock because someone says it looks good. You must look at it and see why it is good. Analyze all potential trades before you execute them. Do not buy stocks because they are running fast in hysteria and do not panic sell a stock when it falls as the public is panic selling. Avoid buying or selling stocks blindly. Do not make CNBC plays, more often than not, you will buy the high of that run.

Stay Away From: IPOs, Penny stocks, Rumor stock plays, and low volume stocks. The odds are not in your favor in any of these cases.

If You Can't Trade, Don't: If for whatever reason you are not 100% there because of distraction, stress, various unrelated problems, etc. DO NOT TRADE! Take the day off and return to trading once you have 100% concentration.

Faith: Probably the most important thing in successful trading. You must believe 100% that you can do this successfully. If you slightly doubt yourself, second guessing your trading methodology, you will find yourself looking for a new job before you know it. Use your will power and believe that you can do it.

Luck: You may lose on a stock that you were in as a result of breaking news which was really negative. This can happen in holding over night positions or a news pending halt intraday. You may be in a trade for all the right reasons, but something out of the ordinary happened and you lost big because of it. This is simply bad luck! There is of course the other side of the coin where you can be long a stock which can be bought out overnight for 80% premium over the closing price. In this case you were lucky to get the extra premium. Luck plays a role in trading. Although we do not want to blame losses on bad luck and gains on good luck, there are those instances in which good or bad luck will determine the outcome. This is also known as catching a break, and catching a bad break. You need to exclude these trades from your track record and regroup fast when these incidents take place. For example, I was in a stock that was trading at $13. I bought the stock at 12:05 PM and the stock was halted, news pending, at 12:09 PM. They did not open the stock for trading for two days. When they finally opened it for trading, the first trade was at $5. Needless to say, I took a big loss. Originally, I was looking for a quick intraday play, without the intention of holding the stock overnight. Unfortunately, I caught a bad break as luck was not on my side, because something I totally did not expect occurred. I had to regroup fast and forget about it as quickly as possible. This is what you need to do in these instances.

Expensive Stocks Versus Cheap Stocks

Many traders fear high priced stocks. I will encourage you all, however, not to fear the higher priced stocks as they will more often than not rank higher in overall success. That means that you can buy fewer shares, if necessary. In fact, I know of one subscriber to bestreturns.com who bought 35 shares of YHOO at $262 and sold at $349 in 3 days. That was 87 points X 35 shares = $3045 profit! (on a $9,170 investment).

I also did a price performance comparison between Low priced stocks and High priced stocks, on 2/23/99. I always enjoy comparing the two. How did they do? In a scan for stocks between $6-$50, which traded more than their 20-day average volume, and traded at least 550,000 that day, we had 211 matches. Now, keep in mind that the market did really well that day. Well, out of 211 stocks in the list, 52 closed in the red. That is 24.6%. Now let us look at the same scan but for stocks priced between $60-$500 a share. There were 78 matches. Out of the 78 matches, only 3 stocks were red, that is 3.8%. So let us summarize it this way, the Dow was up 212 the NASDAQ was up 58. However, 96.2% of the stocks priced between $60-$500 a share which traded 550K+ on higher than their average daily volume were green. Only 76.4% of the stocks priced between $6-$50 a share, which traded 550K+ on higher than their average daily volume, were green. I hope this helps to get my point across. Furthermore, the higher priced stocks had a bigger (percentage) up day, as a group, than the lower priced stocks. **Do not fear trading higher priced stocks!**

Capital Preservation

If I had to state the importance of capital to short-term trading, I would say that capital is like oxygen. We need oxygen to live. You need capital to trade with. Under all circumstances, your number one goal is to protect your capital. It is as simple as that, you can afford to take small losses and stay in the game. However, once you take a big loss, it will decrease your capital substantially. You will now have less money to work with and make it harder on yourself to make it. If you lose 33% on margin, you will actually lose 67% of your capital, in which case you will need to TRIPLE your money to come back to even. Failing to protect and preserve your capital will have you sending out resumes in no time.

Trading Strategies, Entry Points, Where and How

When I find a stock I would like to take a position in, based on a certain technical pattern, I will consider the following strategies. In all of the following examples we will assume that 1200 shares is the position size we want to take in the stock.

Buying A Dip

These different instances will qualify as buying a dip in a stock. I will employ similar strategies in each one of these examples:

1. A stock which is trading in a rising channel or horizontal channel and is at or near the bottom line. I will buy 400 shares at 1/16 to 3/8 over the trendline. I will be more flexible on my stop loss because I took a relative small position and give the stock a chance to bounce. If it falls below a predetermined price, I will sell. If the stock held at the trendline or slightly below it and started to move up, I will add 400 shares at some predetermined point. I will add the final 400 shares as the stock continues to move in the right direction at a predetermined point and complete my 1200 shares desired position. I will trail a stop and tighten it as the stock approaches the top range of the channel.

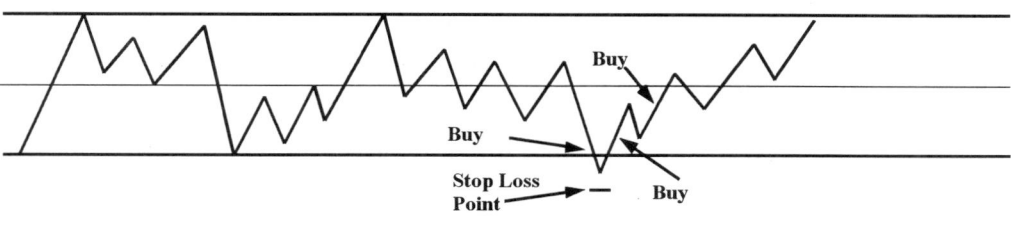

2. A stock which has fallen sharply from recent highs and the outlook for the stock remains bullish. I will use the same strategy here. I will look for the first signs a rally might take place, looking at intraday activity. I would like to see a reversal pattern (such as double bottom, round bottom, falling wedge, etc.) on an intraday chart with heavy volume at the bottom. I will buy 400 shares there, and 400 twice on the way up on predetermined entry points to complete the 1200 shares desired position, as the stock moves in the right direction. I will again let the stock wiggle when I start the position and give it a chance to prove it wants to go back up, I will be more liberal with my stop loss as it is a small position at first.

3. A stock which has sold off and is at support levels. I will buy 400 shares at 1/6 to 3/8 over the support level. I will let the trade wiggle and keep a stop loss just under support. If support holds, I will add the remaining 800 shares as the stock moves up at predetermined entry points, 400 shares at each point and trail a stop.

4. A stock that is testing a previous bottom and might form a double bottom. I will buy 300 shares at the bottom level or close to it, I will add 300 shares on the way up to the previous top. I will add the remaining 600 shares once the stock breakout is over the previous top. The initial stop loss should be liberal as many times a double bottom pattern has a lower second bottom than the first one.

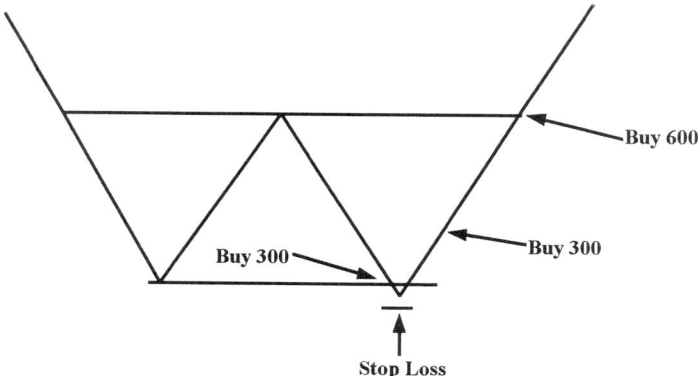

5. A stock in an uptrend which sold off and is at or near its 50-day MA. I will buy 400 shares at or near the 50-day MA. I will keep a liberal stop loss and give the stock a chance to go back up in price. I will add 400 shares twice, at predetermined entry points as the stock moves in the right direction, and I will trail a stop. This play can be made at or near the 200-day MA as well.

You may also consider reversing your position when you buy a stock at support levels and the stock falls through the support. Once you are stopped out, you can take a short position. I will use the same strategy and enter with 400 shares and short sell more as the stock keeps going lower at predetermined entry points and accumulate the balance of the 1200 shares desired position. Because you need an uptick to short sell the stock you, will need to stand in the face of small rallies and take advantage of higher prices to exercise your short sell orders.

Buying Breakouts

These are normally the easiest plays, however, many times a stock can have a fake breakout, as it will breakout over resistance levels, then fall down under and stop you out. Before you know it the stock will breakout again without hesitation and never look back again. The way I like to trade breakouts is to buy 400 shares at 1/4+ over the previous resistance level. I will let the trade wiggle. I will keep a very liberal stop loss as the stock may come down a bit today, tomorrow and take off after that. I will add 400 shares twice, at predetermined entry points as the stock continues to move up and complete the desired 1200 shares position. I will trail a stop and keep evaluating the potential of this next move. I trade all breakout patterns: cup and handle, flags, triangles, etc., the same way. I build my position as the stock is moving in the anticipated direction.

Shorting Stocks Which Break Down Through Support

These plays are tricky as you need an uptick to short sell a stock that is falling down. I use the same system: I will short 400 shares on the first rally the stock has after it violated its support line. I will add to it as it keeps going down, using rallies to get the remainder of the desired 1200 shares position. Some traders also like to short stocks just as they reach resistance levels. They will add more shares as the stock fails to take out the resistance level, on the way down. If the stock takes out the resistance level then they will cover the shorts and go long.

Shorting Stocks In a Double Top Pattern

I use the same system as buying in a double bottom pattern with the difference of short selling at the same points.

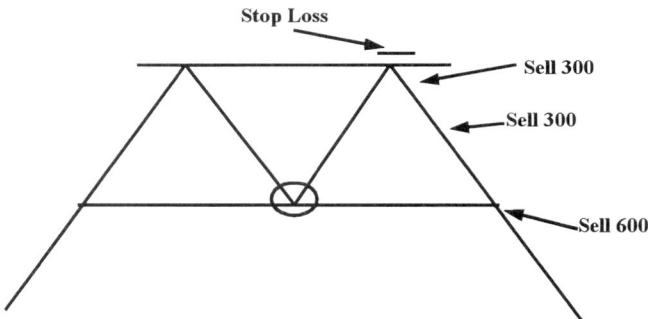

I will short sell 300 shares to start the position, once I see the stock has failed its attempt to take out the previous top. I will short sell another 300 shares at a predetermined entry point as the stock keeps going down. The break through the previous bottom, marked by the circle, is where I would double my position, as I will short sell 600 shares at that point. This will complete my desired 1200 share position. I will use a trailing stop again. In this scenario too, if you are stopped out as the stock is breaking out (where the initial stop loss is set), you may consider reversing your position and go long.

Daytrading Versus Swing Trading

These are both short-term trading strategies. A true daytrader never carries a position overnight. This is known as going to bed FLAT. Swing trading (short-term position trading) is when a trader holds a position anywhere from 2-10 days (at times a position can be held as long as 3 months, if the stock keeps going in the anticipated direction without activating a trailing stop). Daytrading and Swing trading go together hand in hand. There is a difference in the risk management as going flat overnight has no exposure to the market. This is a risk/reward business. One thing that bothers me about the golden rule of daytrading, which says to go flat overnight without exception, is when a daytrader is in a winning position, just before the close of the market, and the stock he is in is at the top 10% of its trading range, and so are the major indexes. However, the daytrader sells his position just to obey the rule. **When a stock closes at the top 10% of its trading range and all the major indexes close at the top 10% of their trading range, there is an 85% chance that the stock will make a higher high the next day.** These are the kind of plays that should be made. So why sell the stock before the close if you have an 85% chance of selling it for a higher price the next trading day? That never made any sense to me. However, if you want to go flat overnight be my guest. You can trade anyway you want to. Traders like me will gladly buy those shares from you, just before the market closes.

Adaptation

The market changes as investors' psychology changes. Past valuations, fundamental analysis, and investors' expectations can drastically change. You must adapt to these changes. These changes will create new market conditions. You need to make the necessary changes to your trading system so it will be compatible with new market conditions. You must also adapt quickly to changes in the overall direction of the market. You must be able to go from being a short-term bull to a short-term bear if a situation justifies it. This is an important element in trading. Many professional traders watched the last big run the stock market had from 1995 to 1999 (Dow 4000 to Dow 11,200), from the sidelines as they shook their head in disbelief. Once they missed the initial run, they waited for a pull back to get back in, which never happened.

Buyers/Sellers Remorse

I don't know how many stories I have heard about traders who owned a stock at a cheap price and sold it very early before a big run, or traders who wanted to buy a stock at a certain price and passed on it. Let's just say they either sold the stock or wanted to buy it at $10 a share. The stock runs up like crazy and it is at $35 a share two months later. These traders shake their heads in disbelief and decide to short the stock for the simple reason that they have missed this big move. Now, they want to make all that money that was left on the table on the short side. They convince themselves that this stock must and will come down to that $10 level. Their philosophy is what goes up must come down right? Not necessarily! I know of a trader who short sold Yahoo at $95 a share. She could not believe that Yahoo ran all the way up from $20 to $95 in a short period of time. Every 10 points Yahoo advanced in price, she short sold another 100 shares. Yahoo went to $225 a share within three weeks. She was completely wiped out. When she told me the story, I could not believe it. I asked her what was her reason in taking the short positions in Yahoo and she told me that about 18 months prior to her taking her initial short position in Yahoo, her daughter-in-law told her to buy it, it was trading at $7 (split adjusted) or so at the time. She did not listen to her and watched Yahoo go up to the sky. She felt that she has passed on the greatest opportunity and she went into denial. This denial phase caused her to short the stock she would have loved to own. Her stubbornness caused her additional losses. She closed her positions when Yahoo hit 150, losing more than 100% of her principle. She was forced to cover the position by her broker. DO NOT SHORT SELL STOCKS BECAUSE YOU WOULD HAVE LOVED TO OWN THEM!

Cost Averaging for Long-Term Growth

I am a firm believer in investing for long-term growth. When you trade stocks for a living it is very difficult to pick the right timing to buy particular stocks in your long-term investment accounts. Needless to say, long-term investment should be more conservative in nature as well as being diversified. I have come to like the spiders offered on the AMEX, SPY which tracks the S&P 500 Index and QQQ which tracks the NASDAQ 100 Index. The way I like to invest in these stocks is by cost averaging. Cost averaging is simply allocating the same amount of money over fixed periods of time. The philosophy behind such method of investing is that you buy fewer shares at or near market tops and more shares near or at market bottoms. I recommend using Brown and Company as they charge $5 commissions on market orders. For example, if I wanted to invest $500 every month in SPY, which trades around $130 a share, I will buy 4 shares. My commission is $5 so I only need SPY to go up 1% to cover the commission. This is cheaper than paying sales load charges and fund expenses. Remember 84% of them cannot outperform the S&P 500. If you stick to this method of investing by allocating $500 a month for 15 years, and if the SPY goes up 12% a year average, you will have $250,519 in 15 years on an investment of $90,000 over the 15 years. If you do not add a penny, your account will go up to $441,500 in 20 years, $778,000 in 25 years and $1,371,000 in 30 years. This is how you can create wealth. If you were to invest $1,000 a month you would have double those numbers. Buying SPY is like buying all the 500 stocks which make the S&P 500 Index. Buying QQQ is like buying 100 stocks which make the NASDAQ 100 Index. It is the most efficient way to spend a small amount of money to buy a big basket of stocks. It is also cost effective as well because you do not pay mutual fund managers their salary and commissions to the sales people. I recommend you read more about these investment vehicles before you make your decision. Just because I like it, it does not mean you will like it too, or that it will fit your investment objectives.

Taxes

Many traders ask other traders about tax-related issues. All questions in regards to incorporating, out of state, off shore, getting a trader status, maintaining investor status, schedule D, schedule C, etc., should be answered only by your OWN tax attorney or accountant. Do not take any tax advise from traders. Your situation is unique and what was a solution for a tax-related problem for one trader, may not be the answer for your problem. Consult your accountant before you make any tax-related decisions.

Mastering the Trading Game

The tools and rules I have featured in this book are the building blocks for a profitable trading system. However, we are all individuals who think and operate differently. Consequently, no one individual can copy someone else's trading system and expect to operate it with the same rate of success. It is a trial and error process to develop a winning system, which may take many years to accomplish. There is one thing that is in common to all winning trading systems and that is a combination of four steps. If you understand these four steps and are able to incorporate them into your trading system, then you are on the right path to develop a winning trading system. In fact, this is probably the simplest, yet most important, lesson in this book.

---

1. Patience: You must wait for the right set-up. You should know which set-ups fit your trading style and which set-ups provide you with the highest percentage of winners. These are the set-ups you should look for, these are the set-ups you should trade.

2. Action: Once you find a set-up that you feel is a high percentage trade, take action and enter a position. Confidence is a key element in taking the action and entering a trade. You must be confidant in your trading system, methodology, your ability to find good set-ups, etc. If you have the confidence, then you won't have any problem to take action and pull the trigger.

3. Trade Management: Ride a profitable trade, and cut a loser quickly. Have big winners and small losers. Do not hold losing positions in your short-term trading account. Do not sell winning trades prematurely.

4. Repeat: Go back to step one and start over.

Section Six

Daytrading Case Study

Charts used in this section are provided by RealTick™ III and are used with the express written permission of Townsend Analytics, Ltd. RealTick™ III is a trademark and copyright of Townsend Analytics, Ltd.

Yahoo Case Study

YHOO		174 13/16	↑	+8 7/16	
High	181	Low		168	
Bid ↓	174 3/4	Ask		174 7/8	

Name	Bid	Size	Name	Ask	Size
BRUT	174 3/4	1	JBOC	174 7/8	10
PRUS	174 3/4	10	ISLD	174 7/8	13
INCA	174 3/4	10	TNTO	175	20
ISLD	174 9/16	9	INCA	175 1/4	9
HRZG	174 1/2	2	REDI	175 1/2	8
SBSH	174 7/16	1	SLKC	175 3/4	1
NITE	174 1/4	5	BRUT	175 7/8	1
COWN	174	4	MASH	175 15/16	2
PURE	174	2			

		----YAHOO INC----	
Date	Time	Price	Volume
4/1/99	15:21	175	200
4/1/99	15:21	174 3/4	100
4/1/99	15:21	175	1000
4/1/99	15:21	174 3/4	100
4/1/99	15:21		
4/1/99	15:21	175 1/8	400
4/1/99	15:21	175	100
4/1/99	15:21	175 1/16	600
4/1/99	15:21		
4/1/99	15:21	174 3/4	1000
4/1/99	15:21	174 3/4	500
4/1/99	15:21	174 3/4	100
4/1/99	15:21	174 3/4	300
4/1/99	15:21	174 3/4	700
4/1/99	15:21	174 13/16	200

Intraday (Left) YAHOO INC (5-Min) Bar
4/01

Reprinted with permission of Townsend Analytics, Ltd.

The basic tools for intraday trading are a level II quote window linked to an intraday chart (1-5 minute bars) and a print report (time and sales report). Combining the three together gives an edge in anticipating a move in a stock. Yahoo was on the most active list when this scenario took place. I entered the ticker into my trading screen and took a snap-shot of the situation. The first thing I did was read the intraday chart from left to right. This gave me an idea as to what Yahoo did all day. It opened around 180 and sold off to 168 within the first hour of trading. From that point, it gradually and consistently rose in price. It topped at 176 1/2 and sold off to 173 1/2, it then attempted to go to 176 1/2 again, but could not break through the resistance level and turned down to 174 3/4, which is the point illustrated in the above diagram. The second thing I noticed was that Yahoo was up over 6 points from yesterday's close, which meant that at the open of trading it was up over 12 points. So, Yahoo gapped open big.

What am I looking for here:
1. Can Yahoo go over 176 1/2 (breakout) successfully and test the morning highs?
2. Is the 173 1/2 level going to hold if Yahoo will attempt to test it?

I had no bias as to which direction the stock will go, so I decided to observe the price action and see if a trade will present itself to me. I will take you step by step as to what occurred in the next 39 minutes.

Observation Phase

YHOO		174 3/4	↑ 6 3/8	
High	181	Low	168	
Bid ↑	174 1/2	Ask	174 9/16	

Name	Bid	Size	Name	Ask	Size
ISLD	174 1/2	2	ISLD	174 9/16	4
SBSH	174 7/16	10	JBOC	174 5/8	10
MASH	174 5/16	4	INCA	174 5/8	9
NITE	174 1/4	5	TNTO	174 3/4	6
AGIS	174 1/4	1	PERT	175 1/8	1
INCA	174 1/8	3	AGIS	175 5/16	2
COWN	174	4	REDI	175 1/2	8
PURE	174	2	MASH	175 1/2	5
REDI	174	2			

	----YAHOO INC----		
Date	Time	Price	Volume
4/1/99	15:21	174 3/4	100
4/1/99	15:21	174 3/4	100
4/1/99	15:21	174 3/4	100
4/1/99	15:21	174 13/16	200
4/1/99	15:21	174 1/2	100
4/1/99	15:21	174 1/2	100
4/1/99	15:21		
4/1/99	15:21	174 3/4	800
4/1/99	15:21	174 1/2	400
4/1/99	15:21	174 1/2	400
4/1/99	15:21		
4/1/99	15:21	174 1/2	200
4/1/99	15:21	174 1/2	700
4/1/99	15:21	174 7/16	100
4/1/99	15:21	174 3/4	900

Reprinted with permission of Townsend Analytics, Ltd.

The stock is not falling down hard, but there are some sellers present. Volume is drying up some, which indicates an indecision time. The Bid and Ask ticked down.

YHOO		174 5/16	↓	+5 15/16
High	181	Low		168
Bid ↓	174 5/16	Ask		174 3/8

Name	Bid	Size	Name	Ask	Size
MASH	174 5/16	1	JBOC	174 3/8	10
ISLD	174 5/16	1	ISLD	174 9/16	4
NITE	174 1/4	5	INCA	174 5/8	9
INCA	174 1/8	3	TNTO	174 3/4	8
COWN	174	4	SBSH	175	1
PURE	174	2	PERT	175 1/8	1
REDI	174	2	AGIS	175 5/16	2
MLCO	174	10	REDI	175 1/2	8
PERT	174	1			

||----YAHOO INC----------			
Date	Time	Price	Volume
4/1/99	15:22		
4/1/99	15:22		
4/1/99	15:22	174 1/2	200
4/1/99	15:22	174 1/2	500
4/1/99	15:22	174 1/2	200
4/1/99	15:22	174 7/16	200
4/1/99	15:22	174 9/16	200
4/1/99	15:22		
4/1/99	15:22	174 5/16	300
4/1/99	15:22	174 1/2	100
4/1/99	15:22	174 5/16	300
4/1/99	15:22	174 5/16	200
4/1/99	15:22		
4/1/99	15:22	174 5/16	500
4/1/99	15:22		

Reprinted with permission of Townsend Analytics, Ltd.

Sellers are still present, as the Bid and Ask tick down, however no big sizes are coming in on the offer, which is a positive.

YHOO		174 7/16	↑	+6 1/16
High	181	Low		168
Bid ↓	174 1/4	Ask		174 7/16

Name	Bid	Size	Name	Ask	Size
ISLD	174 1/4	3	ISLD	174 7/16	3
INCA	174 1/8	3	INCA	174 5/8	9
SBSH	174 1/8	3	TNTO	174 3/4	8
COWN	174	4	SBSH	175	1
PURE	174	2	PERT	175 1/8	1
REDI	174	2	AGIS	175 5/16	2
MLCO	174	10	REDI	175 1/2	8
PERT	174	1	MASH	175 1/2	5
BRUT	174	4			

||----YAHOO INC----------			
Date	Time	Price	Volume
4/1/99	15:22		
4/1/99	15:22	174 5/16	800
4/1/99	15:22	174 5/16	100
4/1/99	15:22		
4/1/99	15:22		
4/1/99	15:22		
4/1/99	15:22	174 1/4	100
4/1/99	15:22	174 7/16	100
4/1/99	15:22	174 1/4	200
4/1/99	15:22	174 5/16	100
4/1/99	15:22	174 1/4	200
4/1/99	15:22	174 1/4	100
4/1/99	15:22	174 5/16	900
4/1/99	15:22	176 3/16	200
4/1/99	15:22	174 7/16	100

Reprinted with permission of Townsend Analytics, Ltd.

At this point, I noticed that the Bid ticked down again, but the Ask ticked up. I also noticed that buyers are lined up at 174, 174 1/8 and 174 1/4. There is depth on the Bid side, which is showing strength.

YHOO		174 5/8	↑	+6 1/4	
High	181		Low	168	
Bid ↑		174 1/2	Ask	174 1/2	

Name	Bid	Size	Name	Ask	Size
BRUT	174 1/2	1	ISLD	174 1/2	1
INCA	174 3/8	5	INCA	174 7/8	6
ISLD	174 3/8	(60)	TNTO	175	4
SBSH	174 1/8	3	SBSH	175	1
REDI	174 1/16	5	PERT	175 1/8	1
TNTO	174 1/16	4	MASH	175 1/2	2
COWN	174	4	SLKC	175 3/4	1
PURE	174	2	AGIS	175 13/16	1
MLCO	174	10			

		----YAHOO INC----	
Date	Time	Price	Volume
4/1/99	15:22		
4/1/99	15:22	174 7/16	200
4/1/99	15:22		
4/1/99	15:22	174 5/16	1000
4/1/99	15:22	174 3/8	100
4/1/99	15:23	174 3/8	500
4/1/99	15:23	174 3/8	1500
4/1/99	15:23	174 3/8	100
4/1/99	15:23	174 3/8	200
4/1/99	15:23	174 3/8	500
4/1/99	15:23		
4/1/99	15:23		
4/1/99	15:23		
4/1/99	15:23	(174 5/8)	200
4/1/99	15:23	174 5/8	700

Reprinted with permission of Townsend Analytics, Ltd.

The buyers are showing more poise. As the Bid strengthens, note the Size on ISLD of 60. This shows buyers with interest to buy the stock. You can also see prints of 174 5/8, which were out of market, as buyers want in. Also, note that the market is locked as the Bid and Ask are the same at 174 1/2.

Taking Action

YHOO		174 11/16	↑	+6 5/16	
High	181		Low	168	
Bid ↑		174 1/2	Ask	174 7/8	

Name	Bid	Size	Name	Ask	Size
BRUT	174 1/2	1	INCA	174 7/8	6
ISLD	174 1/2	(61)	SBSH	175	1
INCA	174 3/8	5	TNTO	175	4
SBSH	174 1/8	3	ISLD	175	2
REDI	174 1/16	5	PERT	175 1/8	1
TNTO	174 1/16	4	MASH	175 1/2	2
COWN	174	4	SLKC	175 3/4	1
PURE	174	2	AGIS	175 13/16	1
MLCO	174	10			

		----YAHOO INC----	
Date	Time	Price	Volume
4/1/99	15:23		
4/1/99	15:23		
4/1/99	15:23	174 5/8	200
4/1/99	15:23	174 5/8	700
4/1/99	15:23	174 1/2	100
4/1/99	15:23		
4/1/99	15:23	174 1/2	100
4/1/99	15:23	172 1/4	100
4/1/99	15:23	174 1/2	100
4/1/99	15:23	174	100
4/1/99	15:23	174 11/16	200
4/1/99	15:23		
4/1/99	15:23	174 11/16	100
4/1/99	15:23		

Reprinted with permission of Townsend Analytics, Ltd.

The Bid is getting stronger as 6100 shares on ISLD have joined the Bid. This was a good time to enter, so I entered a long position on paper at 174 7/8 for 600 shares, taking out the INCA offer using a SelectNet preference order at 15:23.

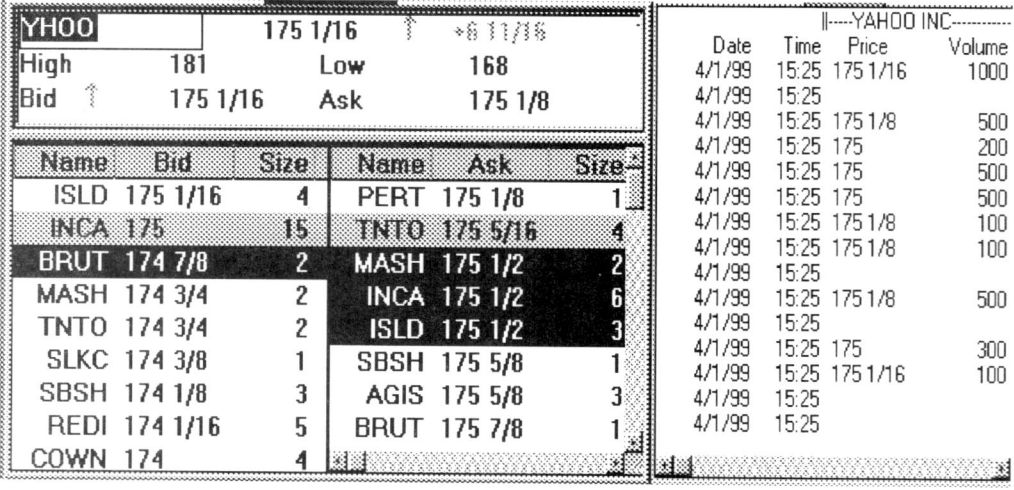

The Bid and Ask are ticking up as the stock is slowly moving up. It is not a buying frenzy or anything like that, but the pause in the action, the low volume, and the strengthening of the Bid suggests a short-term bottom. At this point, I feel that 174 should hold. If it falls below 174, I will sell my position.

Sitting in the Trade

Reprinted with permission of Townsend Analytics, Ltd.

The first few seconds/minutes in a trade are always the hardest ones. You question if you had a good entry or not. You want to see your position in the green. So when Yahoo managed to go over 175 successfully, I felt some relief. This is a psychological element.

YHOO		175	↓	+6 5/8
High	181	Low		168
Bid ↑	175 1/16	Ask		175 1/8

Name	Bid	Size	Name	Ask	Size
TNTO	175 1/16	(12)	PERT	175 1/8	1
ISLD	175 1/16	(14)	TNTO	175 5/16	4
INCA	175	15	MASH	175 1/2	2
BRUT	175	1	INCA	175 1/2	6
MASH	174 3/4	2	ISLD	175 1/2	3
REDI	174 3/4	2	SBSH	175 5/8	1
SLKC	174 3/8	1	BRUT	175 7/8	1
SBSH	174 1/8	3	BEST	176	1
COWN	174	4			

	----YAHOO INC----		
Date	Time	Price	Volume
4/1/99	15:25	175 1/8	100
4/1/99	15:25	175 1/8	100
4/1/99	15:25		
4/1/99	15:25	175 1/8	500
4/1/99	15:25		
4/1/99	15:25	175	300
4/1/99	15:25	175 1/16	100
4/1/99	15:25		
4/1/99	15:25		
4/1/99	15:25	175 1/8	500
4/1/99	15:25	175 1/8	200
4/1/99	15:25	175 1/16	100
4/1/99	15:26	175 1/16	300
4/1/99	15:26	175 1/8	500
4/1/99	15:26	175	100

Reprinted with permission of Townsend Analytics, Ltd.

The second thing that made me feel comfortable in the trade was when I saw other daytraders bidding for the stock on the ECNs. This confirmed that they were feeling the same way that I did. Note the Bid is getting stronger as another 1000 shares came in on ISLD and 1200 on TNTO. It is not a lot of Size, but it is confirming a direction. Traders want to get their hands on the stock.

Market Makers Playing Games

YHOO		175 1/2	↑	+7 1/8
High	181	Low		168
Bid ↑	175 5/16	Ask		175 1/2

Name	Bid	Size	Name	Ask	Size
TNTO	175 5/16	1	INCA	175 1/2	13
ISLD	175 1/4	5	SBSH	175 5/8	1
BRUT	175	1	TNTO	175 3/4	3
INCA	175	15	ISLD	175 3/4	11
HRZG	174 15/16	1	BRUT	175 7/8	1
REDI	174 3/4	2	MASH	175 7/8	1
MASH	174 3/4	1	BEST	176	1
SLKC	174 3/8	1	REDI	176	(500)
SBSH	174 1/8	3			

	----YAHOO INC----		
Date	Time	Price	Volume
4/1/99	15:26		
4/1/99	15:26		
4/1/99	15:26		
4/1/99	15:26	175 5/16	400
4/1/99	15:26	175 5/16	100
4/1/99	15:26	175 1/2	100
4/1/99	15:26	175 1/2	100
4/1/99	15:26	175 5/16	100
4/1/99	15:26	174 1/16	200
4/1/99	15:26	175 1/2	500
4/1/99	15:26	175	100
4/1/99	15:26	174 3/4	100
4/1/99	15:26	175 1/8	100
4/1/99	15:26	175 1/2	100
4/1/99	15:26	175 1/2	200

Reprinted with permission of Townsend Analytics, Ltd.

The stock is ticking up again, but a bad surprise popped up on the screen. Those were the 50,000 shares offered by REDI, ECN at 176. This can be very bad news, in some cases.

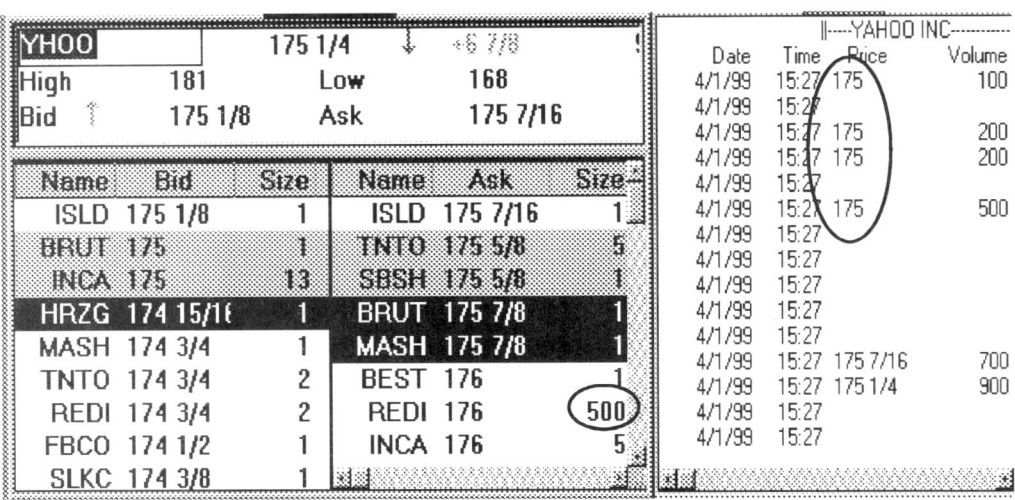

I have to admit, initially, my instinct was saying, sell the stock immediately, below the Bid. "Look at the 50,000 shares for sale at 176. The stock will never get through it," I told myself. And by looking at the print reports I was not alone in thinking that. Note the prints at 175. The Bid never went that low, but traders were bailing out, selling below market. However, not too many of them did. The next thing I noticed was that the Bid size at 175 was not changing, so whoever was buying the stock there at 175 kept refreshing his quote. After thinking for a quick second I decided not to sell. Do you know why? Common sense! What I mean by that is that you need to ask yourself a simple question. If you wanted to sell 50,000 shares of Yahoo, would you really show your hand? I don't think so. Not if you really wanted to sell that many shares without tanking the price of a stock. So I decided to hang in and see what would happen.

It seems like I was not the only trader who did not believe that selling at this point was a good idea. In fact, the Bid size grew and some familiar faces of big Market Makers joined the Bid: SBSH at 175 3/16, MLCO, NITE and HRZG at 175 1/8. The size of 50,000 shares placed on the offer on REDI could have been placed by any one of these Market Makers as they hoped to scare traders into selling their positions. This is done by Market Makers, on a regular basis, with the intention of buying the shares from weak hand traders that are quick to sell as they see the big size on the offer. In the meantime, the same Market Maker who placed the size there is buying from them on the Bid.

YHOO		175 5/8	↓	≈7 1/4	
High	181	Low		168	
Bid ↑	175 1/2	Ask		175 5/8	

Name	Bid	Size	Name	Ask	Size
INCA	175 1/2	1	SBSH	175 5/8	2
ISLD	175 1/2	1	MASH	175 3/4	2
MASH	175 1/4	9	ISLD	175 3/4	10
HRZG	175 1/4	1	TNTO	175 3/4	3
NITE	175 1/8	5	BRUT	175 7/8	1
MLCO	175 1/8	10	BEST	176	1
BRUT	174 7/8	2	PERT	176	1
REDI	174 3/4	2	INCA	176	5
TNTO	174 3/4	2			

YAHOO INC

Date	Time	Price	Volume
4/1/99	15:30	175 5/8	100
4/1/99	15:30		
4/1/99	15:30		
4/1/99	15:30	175 5/8	100
4/1/99	15:30	175 5/8	100
4/1/99	15:30	175 5/8	100
4/1/99	15:31	175 5/8	100
4/1/99	15:31	175 3/4	200
4/1/99	15:31	175 5/8	100
4/1/99	15:31	175 5/8	500
4/1/99	15:31	175 5/8	100
4/1/99	15:31	175 5/8	800
4/1/99	15:31	175 5/8	500
4/1/99	15:31	175 5/8	100
4/1/99	15:31	175 5/8	500

Reprinted with permission of Townsend Analytics, Ltd.

Guess what, the 50,000 on REDI disappeared before the price even hit 176. So, where did the 50,000 shares offered at 176 go? Good question. This is an example of how the Market Makers play tricks in trying to fool daytraders. Remember, we are all competing to make money out there. I am glad I escaped their trick this time. At this point, Yahoo shares look extra strong. Note that all prints are at or above the current Ask. SBSH is selling more than he is showing as size, which is normal, but even he can't hold the momentum back. The stock is printing 175 3/4 as traders are going around SBSH to get the shares. As soon as the 500 size disappeared on REDI, traders are jumping in to buy. My trade is looking much better now ...

Modifying the Strategy Behind the Trade

YHOO		175 3/4	↓ +7 3/8	
High	181	Low	168	
Bid ↑	175 9/16	Ask	175 3/4	

Name	Bid	Size	Name	Ask	Size
SLKC	175 9/16	1	MASH	175 3/4	1
INCA	175 9/16	5	MWSE	175 3/4	1
ISLD	175 9/16	8	BRUT	175 7/8	1
HRZG	175 1/4	1	BEST	176	1
MASH	175 1/4	9	PERT	176	1
NITE	175 1/8	5	INCA	176	5
MLCO	175 1/8	10	ISLD	176	2
BRUT	174 7/8	2	NITE	176 1/8	10
REDI	174 3/4	2			

		---YAHOO INC---	
Date	Time	Price	Volume
4/1/99	15:31	175 5/8	800
4/1/99	15:31	175 5/8	500
4/1/99	15:31	175 5/8	100
4/1/99	15:31	175 5/8	500
4/1/99	15:31	175 1/2	100
4/1/99	15:31		
4/1/99	15:31	175 3/4	100
4/1/99	15:31	175 5/8	200
4/1/99	15:31		
4/1/99	15:31	175 3/4	900
4/1/99	15:31	175 5/8	100
4/1/99	15:31	175 5/8	300
4/1/99	15:31	175 7/8	100
4/1/99	15:31	175 3/4	100
4/1/99	15:31	175 3/4	100

Reprinted with permission of Townsend Analytics, Ltd.

At this point, volume is picking up. SBSH is out of the way and my trade is looking really good. Things are happening really quickly. In the last 4 minutes, the 500 size show up, weak hands get shaken out. The big size disappears and volume is coming in. At this point, the stock is ready to fly. So I am trying to set my sell strategy.

1. Do not let a profit turn into a loss.

2. Do not sell too early if the momentum is still there.

3. Consider exiting in two or three phases as profit opportunities present themselves, without giving up too much opportunity cost should Yahoo have more strength.

I decided to wait and see how Yahoo does. If it gets to 176 1/2 where it had troubles earlier, thinking that if there is a pause in the action there, I would sell 200-300 shares.

YHOO		175 3/4	↓	+7 3/8	
High	181	Low		168	
Bid ↑	175 11/16	Ask		175 7/8	

Name	Bid	Size	Name	Ask	Size
SLKC	175 11/16	1	MASH	175 7/8	6
REDI	175 5/8	7	BRUT	176	7
ISLD	175 5/8	2	NITE	176 1/8	10
INCA	175 9/16	5	TNTO	176 1/8	18
MASH	175 1/2	8	ISLD	176 1/8	3
NITE	175 1/8	5	SBSH	176 1/4	1
MLCO	175 1/8	10	MLCO	176 3/8	10
HRZG	175	1	HMQT	177	10
BRUT	174 7/8	2			

|----YAHOO INC----|
Date	Time	Price	Volume
4/1/99	15:31	176	100
4/1/99	15:31	173 1/2	200
4/1/99	15:31	175 7/8	100
4/1/99	15:31	175 1/2	200
4/1/99	15:31		
4/1/99	15:31	175 3/4	100
4/1/99	15:31	175 3/4	100
4/1/99	15:31	175 3/4	100
4/1/99	15:31	176	100
4/1/99	15:31	175 3/4	300
4/1/99	15:31	176	500
4/1/99	15:31	175 3/4	100
4/1/99	15:31	173 7/8	200
4/1/99	15:31		
4/1/99	15:31	175 11/16	100

Reprinted with permission of Townsend Analytics, Ltd.

Yahoo is still showing strength as the Bid and Ask are ticking up. Also note that there are prints at 176, this indicates that buyers are going out of market (higher than the best offer) to buy Yahoo shares.

YHOO		176 1/2	↑	+8 1/8	
High	181	Low		168	
Bid ↑	176 7/16	Ask		176 1/2	

Name	Bid	Size	Name	Ask	Size
ISLD	176 7/16	10	BRUT	176 1/2	8
AGIS	176 5/16	1	TNTO	176 1/2	5
TNTO	176 1/4	4	SLKC	176 9/16	1
HRZG	176 1/4	1	ISLD	176 5/8	5
FBCO	176 1/4	1	SBSH	176 7/8	1
INCA	176 1/8	2	HMQT	177	10
REDI	176 1/8	9	COWN	177	1
MASH	175 1/2	8	HRCO	177	1
NITE	175 1/8	5			

|----YAHOO INC----|
Date	Time	Price	Volume
4/1/99	15:32	176 3/8	500
4/1/99	15:32	176 3/8	100
4/1/99	15:32	176 3/8	400
4/1/99	15:32	176 3/8	100
4/1/99	15:32	176 1/2	1000
4/1/99	15:32	176 3/8	100
4/1/99	15:32	176 5/16	500
4/1/99	15:32	175 3/16	200
4/1/99	15:32	176 5/16	1200
4/1/99	15:32	176 5/16	500
4/1/99	15:32		
4/1/99	15:32	176 1/2	400
4/1/99	15:32		
4/1/99	15:32	176 1/2	400
4/1/99	15:32		

Reprinted with permission of Townsend Analytics, Ltd.

Yahoo is demonstrating continued strength on rising volume as the stock goes up over a point in 3 minutes. We have reached the resistance level at 176 1/2 and I am watching carefully. I am ready to sell 200 shares if the stock starts pulling back.

The Breakout

YHOO		176 11/16	↓ -0 5/16	
High	181	Low	168	
Bid ↑	176 11/16	Ask	176 7/8	

Name	Bid	Size	Name	Ask	Size
ISLD	176 11/16	5	SBSH	176 7/8	10
HRZG	176 1/4	1	INCA	176 7/8	1
FBCO	176 1/4	1	TNTO	176 15/16	7
TNTO	176 3/16	2	HMQT	177	10
REDI	176 1/8	5	COWN	177	1
AGIS	175 15/16	1	HRCO	177	1
JBOC	175 7/8	5	BRUT	177	3
INCA	175 3/4	3	ISLD	177	12
MASH	175 5/8	1			

YAHOO INC

Date	Time	Price	Volume
4/1/99	15:33	176 13/16	400
4/1/99	15:33	176 3/4	100
4/1/99	15:33	176 3/4	100
4/1/99	15:33	176 3/4	900
4/1/99	15:33	176 13/16	100
4/1/99	15:33	176 11/16	100
4/1/99	15:33	176 13/16	100
4/1/99	15:33	176 7/8	200
4/1/99	15:33	176 13/16	500
4/1/99	15:33	176 7/8	200
4/1/99	15:33	176 13/16	100
4/1/99	15:33	176 13/16	100
4/1/99	15:33	176 11/16	300
4/1/99	15:33	176 11/16	200
4/1/99	15:33		

Reprinted with permission of Townsend Analytics, Ltd.

The strength is there and Yahoo goes through the resistance without hesitation. This is actually a good entry point if I wanted to add more shares to my position. Technical traders see the opportunity and jump on board the Yahoo ship.

YHOO		177	↑ +0 5/8	
High	181	Low	168	
Bid ↑	176 15/16	Ask	177	

Name	Bid	Size	Name	Ask	Size
ISLD	176 15/16	10	REDI	177	8
REDI	176 13/16	9	SLKC	177 3/16	1
PRUS	176 3/4	1	ISLD	177 3/16	4
TNTO	176 9/16	2	BRUT	177 1/4	1
FBCO	176 1/2	1	INCA	177 1/4	5
BRUT	176 1/2	2	COWN	177 1/4	10
HRZG	176 1/4	1	PERT	177 1/2	1
AGIS	176 3/16	1	HRCO	177 1/2	1
JBOC	175 7/8	5			

YAHOO INC

Date	Time	Price	Volume
4/1/99	15:33		
4/1/99	15:33	177	700
4/1/99	15:33	177	200
4/1/99	15:33	177	200
4/1/99	15:33	177	900
4/1/99	15:33	177	200
4/1/99	15:33	177	300
4/1/99	15:33	177	300
4/1/99	15:33	177	300
4/1/99	15:34	177	300
4/1/99	15:34	177	200
4/1/99	15:34		
4/1/99	15:34	176 15/16	400
4/1/99	15:34	177	300
4/1/99	15:34		

Reprinted with permission of Townsend Analytics, Ltd.

Yahoo is taking out the 177 level. Note that in two minutes it went up from 175 1/2 to 177.

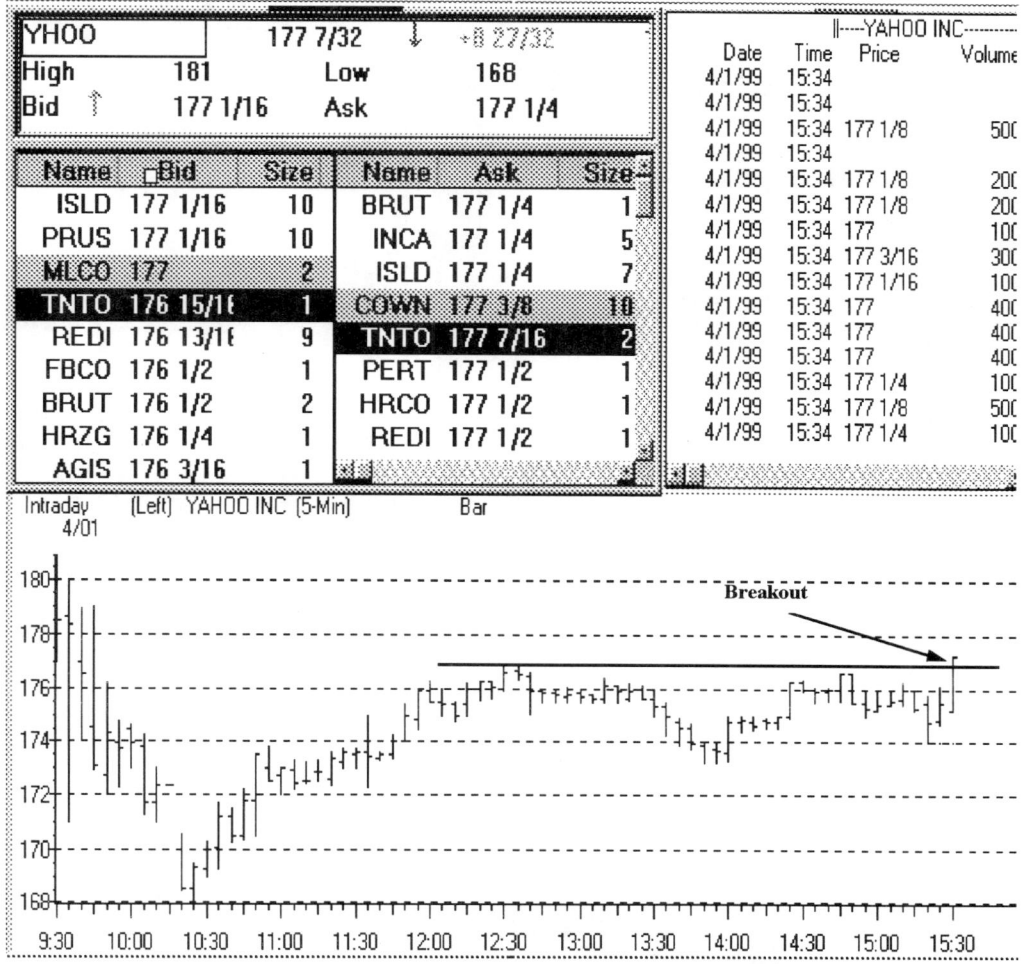

Reprinted with permission of Townsend Analytics, Ltd.

This is what the breakout looks like on the intraday chart. Yahoo is looking strong, and should try to test the next resistance level, the opening price of 180. Notice that it took the 177 price level out. Now, I am trailing a mental stop. My price target is 180 and if Yahoo goes below 176 1/2 I will sell 300 shares, and if it goes below 175 1/2 I will sell the remaining 300 shares.

YHOO		177 5/8	↑ +9 1/4	
High	181	Low	168	
Bid ↑	177 9/16	Ask	177 11/16	

Name	Bid	Size	Name	Ask	Size
ISLD	177 9/16	3	REDI	177 11/16	5
BRUT	177 1/2	2	ISLD	177 11/16	5
FBCO	177 1/2	1	INCA	177 3/4	10
INCA	177 1/2	9	SWST	177 13/16	1
TNTO	177 1/2	7	BRUT	177 7/8	1
AGIS	177 1/16	1	FCAP	177 15/16	1
MLCO	177	2	LEHM	178	1
MASH	177	5	DLJP	178	1
PURE	177	2			

||----YAHOO INC----------

Date	Time	Price	Volume
4/1/99	15:35		
4/1/99	15:35		
4/1/99	15:35	177 9/16	800
4/1/99	15:35	177 5/8	200
4/1/99	15:35	177 5/8	300
4/1/99	15:35	177 9/16	100
4/1/99	15:35	177 5/8	300
4/1/99	15:35	177 9/16	100
4/1/99	15:35		
4/1/99	15:35		
4/1/99	15:35	177 9/16	100
4/1/99	15:35	177 9/16	100
4/1/99	15:35	177 5/8	200
4/1/99	15:35		
4/1/99	15:35		

Reprinted with permission of Townsend Analytics, Ltd.

The stock keeps on rising with no hesitation. At this point, I raise the mental stop to 176 1/2 for all 600 shares. I am trailing a stop one point behind the bid.

Trailing a Stop

YHOO		177 7/8	↓ +9 1/2	
High	181	Low	168	
Bid ↑	177 13/16	Ask	177 15/16	

Name	Bid	Size	Name	Ask	Size
ISLD	177 13/16	3	FCAP	177 15/16	1
INCA	177 3/4	10	INCA	177 15/16	2
SLKC	177 3/4	1	LEHM	178	1
FBCO	177 3/4	1	DLJP	178	1
JBOC	177 3/4	10	PRUS	178	3
NITE	177 5/8	5	NITE	178	10
BEST	177 5/8	1	BEST	178	1
BRUT	177 1/2	2	HRZG	178	2
MASH	177 7/16	10			

||----YAHOO INC----------

Date	Time	Price	Volume
4/1/99	15:35		
4/1/99	15:35	177 13/16	100
4/1/99	15:35	177 13/16	100
4/1/99	15:35	177 3/4	100
4/1/99	15:35	177 9/16	100
4/1/99	15:35		
4/1/99	15:35		
4/1/99	15:35		
4/1/99	15:35		
4/1/99	15:35	178	700
4/1/99	15:35	178	700
4/1/99	15:35	177 7/8	200
4/1/99	15:35		
4/1/99	15:35		
4/1/99	15:35	177 7/8	100

Reprinted with permission of Townsend Analytics, Ltd.

Yahoo is still rising, the Bid and Ask keep ticking up. It is trading out of market at 178. At this point, I am ready to sell 300 shares at the first sign of weakness. I moved the mental stop loss for the remainder 300 shares to 177.

YHOO		178	↑	+9 5/8			Date	‖----YAHOO INC---------- Time Price	Volume
High	181	Low		168			4/1/99	15:36 178	1000
Bid ↑	177 15/16	Ask		178			4/1/99	15:36 178	1000
							4/1/99	15:36 178	500
Name	Bid	Size	Name	Ask	Size		4/1/99	15:36 178	1500
SLKC	177 15/16	1	REDI	178	8		4/1/99	15:36	
AGIS	177 15/16	1	BEST	178	1		4/1/99	15:36	
JBOC	177 7/8	10	BRUT	178	13		4/1/99	15:36 178	1500
ISLD	177 7/8	12	ISLD	178	(122)		4/1/99	15:36 178	500
FBCO	177 3/4	1	MASH	178	33		4/1/99	15:36 178	1000
INCA	177 3/4	10	SWST	178 5/16	1		4/1/99	15:36 177 15/16	200
BEST	177 5/8	1	MLCO	178 3/8	10		4/1/99	15:36	
NITE	177 5/8	5	HRZG	178 3/8	1		4/1/99	15:36	
MASH	177 7/16	8					4/1/99	15:36 178	200
							4/1/99	15:36	
							4/1/99	15:36	

Reprinted with permission of Townsend Analytics, Ltd.

The Ask reached 178. This is another time I was getting ready to sell the stock, because I was getting a little nervous as there was a fair amount of Size for sale, 122 on ISLD. However, the 178 prints kept on printing and the ISLD Size was gone very quickly.

YHOO		178	↑	+9 5/8			Date	‖----YAHOO INC---------- Time Price	Volume
High	181	Low		168			4/1/99	15:37 178	100
Bid ↑	177 15/16	Ask		178			4/1/99	15:37 178	300
							4/1/99	15:37 177 15/16	600
Name	Bid	Size	Name	Ask	Size		4/1/99	15:37 178	1000
INCA	177 15/16	3	MASH	178	21		4/1/99	15:37	
ISLD	177 7/8	4	BRUT	178 1/16	4		4/1/99	15:37	
TNTO	177 13/16	3	INCA	178 1/16	10		4/1/99	15:37 178	800
MASH	177 3/4	2	TNTO	178 3/16	4		4/1/99	15:37 177 29/32	200
BEST	177 5/8	1	MLCO	178 3/8	10		4/1/99	15:37 178	1000
FBCO	177 5/8	1	HRZG	178 3/8	1		4/1/99	15:37 177 7/8	100
HRZG	177 9/16	1	HRCO	178 1/2	1		4/1/99	15:37	
SLKC	177 9/16	1	REDI	178 1/2	2		4/1/99	15:37	
AGIS	177 5/16	1					4/1/99	15:37	
							4/1/99	15:37	
							4/1/99	15:37 178	500

Reprinted with permission of Townsend Analytics, Ltd.

The momentum was still there as buyers continue to buy. The 122 Size on ISLD was taken out. Yahoo wants to go higher, and I am enjoying the ride.

Yahoo took the 178 level out and SBSH, a big seller earlier, has joined the best Bid. This was somewhat comforting.

Here is a full snap-shot of my trading screen. Note, the intraday chart remains positive and Yahoo is looking really strong. I am a point and a half away from my price target, I have moved up my mental stop loss to 177 7/8.

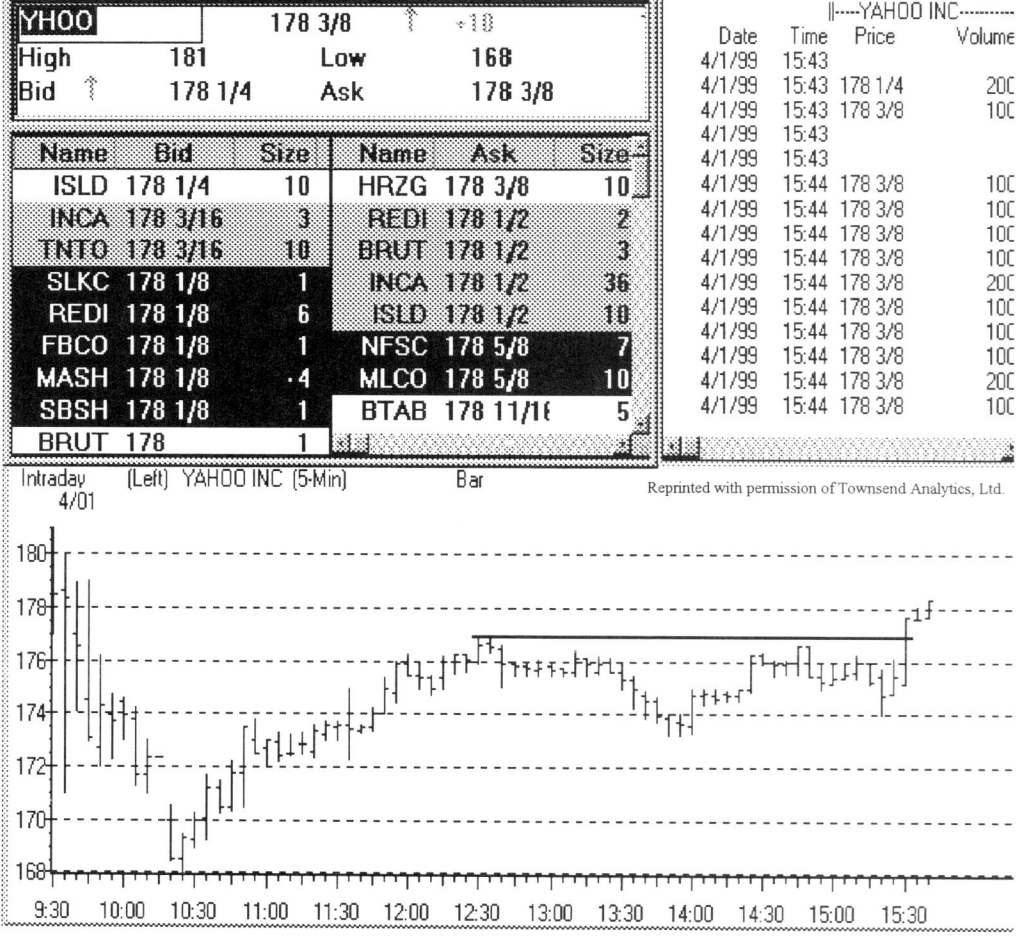

YHOO	178 1/2 ↓ -10 1/8			
High 181	Low 168			
Bid ↑ 178 9/16	Ask 178 5/8			

Name	Bid	Size	Name	Ask	Size
ISLD	178 9/16	10	NFSC	178 5/8	7
INCA	178 1/2	8	BTAB	178 11/16	5
SBSH	178 1/2	1	HRZG	178 3/4	1
TNTO	178 1/2	4	BEST	178 3/4	10
NITE	178 3/8	5	INCA	178 3/4	20
REDI	178 3/8	1	ISLD	178 3/4	5
SLKC	178 1/8	1	TNTO	178 3/4	2
FBCO	178 1/8	1	PERT	178 7/8	1
MASH	178 1/8	4			

‖----YAHOO INC----------			
Date	Time	Price	Volume
4/1/99	15:45		
4/1/99	15:45		
4/1/99	15:45		
4/1/99	15:45	178 9/16	500
4/1/99	15:45	178 9/16	100
4/1/99	15:45	178 9/16	100
4/1/99	15:45	178 1/2	100
4/1/99	15:45		
4/1/99	15:45		
4/1/99	15:45		
4/1/99	15:45		
4/1/99	15:45		
4/1/99	15:45		
4/1/99	15:45		

Reprinted with permission of Townsend Analytics, Ltd.

Yahoo moves over 178 1/2, volume seems to dry up a little. I moved my mental stop loss to 178 1/4 for 300 shares and 178 for the remainder 300 shares.

YHOO	179 ↑ +10 5/8			
High 181	Low 168			
Bid ↑ 178 3/4	Ask 179			

Name	Bid	Size	Name	Ask	Size
INCA	178 3/4	5	SWST	179	1
ISLD	178 3/4	13	MLCO	179	10
REDI	178 3/4	5	NITE	179	8
SLKC	178 3/4	1	BRUT	179	21
FBCO	178 11/16	1	HRZG	179	7
SBSH	178 11/16	1	INCA	179	13
PURE	178 1/2	2	PRUS	179	5
MASH	178 1/2	6	MASH	179 1/8	1
TNTO	178 1/4	4			

‖----YAHOO INC----------			
Date	Time	Price	Volume
4/1/99	15:46	179	100
4/1/99	15:46	179	100
4/1/99	15:46		
4/1/99	15:46		
4/1/99	15:46	179	200
4/1/99	15:46	179	100
4/1/99	15:46	179	100
4/1/99	15:46	179	600
4/1/99	15:46	179	300
4/1/99	15:46		
4/1/99	15:46		
4/1/99	15:46	179	100
4/1/99	15:46	179	900
4/1/99	15:46		
4/1/99	15:46		

Reprinted with permission of Townsend Analytics, Ltd.

Yahoo manages to go up to 179. Note, there is a 1/4 spread at this point. All the prints are 179 but the Bid has not moved up yet.

At this point, the stock actually pulled back to 178 3/8 and traded within 5/8 of a point range between 178 3/8 to 179, for 8 minutes. I was sitting on my heals, waiting to see what would happen next. I managed to survive the 8 minutes as the stock never went down far enough to trigger my mental stops.

Buyers came back and Yahoo went over 179 again. I have moved my mental stop to 178 1/2.

Selling 1/2 of the Position

Sellers came in, at this point, and Yahoo went back under 179. Look at the Size of 99 on INCA and 23 on ISLD showing daytraders want to get out of Yahoo. I am getting ready to sell.

Name	Bid	Size	Name	Ask	Size
SLKC	178 7/8	1	INCA	178 15/16	(99)
ISLD	178 7/8	10	ISLD	178 15/16	8
TNTO	178 13/16	4	NITE	179	9
REDI	178 5/8	8	HRZG	179	1
MLCO	178 1/2	4	AGIS	179	1
BRUT	178 1/2	1	BRUT	179 1/4	4
HRZG	178 1/2	1	MASH	179 1/4	2
MASH	178 3/8	1	COWN	179 3/8	1
INCA	178 3/8	3			

YHOO 179 1/16 ↑ +10 11/16
High 181 Low 168
Bid ↓ 178 7/8 Ask 178 15/16

Date	Time	Price	Volume
4/1/99	15:55	178 7/8	1000
4/1/99	15:55	178 7/8	100
4/1/99	15:55	178 7/8	300
4/1/99	15:55	178 15/16	400
4/1/99	15:55	179 3/16	100
4/1/99	15:55		
4/1/99	15:55		
4/1/99	15:55	178 15/16	1000
4/1/99	15:55	179	2500
4/1/99	15:55		
4/1/99	15:55		
4/1/99	15:55	178 7/8	1000
4/1/99	15:55	178 15/16	100
4/1/99	15:55	178 15/16	5000
4/1/99	15:55	179 1/16	100

Reprinted with permission of Townsend Analytics, Ltd.

The Ask ticks down and the 99 Size on INCA follows. This is normally the signal I look for and I decided to sell 1/2 my position at this point. I sold 300 shares at 178 5/8 on REDI via a SelectNet Preference order at 15:55. It was out of market by 1/4 of a point, but I wanted a fill, so I went out of market.

Bouncing Back Up

YHOO 178 5/8 ↓ +10 1/4
High 181 Low 168
Bid ↓ 178 1/2 Ask 178 9/16

Name	Bid	Size	Name	Ask	Size
NITE	178 1/2	5	SLKC	178 9/16	1
FBCO	178 7/16	1	INCA	178 9/16	15
MASH	178 3/8	1	ISLD	178 9/16	1
INCA	178 3/8	3	REDI	178 15/16	7
TNTO	178 3/16	4	HRZG	179	2
PRUS	178	1	BRUT	179	3
PURF	178	2	TNTO	179	1
BRUT	178	3	PERT	179 1/8	2
AGIS	178	1			

Date	Time	Price	Volume
4/1/99	15:56		
4/1/99	15:56		
4/1/99	15:56		
4/1/99	15:56		
4/1/99	15:56	178 5/8	600
4/1/99	15:56		
4/1/99	15:56		
4/1/99	15:56	178 5/8	500
4/1/99	15:56	179	100
4/1/99	15:56	178 1/2	400
4/1/99	15:56		
4/1/99	15:56		
4/1/99	15:56	179 1/2	500
4/1/99	15:56	179 1/2	500
4/1/99	15:56	178 5/8	900

Reprinted with permission of Townsend Analytics, Ltd.

Yahoo came down to 178 1/2 Bid and I was ready to sell the remainder 300 shares if the Bid fell below 178 1/4. I had a SelectNet Preference BRUT, sell order ready to go with one click of a mouse watching the activity very closely.

YHOO		178 3/8	↓	+10		|---YAHOO INC---		
					Date	Time	Price	Volume
High	181	Low		168	4/1/99	15:57	178 15/16	1700
Bid ↑	178 7/8	Ask		179	4/1/99	15:57	178 3/4	5000

Name	Bid	Size	Name	Ask	Size
AGIS	178 7/8	1	HRZG	179	10
ISLD	178 13/16	10	BRUT	179	3
INCA	178 3/4	2	TNTO	179	1
REDI	178 9/16	5	SLKC	179 1/16	1
FBCO	178 9/16	1	PERT	179 1/8	2
NITE	178 1/2	4	ISLD	179 1/8	1
MASH	178 3/8	1	COWN	179 3/8	1
PRUS	178	1	INCA	179 3/8	20
PURE	178	2			

Right panel (YAHOO INC prints at 15:57): 178 3/8 / 100; 178 7/8 / 200; 178 9/16 / 500; 178 1/2 / 500; 178 9/16 / 200.

Reprinted with permission of Townsend Analytics, Ltd.

The 178 1/2 level held and Yahoo went back up to 179 Ask. Note that the prints are all below the bid price, yet the bid ticked up. The big sizes previously seen on INCA and ISLD at 179 and 178 15/16 are gone. This is a big positive.

Closing the Position

YHOO		179 1/4	↑	+10 7/8		|---YAHOO INC---		
					Date	Time	Price	Volume
High	181	Low		168	4/1/99	15:58		
Bid ↑	179 3/16	Ask		179 3/8	4/1/99	15:58	179	100

Name	Bid	Size	Name	Ask	Size
ISLD	179 3/16	14	HRZG	179 3/8	1
AGIS	179 1/8	6	TNTO	179 3/8	4
REDI	179	3	MLCO	179 7/16	10
SLKC	179	1	ATTN	179 1/2	10
INCA	179	25	NITE	179 1/2	10
MASH	179	1	SBSH	179 1/2	1
NITE	178 7/8	5	INCA	179 1/2	1
TNTO	178 13/16	2	BRUT	179 1/2	14
PRUS	178	1			

Right panel prints at 15:58: 179 1/8 / 100; 179 1/4 / 200; 179 1/16 / 200; 179 1/8 / 600; 179 3/16 / 1000; 179 1/4 / 100; 179 1/4 / 100; 179 1/4 / 100.

Reprinted with permission of Townsend Analytics, Ltd.

Yahoo moves over 179 1/4, it is the highest level of this run so far, 2 minutes left to the closing bell. I am getting ready to sell the remaining 300 shares.

One minute left to the bell, trades are flying at 180. I enter a sell order at 179 7/8 on ISLD. The bid hits 179 7/8 and my order gets executed.

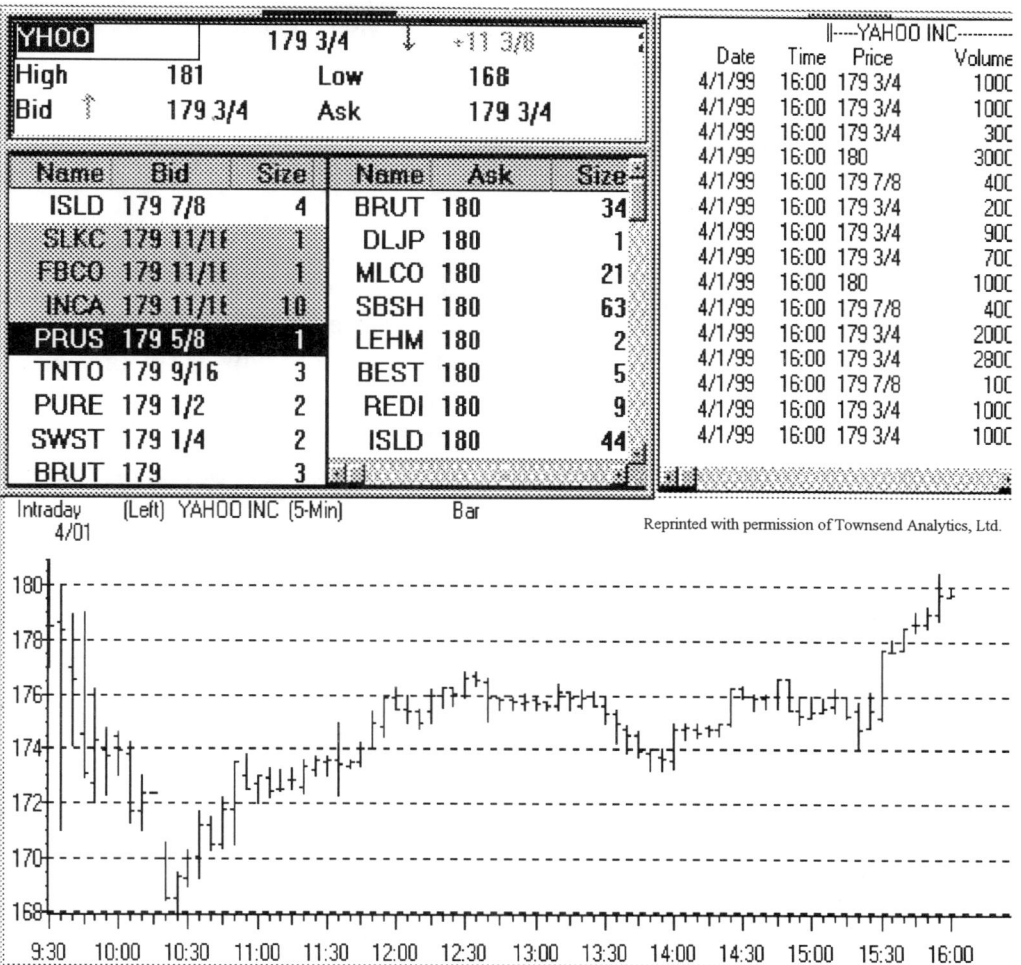

I sold the remaining 300 shares at 179 7/8 and went to bed flat. As a true daytrader in this case, I did not want to carry a position overnight and expose myself to additional risk.

How did I do on this trade?

I bought 600 shares at 174 7/8.
I sold 300 shares at 178 5/8.
I sold the remaining 300 shares at 179 7/8.

1. (178 5/8-174 7/8) X 300 = 3.75 X 300 = 1125
2. (179 7/8-174 7/8) X 300 = 5 X 300 = 1500

Total profit of $2,625 less commissions.

In analyzing this trade further, the key to success was the strategy behind the trade. I had a price target in mind and I raised my mental stops as the stock moved up. Once the price target was reached (176 1/2), I was willing to see if the stock would go higher, raising the bar to the next resistance level of 180, which was the opening price. I was mentally stopped out, selling half my position at 178 5/8. I held the remaining half of my position and sold it at the close. I stuck to my strategy and money management. I did not panic sell when the 50,000 shares showed up on REDI at 176, and I sold the entire position before the close of market. But what really made this trade successful was the good entry I had. When you have a good entry, you can sit in a trade and make money a lot easier than if you have a bad entry. This is why I posted every level II chart and posted my thinking at the time. In your practice phase, it is important to record these feelings, train of thought, strategies and changes as they occur in real time. So, when you analyze them later on, you will understand and learn from your own successful and unsuccessful decisions and actions.

The Next Trading Day

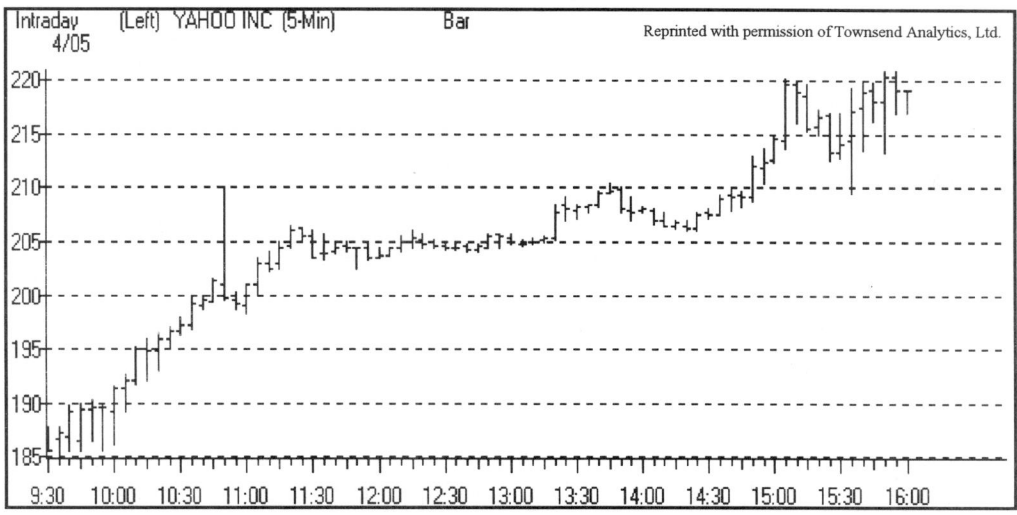

In case you wondered what Yahoo did on its next trading day, I will include an intraday chart. Yahoo went to 220, up 40 points from where we sold the last 300 shares. This is why I normally will hold some of my position if the stock was showing strength at day end. I will, at times, even add to my position if I see strength. However, this example of Yahoo, was to illustrate an intraday trade, in which traders go flat to bed. You do, however, leave a lot of money behind. If you want to trade intraday exclusively, successfully, not carrying any positions over night, you must have a very special personality, because you can't look back. You can never look at the fact you sold Yahoo at 179 7/8 and it went up 40 points the next day. If you do, you will have a higher failure rate, because your trading will become emotional. **The secret is to keep focus on new opportunities and forget about past trades,** especially the ones you got out of with a profit, small or big, and the stock kept going up (or down in a short position). This statement is also true for short term position trading (short-term hold, 2-10 days), as you will leave money behind.

There are always new opportunities. In fact, I could have bought back into Yahoo the next day at 185-190 and still manage a nice profit. This brings another hard task. Buying back into a stock which you just sold for a profit or loss, that has a good potential to be a winning trade. If you took action on selling it, for whatever reason, how can you justify buying it again. This is one of the hardest things to do, because you have to admit that you were wrong to sell the stock. This is not the case though! **When you enter your sell order, it is always the right decision, because your sell is a part of your trading strategy**. Unless you did not stick to your trading strategy, your sell order can never be wrong! Keep that in mind. If you did not estimate good price targets, or stop loss, it is a different issue. If you stuck to your strategy and sold according to your plan at a profit, or a loss, you can never get upset about it. This is a part of your discipline and mental state of mind. Now, if you want to buy back into a stock, make sure to ask yourself the same exact questions, why am I buying in? What are my price target, stop loss price, and entry point? Is the risk/reward ratio in my favor? Is it a good trade? **Never, ever buy back into a stock because of emotional reasons, whatever they may be! Buy back into a stock if the trade that is represented to you justifies it!**

Appendix A

Note if you are using RealTick™ III, you might need to type in a period followed by the letter X to get a quote or a chart for the index, following the symbols on this list. Example, if you want to look up the NASDAQ 100 index, $NDX you need to type $NDX.X

Market Indexes

$INDU Dow Jones Industrial Average™
$TRAN Dow Jones Transportation Average™
$UTIL Dow Jones Utilities Average™
$COMPQ NASDAQ Composite Index
$NDX NASDAQ 100 Index
$SPX S&P 500 Stock Index
$OEX S&P 100 Stock Index
$WSX Wilshire Small Cap Index
$TYX 30 Year T-Bond Interest Rate (x .10)
$RUI Russell 1000
$RUT Russell 2000
$RUA Russell 3000

Industry Indexes

$XAL AIRLINE (AMEX)
$AUX AUTOMOTIVE (CBOE)
$BANK BANKING (NASDAQ)
$BKX BANK PHLX/KBW (PHLX)
$BIX BANK S&P (CBOE)
$BTK BIOTECH (AMEX)
$IXBT BIOTECH (NASDAQ)
$CEX CHEMICAL S&P (CBOE)
$IXCO COMPUTER NASDAQ
$GHA COMPUTER HARDWARE GOLDMAN/SACHS
$GSV COMPUTER SERVICES GOLDMAN/SACHS
$CWX COMPUTER SOFTWARE (CBOE)
$GSO COMPUTER SOFTWARE GOLDMAN/SACHS
$XCI COMPUTER TECHNOLOGY (AMEX)
$CMR CONSUMER MORGAN STANLEY (AMEX)

$EVX ENVIRONMENTAL (CBOE)
$NF FINANCIAL (NYSE)
$IXF FINANCIAL (NASDAQ)
$OFIN FINANCIALS OTHER (NASDAQ)
$FPP FOREST & PAPER PRODUCTS (PHLX)
$GAX GAMING (CBOE)
$GOX GOLD (CBOE)
$XAU GOLD AND SILVER (PHLX)
$HCX HEALTH CARE S&P (CBOE)
$MSH HIGH TECH 35 MORGAN STANLEY (AMEX)
$ND INDUSTRIAL (NYSE)
$INDS INDUSTRIAL (NASDAQ)
$NIND INDUSTRIAL NASDAQ NATIONAL MARKET
$INSR INSURANCE (NASDAQ)
$IUX INSURANCE S&P (CBOE)
$IIX INTERNET (AMEX)
$INX INTERNET (CBOE)
$GIN INTERNET GOLDMAN/SACHS
$XNG NATURAL GAS (AMEX)
$NWX NETWORKING (AMEX)
$GIP NETWORKING MULTIMEDIA (GOLDMAN/SACHS)
$XOI OIL (AMEX)
$XOI OIL AND GAS (AMEX)
$OIX OIL (CBOE)
$OSX OIL SERVICE
$DRG PHARMACEUTICAL (AMEX)
$RIX REIT (real estate) (CBOE)
$RLX RETAIL S&P (CBOE)
$GSM SEMICONDUCTOR GOLDMAN/SACHS
$SOX SEMICONDUCTOR (PHLX)
$XBD SECURITIES BROKER/DEALER (AMEX)
$TXX TECHNOLOGY (CBOE)
$PSE TECHNOLOGY (PSE)
$IXTC TELECOMMUNICATIONS (NASDAQ)
$PNX TELECOM PHONE (PHLX)
$TRANQ TRANSPORTATION (NASDAQ)
$NV TRANSPORTATION (NYSE)
$TRX TRANSPORTATION S&P (CBOE)
$NNA UTILITIES (NYSE)
$UTY UTILITIES (PHLX)

Appendix B

Trading Station Setup

It is important to have a good computer, monitor and internet connection setup. If you plan on trading with software like RealTick™ III and be able to monitor the market and execute orders professionally, I recommend that you invest in your trading station setup. I currently use a 400 MHz, 128 RAM computer with dual 21" monitors. I use a high-speed internet connection via cable modem. I have DSL service as a back up internet connection. Screen size is a commodity in this business as you need to see what is going on in the market with relative ease. If you are a beginner, I recommend you start with:

1. 350 MHz, 128 RAM or better computer
2. A 21" monitor (do not buy anything smaller, you will want to buy at least one more 21" monitor, later, mark my words).
3. Cable modem or DSL internet connection, if available in your area.
4. A backup internet connection service, may be a dial up.

I run two independent computer systems side by side. I use one to run my scanning programs, which is connected to the internet via DSL. The other system is my trading system, which I run RealTick™ III on, exclusively. This system is connected to the internet via cable modem. If the network goes down, I can turn around to my other computer and run the trading program there, without having to dial up for connection. This saves me time and money if I lose the connection to the internet on either system. I am not encouraging you to go and spend all this money on a trading station, now. Once you have demonstrated success in your trading, you can expand your setup. Do not spend money on cheaper equipment right now, as you will trash it later. If your existing computer is not up to the task, buy a computer that is at least 400 MHz and 128 RAM. Do not buy 17" or 19" monitors as you will want 21" later on. You might as well start there. If you plan on running a dual/multi monitor setup, I recommend you get the exact same monitors, size and brand, for ultimate results.

Glossary

Accumulation: The first phase in a bull market when investors buy shares from other investors who are uncertain about the stock market. Volume is increasing slightly during rallies.

After-Hours Trading: Trading activity in a stock after the market closed.

Arbitrage Activity: Traders who try to profit from buying and selling two related securities, at the same time.

Ascending Triangle: A bullish continuation pattern in an uptrending stock. Drawing a line over the price tops and a line under the bottoms creates a right-angle triangle, where the slope is rising (from left to right.) Successful penetration of the horizontal line (over the tops) can indicate a continuation of the trend and generates a buy signal.

Ask: The lowest price sellers are willing to sell a stock.

Back Testing: Using historical data to test a strategy.

Basing Pattern: A stock that is trading in a relative narrow range over a period of time.

Bear: An investor who believes the market or a stock will go down.

Bear Market: A period of time in which stock prices decline 20% or more from the top.

Beta: A measurement of the sensitivity a stock has to the movement of the broader market. High beta stocks rise more in price or decline more in price in direct relationship to the broader market. Low beta stocks do not rise or decline as much as the broader market does. Negative beta stocks move in inverse relationship to the broader market. They can decline when the market goes up or rise when the broader market goes down.

Bid: The highest price buyers are willing to pay for a stock.

Block Trade: A transaction reflecting a large quantity of stock, normally 10,000 shares or more, bought or sold as one unit.

Bottom: The lowest trading price a stock traded at, over a period of time.

Breadth: The difference between advancing issues and declining issues in the market. If there are more advancing issues then breadth is positive, if there are more declining issues then breadth is negative.

Breakout: When a stock successfully penetrates through support or resistance, or any technical pattern.

Bull: An investor who believes the market or a stock will go up.

Bull market: A period of time in which stock prices rise 20% or more from the bottom.

Channel Pattern: A stock that trades in a pattern in which drawing straight lines under the bottoms and over the tops result two parallel lines.

Chart: The display of price data over a period of time in a chart format. Price is on the Y axis and time is on the X axis.

Confirmation: When a technical indicator agrees with a certain price movement.

Congestion: Consecutive periods with no real progress in price.

Continuation Pattern: A technical pattern that suggest a continuation of an existing trend such as ascending and descending triangles.

Consolidation: A period of time in which a stock is changing hands with no real direction. Normally, it is indecision time between bulls and bears.

Correction: A reversal price movement from the ongoing trend which is not significant enough to reverse the over all trend. Corrections are also called a pullback in bull markets or rallies in bear markets.

Depth: The number of shares on the bid or ask that can be purchased or sold without dramatically changing the price of a security.

Declining Trendline: A trendline drawn over the top prices a security traded in and is sloping downward.

Declining Trading Channel: A stock that trades in a pattern in which drawing straight lines under the bottoms and over the tops result two downward-sloping parallel lines.

Descending Triangle: A bearish continuation pattern in a downtrending stock. Drawing a line over the price tops and a line under the bottoms creates a right-angle triangle, where the slope is declining (from left to right.) Successful penetration of the horizontal line (under the bottoms) can indicate a continuation of the trend and generates a sell signal.

Distribution Phase: This takes place near market tops, or at the end of a bull market, when lucky investors sell their shares to bag-holding investors. In this phase, rallies normally occur on lower volume.

Divergence: When a technical indicator disagrees with a certain price movement.

Dividend: Distribution of profits by a corporation to its stockholders.

Dollar Cost Averaging: A popular investment approach which consists of investing the same amount of money at regular time intervals.

Double Bottom: A reversal technical pattern where one bottom is formed on high volume followed by a rally. The stock then declines in price to test the bottom and forms a second bottom, normally on lower volume than the first bottom. If the second bottom holds successfully, followed by a rally that rises over the tops of the rally from the first bottom, a reversal is taking place. This generates a buy signal.

Double Top: A reversal technical pattern where one top is formed on high volume followed by a correction. The stock then rallies to test the high and forms a second top, normally, on lower volume than the first top. If the second top is not penetrated successfully followed by another correction in which price declines lower than the lows of the correction from the first top, a reversal is taking place and a sell signal is generated.

Dow Jones Industrial Average: A price weighted average of 30 industrial stocks.

Downtick: On NYSE, a trade taking place at a lower price than the previous trade. On NASDAQ, a lowering in price of the best bid.

ECN: Electronic Communications Network. It matches orders from buyers and sellers together, and executes them against each other, in lightning speed. This order execution vehicle is available to subscribers of the ECN only, or via SelectNet preference orders. Examples are: INCA, ISLD, REDI, BTRD,

ARCA, ATTN, STRK, NTRD, and BRUT.

Ex-Dividend: The day the dividend is subtracted from the price of a stock, it is now trading without its dividend.

Float: Number of shares available for trading. A company can have 10 million shares outstanding and only 1 million float.

Fundamental Analysis: Analyzing a company's performance based on financial data related to sales, earnings, growth potential, balance sheet, management, new products, R&D etc.

Gap Open: The difference between a closing price and the next trading session opening price. The gap is the price range in which no shares were traded during market hours. A gap up occurs when the opening price is higher than previous day's closing price. A gap down occur when the opening price is lower than previous day's closing price.

Horizontal Trading Channel: A stock that trades in a pattern in which drawing straight lines under the bottoms and over the tops result two horizontal parallel lines.

Index: Average price of a group of stocks used to study the overall market, industry, sector, etc. Famous indexes are the Dow 30, S&P 500, NASDAQ Composite, Dow Transport, Dow Utility.

Inside Market: The highest bid and lowest offer (ask) make the inside market.

Insider: Someone with at least 10% ownership in a company, an officer, or a director.

Instinet: An ECN that allows subscribers to display quotes and trade during, before, and after market hours.

Island: An ECN that allows subscribers to display quotes and trade during, before and after market hours.

Limit Order: An order to buy or sell a stock at a specific price.

Margin: Extended credit granted by a broker to an investor which is governed by the NASD.

Market Maker: A participating firm publishing a quote for a NASDAQ security. Market Makers are required to honor their quote should they receive an order to buy or sell at their published quote price. Market Makers are only required to honor orders up to the size they are quoting. The size can be seen on a level II quote screen.

Market Order: An order to buy or sell a stock at the current market price.

NASD: National Association of Securities Dealers which is responsible for the operations and regulations of the NASDAQ.

Odd Lot: A transaction of less than 100 shares.

Open Order: An order to buy or sell a security which remains open until it is filled or cancelled by the customer.

Order Flow: Orders sent by brokers to market makers to buy or sell a security.

Overbought: A stock that has been rising in price and is considered overvalued at this point of time.

Oversold: A stock that has been declining in price and is considered undervalued at this point of time.

Panic Selling: A situation where sellers are in abundance rushing to sell their stocks, causing sharp decline in stock prices.

PE Ratio: Price-to-earnings ratio is calculated by dividing the price of a stock by its annual earnings per share. It is normally calculated based on earnings from the latest fiscal year. However, earnings estimates for the next fiscal year can be plotted into the formula as well, often referred to as **forward PE ratio**.

Penetration: The point at which a stock price penetrates through support, resistance or technical pattern lines.

Program Trading: Computerized trading decision based on a particular formula sent to the market electronically.

Range: The difference between the high price and the low price for the studied period of time. High – Low = Range.

Resistance: A price level which a stock has difficulty rising over due to the forces of supply and demand.

Reversal Pattern: A technical pattern suggesting that the existing trend is changing. Examples: Head and Shoulders, Reverse Head and Shoulders, Double Bottom, Double Top, Triple Bottom, Triple Top, Rounding Bottoms, Rounding Tops, Falling Wedges in downtrending stocks, Rising Wedges in uptrending stocks, etc.

Rising Trading Channel: A stock that trades in a pattern in which drawing straight lines under the bottoms and over the tops result two upward-sloping parallel lines.

Rounding Bottom: If you draw a line under the lows it will form a concave shape similar to a saucer. It is important for the volume bars to form a similar pattern as volume declined as the stock moved lower, to the lowest point, and started rising as the stock price move higher from its lowest point.

Rounding Top: If you draw a line over the tops it will form a convex shape pattern similar to a pitcher mound. It is important for the volume bars to form a concave pattern as volume declined as the stock moved higher, to the highest point, and started rising as the stock price decline from its highest point.

SEC: Security and Exchange Commission. It is a governing agency which deals with protecting the public (as much as they can) from fraud and stock manipulation.

Section (area) Pattern: A time period in which a stock forms a technical pattern such as continuation or reversal patterns, triangles, wedges, round top, etc.

SelectNet: This is an automated service which is employed by NASDAQ exclusively. It allows traders to route orders to market makers in which they can negotiate terms and prices and execute trades electronically. It eliminates all human contact from the trade, which is different from NYSE trades routing.

Short Sale: Selling a stock which is not owned. This is done with anticipation that the stock price is to decline in the future at which time an investor can buy the stock back cheaper and profit from it. It is done by borrowing the stock from a broker (if he has it) and selling it. This opens a short position. To close the position, a purchase of a stock takes place and the stock is returned to the lending broker. A profit or a loss will be the difference between the sale price and the purchase price. You may only short sell a stock on an uptick.

Short Interest: The total number of shares that will have to be bought to close all short positions in a stock. It is the total number of shares reflecting short open positions by investors.

Specialist: An exchange market member who deals in one or more stocks in which all trades pass through him.

Spread: The difference between the bid and the ask. Ask – Bid = Spread.

SOES: Small Order Execution System. It is an automated order execution system of up to 1000 shares of stock offered by the NASDAQ stock market. It was implemented after the 1987 crash.

Stair Stepping Pattern: A pattern which is similar to a stairway in appearance. In an uptrending stock, it presents itself as an upswing followed by sideways movement, followed by an upswing followed by sideways movement and so on. In a downtrending stock, it presents itself by a downswing followed by sideways movement followed by downswing followed by sideways movement and so on.

Stock Split: A company which increases the number of shares outstanding by issuing more stock. It is also looked at as a stock dividend, where share holders will receive additional shares without changing the existing ownership ratios of the company. A 2 for 1 Stock Split, means that each shareholder will receive an additional share of stock for each share he owns now. The price of the stock will be adjusted accordingly, so if John had 100 shares of XYZ Corp at $10 a share the day of the split. After market closes, he will receive additional 100 shares and the price of the stock will be adjusted to $5 a share. 100 X 10 = 1000 = 200 X 5. There is no monetary gain.

Stop Orders: These are orders that have an activation price which is out of the current inside market. They are most often used to limit losses. **Stop Buy** is an order is to buy a stock once it reached a certain price which is **above** the current market price. **Stop Sell** is an order to sell a stock once it reached a certain price which is **below** the current market price.

Support: A price level in which quantity demanded is greater than quantity supplied, preventing the stock from going lower. This can change, but until it does, this price level will be considered support.

Symmetrical Triangle: A period of sideways congestion where the latest tops fail to reach previous tops and latest bottoms fail to reach previous bottoms causing the range to narrow down, eventually a breakout should occur.

Technical Analysis (TA): Analysis of stock prices over a period of time.

Technical Indicators (Studies): These are derived by applying mathematical formulas to historical price and volume data. Examples include: Moving Averages, RSI, etc.

Time and Sales: A transaction print report in which the time, the number of shares, and price are printed within 90 seconds of the actual time the trade took place.

Top: The highest trading price a stock traded at, over a period of time.

Trend: The general direction a stock is moving in over a certain period of time.

Trendline: A straight line drawn over the tops or under the bottoms which illustrates the general trend for that period of time.

Uptick: On NYSE, a trade taking place at a higher price than the previous trade. On NASDAQ, a rise in price of the best bid.

Volatility: A measurement of price fluctuation for a stock. When stocks move sharply they are more volatile.

Volume: The total number of shares traded over a period of time.

Whipsaw: Buying and/or Selling a stock at the wrong time. The closing of a relatively new stock position due to price fluctuation at a loss, only to watch the stock move in the anticipated direction shortly after.

StockJunkie.com
I Trade Stocks For A Living

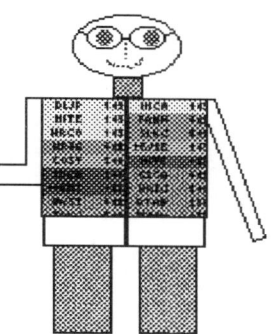

U.S. Stock Market
- Detailed Quote
- Market Quote
- Market Breadth
- NYSE Winners
- Nasdaq Winners
- AMEX Winners
- NYSE Losers
- Nasdaq Losers
- AMEX Losers
- NYSE Actives
- Nasdaq Actives
- AMEX Actives
- 52-Week Highs
- 52-Week Lows
- Volume Alert
- Top 50 Options
- Fair Value
- S&P Futures

The StockJunkie Column

Advanced Short-Term Trading Seminar StockJunkie is now holding two and three day seminars focusing on advanced trading strategies. For more information Click Here

New Release: The book "Stock Trading Wizard" *Advanced Short-Term Trading Strategies* by Tony Oz. For more information Click Here

Educational Section: Daytrading case studies. Actual trades executed by Tony Oz, featured step by step. To view these daytrading case studies click on the links below.

Case Study One
Case Study Two
Case Study Three
Case Study Four

Trader's Resources
- Research
- Book Store
- Quotes & Charts
- Discount Brokers
- Daytrading Brokers
- Market News
- Commentary
- Earnings Calendar
- Stock Splits
- IPOs
- U.S. Economy
- After-Hours Trading
- Pre-Market Trading
- Short Interest
- Trading Games
- SEC Filing
- Trading Software
- Mutual Funds
- Technical Analysis
- Stock Picks

I have created the StockJunkie free website to provide serious traders with links to the best financial sites. Since these links are constantly updated, it was useless to list them in the book. I also feature daytrading case studies on the site. You are more than welcome to join the StockJunkie group.

Tony Oz's
Advanced Short-Term Trading Seminars

Seminar Overview

This seminar is designed for anyone who wants to learn about trading stocks for a living. The seminar covers everything from the basics to the most advanced trading strategies and tools. Our goal is to teach traders how they can be more successful. We will achieve our goal once a student looks back in time, 5 years after attending the seminar, and says: "Attending the Stock-Junkie Seminar was the BEST investment decision I have made in the last five years!"

Qualifications

Online stock trading experience of at least 30 executed trades. A burning desire to learn about advanced short-term trading strategies. You need to pass a mini interview session with Tony Oz in which you will be asked to answer questions related to short-term trading. **Please note that you may not qualify to take this seminar!**

Seminar Outline

<u>About The Stock Market:</u> Investment/Trading Objectives, Exchange Market, OTC, Risks Factors Affecting the Stock Market, General Market Psychology, Supply and Demand, Supply and Demand in the Stock Market, Bid and Ask, Spread, Short Sale.

<u>Technical Analysis:</u> Basics of TA, Volume, Identifying the Trend, Support and Resistance, Trendlines, Moving Averages, Using Moving Averages in Trading, Breakouts, Characteristics of Price Movements, Technical Patterns, Double Bottom, Double Top, Head and Shoulders, Reverse Head and Shoulders, Cup and Handle, Trading in a Channel, Continuation Patterns, Triangles, Flags, Wedges, Stair Stepping, RSI, Using Intraday Charts. Visual demonstrations.

<u>Introduction to Level II:</u> Bid and Ask, Multiquote Window, What Does Level II Tell Us? The Big Market Makers, Who is the AX? Time and Sales Print Report, Using Time and Sales with Level II, Illustration of an AX in Action, Dynamics of Level II. (Visual and recorded demonstrations.)

Advanced Order Execution Systems: SOES, SelectNet, SelectNet Preference Orders, ECNs, Trading Like a Market Maker, More ISLD Stuff, Arca, Market Maker's Tricks, Which Execution System to Use? Pre-Market and After-Hours Trading. (Visual and recorded demonstrations.)

Trading For A Living: Research, Trading Strategy, Trading Strategy Table, Execution, Trade Records, Trade Records Table, Ego, Money Management, Winning Streaks, Losing Streaks, You Don't Have to Trade Everyday, Dealing With Pressure, Supervising Your Trades, Finding Stocks to Trade, Real Time Scans, Learning Curve, Paper Trading, Chat Rooms, Secrets to Successful Trading-What Does it Take? Expensive Stocks Versus Cheap Stocks, Capital Preservation, Trading Strategies, Buying Points, Where and How, Daytrading Versus Swing Trading, Adaptation, Buyers/Sellers Remorse, Cost Averaging For Long-Term Growth, Taxes. (Visual and recorded demonstrations).

Daytrading Strategy Illustrations: Case Studies which will show recorded **actual** executed trades. We will study the thought process behind entering the trades and answer the where, why and how questions in regards to each case we study. (Visual and recorded demonstrations.)

Using RealTick™ III and the Internet as a tool for research and execution: Why and how can we use free Internet services to do our research. Why and how can we use the trading software RealTick™ III in our advantage. (Visual and recorded demonstrations.)

Testimonial

"Tony, What a GREAT seminar !! I really enjoyed learning how to trade from a PRO such as yourself. The best part was showing us exactly how to set up our screens, what technical analysis tools to use and actual case studies of your trades. It is very clear to me that you are truly concerned that your students learn the right way to trade and are successful down the road. Obviously, you are not into teaching for the money but to pass on this burning passion you have to others. I think I have the bug also and with your book as guidance I will also become successful." -- E. James, CA.

To get more info about the seminar go to:

http://www.stockjunkie.com/seminar.htm

Interest Form

Please fill out this form if you are interested in attending the Advanced Short-Term Trading Seminar. Please Fax to: 1-949-360-1558.

Name: _____ E Mail: _____

Tel # _____ Best Time to Call: _____

Your goal in attending the seminar: _____

_____

_____

_____

_____

Investment Experience: _____

_____

_____

_____

_____

Your Broker: _____

On a scale of 1-10 how would you rate your broker _____

Why? _____

_____

_____

All information will be kept confidential. It will not be given out or sold to anyone!

BestReturns.com

What is our service all about?

Our service is about saving you time. We follow thousands of securities on a daily basis as we scan the market for high percentage short-term plays. Our goal is to scan the market for high percentage set-ups and place our results in front of your eyes prior to market open. Stock picking and trading is fun, so we want you to make the final decision and play a stock pick you like. We don't want to take the fun of stock picking away from you. We just want to open your eyes to additional high percentage plays. You still get to do some research and of course place the orders.

Daily Stock Picks- This area features individual stock picks that have a probability of 70% or higher to be winners. We rate our picks based on historical technical data and we only post high percentage plays. We do not force plays just so we have a pick listed on the page! This may result no picks for the day if nothing rates over 70%.

Market Outlook- This is a general analysis and overview of the entire stock market. This analysis is based on fundamental, psychological and technical elements.

The Final List- The final list will feature an additional list of up to 30 stocks for you to look at before the market opens. The trick is that you will need to decide if you want to go long or short and at which entry and exit price.

7-Day Free Trial

We will give you no sales pitch here because we truly believe that our service is very valuable. If you are interested you may try it for one week free of charge. Log onto the site and click on the Free Trial link.

http://www.BestReturns.com

About the Author

Tony Oz is a professional short-term trader who lives and breathes stocks on a daily basis. In 1998, he has made a name for himself when he won 3 stock picking contests beating as many as 2300 contestants over a 4-week period of time. Competition returns were as high as 106% in 4 weeks, and the compounded return for the 5 contests was 822%. He was contracted by a stock picking site, *bestreturns.com*, to make stock picks for their subscribers. He is one of the founding members and popular traders of Day Traders of Orange County. His experience in teaching Short-Term Trading Seminars has contributed to the writing of what is promised to be one of the best Short-Term Trading Strategies ever published.

Tony lives with his wife and son, in Southern California.